S-BPM in the Wild

Albert Fleischmann · Werner Schmidt
Christian Stary

Editors

S-BPM in the Wild

Practical Value Creation

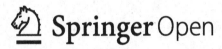

Editors
Albert Fleischmann
Interaktiv Expert
Pfaffenhofen
Germany

Christian Stary
Kepler University of Linz
Linz
Austria

Werner Schmidt
Technische Hochschule Ingolstadt
Ingolstadt
Germany

ISBN 978-3-319-36498-8   ISBN 978-3-319-17542-3   (eBook)
DOI 10.1007/978-3-319-17542-3

Printed on acid-free paper

Springer International Publishing AG Switzerland is part of Springer Science+Business Media
(www.springer.com)

Preface

While S-BPM has received attention and acceptance in the research and innovative development community, its reception and uptake in business practice and organizational development is still a challenge for management and operation. Several case studies have been provided in the annual S-BPM ONE events, in order to demonstrate capabilities and implementation approaches. We follow this tradition by providing a dedicated volume with recent field studies.

Targeting developers, educators, and practitioners, we have structured the latest key methodological and technological S-BPM developments in training, research, and application. They have been carefully selected and thoroughly peer-reviewed by at least three experts in the field.

We need to thank all relevant people for their active engagement facilitating the editing of this book, in particular

- the authors of the various contributions sharing their expertise in a narrative way,
- the reviewers reflecting on each of the contributions thoroughly, and
- the European Commission funding this IANES[1] outreach activity.

Finally, we cordially thank Ralf Gerstner and Viktoria Meyer from Springer for their assistance and support when publishing this volume.

Pfaffenhofen   Albert Fleischmann
Ingolstadt   Werner Schmidt
Linz   Christian Stary

[1]IANES is a European FP 7 project on Interactive Acquisition, Negotiation and Enactment of Subject-Oriented Business Process Knowledge supported by contract no. PIAP-GA-2011-286083 (EU-FP7-IAPP); see also www.ianes.eu.

Contents

About the Authors

Martina Augl is in charge of the Department of Organizational Development at TILAK, Tirol Landeskrankenanstalten GmbH, the Tyrolean operator of public hospitals, and is responsible for organizational development projects. Her main focus is to change management, leadership, communication, and process design based on a systemic approach. Her experience is on consultancy for strategy, marketing, cultural issues, and knowledge management. Martina Augl is also a lecturer in the master study programs Operation Management, Quality and Process Management, and Controlling for Knowledge and Change Management. Medical Department, Organizational Development Unit, Tiroler Landeskrankenanstalten GmbH. (TILAK), Innsbruck, Austria, e-mail: martina.augl@tilak.at

Ross Brown Member of the Business Process Management (BPM) Discipline at QUT his main research interests are in the application of virtual environment technology to the representation of business processes. He uses 3D virtual worlds to enable people to easily visualize business processes and to obtain insight into complex processes for all stakeholders. A number of projects are currently underway, including the embedding of executable workflows in 3D virtual worlds, a remote collaborative 3D BPMN editor, and the development of 3D agent architectures for process emulation, logging, and interaction. The Smart Services Collaborative Research Centre in Australia is actively supporting this research. He has published over 60 papers in various academic research and industry fora. He has reviewed papers for international conferences and journals (APCCM, ISCV, EuroVis, CBPSM, Future Generation Computer Systems, Computers in Entertainment, Transactions on Computer Graphics and Visualization, SIGCHI, Transactions on Computational Intelligence and AI in Games, among others) and has examined theses from Australian universities in the fields of games technology, computer graphics, and visualization. He is a reviewer of Australian Research Council funding grants, the peak research funding body in Australia. Information Systems School, Science and Engineering Faculty, Queensland University of Technology, Brisbane, QLD, Australia, e-mail: r.brown@qut.edu.au

Max Dirndorfer is a scientific assistant and lecturer in the field of business information technology at Technische Hochschule Deggendorf (University of Applied Sciences). He has wide work experience in the design and implementation of (subject-oriented) business processes. Prior to that, he worked as a technical employee at a large publishing house. Technische Hochschule Deggendorf, Deggendorf, Germany, e-mail: max.dirndorfer@th-deg.de

Albert Fleischmann is an independent scientific advisor. He has been an accomplished software engineer for over 30 years and has extensive experience in business process management. In theory and practice, he successfully realizes initiatives of projects, processes, and quality management in enterprises. Based on his experience in process management and software development, he developed the subject-oriented business process management (S-BPM) approach. Together with some friends, he founded a company now called Metasonic. This company offers a complete product suite based on S-BPM. Currently, he is working on further enhancements of the S-BPM concept, and, together with researchers from universities, he publishes regularly the corresponding results at several conferences. Albert Fleischmann is a lecturer at several universities. He holds a doctoral degree in computer science. Interaktiv Expert, Pfaffenhofen, Germany, e-mail: albert.fleischmann@interaktiv.expert

Christoph Fleischmann was born in 1986 in California, USA, and grew up in Bavaria, Germany. He studied Industrial Engineering at Vienna University of Technology with specialization in the fields of production and process management. Since 2014, he is working as an assistant for production and logistics at ENGEL AUSTRIA in Schwertberg, Austria. St. Pölten, Austria, e-mail: chris.fleischmann@gmx.net

Joel Harman is a research student in the Science and Engineering Faculty at the Queensland University of Technology. He has completed a Bachelor of Games and Interactive Entertainment with an Honours in Information Technology. His research interests are in the application of immersive game technologies within other domains, in particular how these technologies can assist in role-playing and simulating complex tasks. Science and Engineering Faculty, Queensland University of Technology, Brisbane, QLD, Australia, e-mail: joel.harman@connect.qut.edu.au

Lothar Hübner is an independent management consultant. After his training as a banker, he worked very early in IT. For over ten years, he was a member of the management board of the large consulting company Roland Berger and Partner and responsible for the establishment of large American SW providers in the German-speaking area. He gained experience specifically in the IT environment in the financial service management area. As head of an entrepreneurs organization and internal IT at a major IT service provider in the banking sector, he designed the business processes and thus successful structures for modern service management. Balingen, Germany, e-mail: lothar.huebner@lhci.de

Udo Kannengiesser is a research engineer at Metasonic GmbH, a commercial vendor of S-BPM software. Previously, he worked as a research scientist at National ICT Australia and as a research consultant for universities in Australia and the USA. He holds a Ph.D. from the University of Sydney. His current research interests include extensions of the S-BPM methodology and its application to production processes and agent-based systems. He is also an active researcher in the fields of design computing and design cognition. He is among the principal contributors to research in the function–behaviour–structure (FBS) framework, one of the most widely used models of designing. Metasonic GmbH, Pfaffenhofen, Germany, e-mail: udo.kannengiesser@metasonic.de

Matthias Kurz is an IT architect at QUA-LiS NRW, a think tank of the school administration of North Rhine-Westphalia. He publishes research papers on business process management, adaptive case management, and the connection between strategy design and strategy implementations at several international conferences. Before joining the public service, he was a cloud architect at DATEV eG and the head of the BPM research group at the Chair of Information Systems II of the Friedrich-Alexander University of Erlangen-Nuremberg. QUA-LiS NRW, Soest, Germany, e-mail: Matthias.kurz@qua-lis.nrw.de

Alexander Lawall graduated with a diploma in computer science from Hof University in 2005. His studies focused on multimedia applications. After the diploma, he enrolled in the master's program "Software Engineering for Industrial Applications" at Hof University which he completed with master's degree (M.Eng.) in 2007. During the studies, he gathered experience in companies such as Sandler AG and Textilgruppe Hof AG, where he developed a quality management system. Afterward, he worked as a research assistant at Bayreuth University in the department of business mathematics. Since then, he has been working as a research assistant for the Institute of Information Systems at Hof University. Institut für Informationssysteme der Hochschule für Angewandte Wissenschaften Hof, Hof, Germany, e-mail: alexander.lawall@hof-university.de

Matthias Lederer Chair for Information Systems is a research assistant at the University of Erlangen-Nuremberg and BPM consultant at the German industrial manufacturing company REHAU. His major field of research and teaching is business process management and especially the strategy alignment as well as performance and compliance management of IT-enabled workflows. Mr. Lederer holds a master's degree in international information systems. In several work placements and in a trainee program, he earned practical experiences in the fields of workflow management and software engineering. Services-Processes-Intelligence, University of Erlangen-Nuremberg, Nuremberg, Germany, e-mail: matthias.lederer@fau.de

Harald Lerchner is a member of the research and teaching staff at the Department of Business Information Systems—Communications Engineering at the Johannes Kepler University in Linz. His research interests focus on organizational learning and also on business process management and modeling. Previously, he had been working many years in the industry and was responsible as CIO for IT across groups. Department of Business Information Systems—Communications Engineering, Johannes Kepler University of Linz, Linz, Austria, e-mail: harald.lerchner@jku.at

Frank Lorbacher is Managing Consultant at Detecon International. He has over 20 years of experience in BPM projects in different branches. His main focus is modeling and execution of processes within the service-oriented architecture. He is an expert in digitalized processes and corresponding process transformation. Detecon International GmbH, Cologne, Germany, e-mail: frank.lorbacher@detecon. com

Nils Meyer CTO, Chief Technology Officer, Director Software Production Since the organization was founded, Nils Meyer has been working for Metasonic GmbH. Today, he is the head of software production and research and development. Furthermore, he is responsible for the software development of the Metasonic Suite and Metasonic Touch as well as for all the entire research initiatives of the company. Nils Meyer studied information management and has a bachelor's degree in business information systems from the university in Ingolstadt. In 2009, Nils Meyer gained an MBA with a focus on knowledge management. In addition, he graduated with a master's degree in computer sciences in 2007. Research and Development, Metasonic GmbH, Pfaffenhofen, Germany, e-mail: nils.meyer@metasonic.de

Christoph Piller studied business and engineering at UAS Technikum Wien in Vienna. He was the department head of a metalworking shop for five years and gave several lectures about his research at process management conferences. Today, Christoph Piller is working in the automotive industry as project coordinator. UAS Technikum Wien, Ingolstadt, Germany, e-mail: chpiller@gmx.net

Stefan Raß has worked from 2005–2013 as a management and IT consultant in an international consulting firm, responsible for several IT and BPM projects. He has many years of theoretical and practical experience in the field of S-BPM and is currently CEO of StrICT Solutions GmbH, a Styrian IT company in the field of structured communication and S-BPM. CEO, StrICT Solutions GmbH, Graz, Austria, e-mail: rass@strict-solutions.com

Dominik Reichelt completed his master's degree at Hof University in 2010 and is a member of the research group Information Management of the Institute of Information Systems at Hof University. He participated as a software engineer in various projects ranging from cost reporting solutions to the development of systems for automated testing. His main research interest lies in the correlation between business documents, business processes, and process stakeholders. Institut für Informationssysteme der Hochschule für Angewandte Wissenschaften Hof, Hof, Germany, e-mail: dominik.reichelt@hof-university.de

Thomas Rothschädl graduated from the Johannes Kepler University in Linz, Austria, in Business Informatics. In 2011, he joined the Metasonic Research and Development team. His major topics have been cross-organizational business processes, ad/hoc adaptation of subject-oriented business processes, and the tangible modeling table "Metasonic Touch." From October 2012 to June 2013, he was visiting researcher at the Research Exchange Project IANES: Interactive Acquisition, Negotiation and Enactment of Subject-oriented Business Process Knowledge. Ruxit, Linz, Austria, e-mail: Thomas.rothschaedl@ruxit.com

Thomas Schaller studied business computer science focusing on system development, office automation, and operational production systems at the University of Bamberg, where he also graduated in the field of workflow management systems. Having worked for Bertelsmann AG and Loewe AG, where he was able to gather practical experience, he was appointed to Hof University as a lecturer in the field "Computer-assisted Business Processes." Since then, he has been heading the course "Administrative IT," which is carried out together with the Fachhochschule für Öffentliche Verwaltung und Rechtspflege (University of Public Administration and Administration of Justice) in Hof. Generally, his field of research includes the automation of business processes in corporations and administrations. Institut für Informationssysteme der Hochschule für Angewandte Wissenschaften Hof, Hof, Germany, e-mail: thomas.schaller@iisys.de

Werner Schmidt is a Professor of Business Informatics at Technische Hochschule Ingolstadt (THI) Business School, Germany. His teaching and research areas include business process management and IT management. In these areas, he is (co-)author/editor of some books, conference proceedings, and numerous research papers. He has organized and chaired several academic events and is regularly serving on the program committee of several conferences (e.g., www.s-bpm-one.org). Werner is co-founder and chairperson of the Institute of Innovative Process Management (www.i2pm.net). He has many years of industry experience in BPM and software development projects, gained while working for software and service providers such as Datev eG. Technische Hochschule Ingolstadt Business School, Ingolstadt, Germany, e-mail: Werner.schmidt@thi.de

Peter Schott Chair for Information Systems holds a master's degree in Industrial Engineering and Management. Currently, he works as a research assistant and Ph.D. student at the Chair of Information Systems II at the University of Erlangen-Nuremberg. His research emphasizes process and production optimization and complexity management, especially in the context of Industry 4.0. During several work placements, he gained insights into the process and production departments of globally active, large-scale enterprises and was able to underpin his theoretical knowledge with practical know-how. Services-Processes-Intelligence, University of Erlangen-Nuremberg, Nuremberg, Germany, e-mail: peter.schott@fau.de

Robert Singer is a Professor of Business Management at the Department of Computer Sciences, FH JOANNEUM—University of Applied Sciences in Graz, Austria. In 1988, he started his career as researcher at the Institute of Experimental Physics at the University of Graz. Afterward, he was a senior consultant in a multinational company, and from 1996 until the end of 1998, he held the position of a department head (production and logistics) at a manufacturing facility in Hungary.

Later, he was CEO of several companies in the field of IT and business consulting and founder of a consulting firm. His research interests are in operations and business process management, socio-technical systems, and management. FH-Joanneum—University of Applied Sciences, Graz, Austria, e-mail: robert.singer@fh-joanneum.at

Marc Sprogies IT Business and Client Engineer is a bachelor student of Business Informatics at Technische Hochschule Ingolstadt (THI). He works part-time as an IT Business and Client Engineer at WK EDV GmbH, a medium-sized IT service provider well established in the regional market. In this position, Marc is involved in many facets of ITIL-based service delivery and improvement. Before joining the bachelor program at university, he first completed an apprenticeship as "Informatik-Kaufmann" in the German dual education system. After that, he worked as an assistant to the CIO in the headquarters of a large grocery store with many outlets, where he gained comprehensive insights into managing an IT department. WK EDV GmbH, Ingolstadt, Germany, e-mail: marc.sprogies@t-online.de

Christian Stary as a computer scientist, he completed his Ph.D. in Usability Engineering in 1988 at the Vienna University of Technology, while studying Philosophy of Science and Psychology at the University of Vienna. He was promoted in Applied Computer Science for associate professorship at the Vienna University of Technology before holding a visiting position at Florida International University and being appointed in Linz in 1995. His research interests are interactive knowledge elicitation, learning, and knowledge processing. Besides teaching fundamentals and applications of interactive knowledge management techniques and distributed technologies, he is a principal investigator in national and international research and development projects, such as TwinTide (design and evaluation method transferability across industry sectors) and SoPCPro (Subject-Orientation for People-Centered Production). Department of Business Information Systems—Communications Engineering, Knowledge Management Competence Center, Johannes Kepler University of Linz, Linz, Austria, e-mail: christian.stary@JKU.at

Introduction

1

Albert Fleischmann, Werner Schmidt and Christian Stary

Subject orientation, as introduced in (Fleischmann et al. 2012), aims for contextual design of socio-economic and socio-technical systems primarily from an interaction perspective. The S-BPM (Subject-oriented Business Process Management) modeling language reflects the trend towards semantic specification and processing. Although S-BPM is a domain-independent approach, each application is case-sensitive, even when validated models can be executed automatically, thus enabling seamless roundtrip engineering. Infrastructures, in terms of both organizational and technical characteristics, such as project-like organization of work, service-oriented architectures and cloud computing, need to be integrated along each life cycle.

While traditional approaches to modeling are mainly driven by functional and hierarchical decomposition of value chains, S-BPM considers behavior primarily emerging from the interaction between active system elements termed subjects, based on behaviors encapsulated within the individual subjects. Particular bundles of activities and their iterations enable adapted or novel organizational behavior, becoming manifest in the various levels of organizational development. Each level corresponds to a certain level of organizational maturity, and can be achieved either

A. Fleischmann
Interaktiv Expert, 85276 Pfaffenhofen, Germany
e-mail: albert.fleischmann@interaktiv.expert

W. Schmidt
Technische Hochschule Ingolstadt Business School, Ingolstadt, Germany
e-mail: Werner.schmidt@thi.de

C. Stary (✉)
Department of Business Information Systems—Communications Engineering Knowledge Management Competence Center, Johannes Kepler University of Linz, Linz, Austria
e-mail: christian.stary@JKU.at

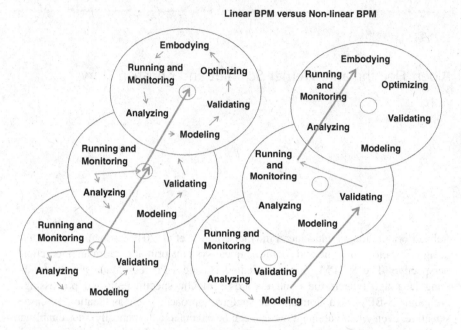

Fig. 1.1 Patterns of organizational development driven by S-BPM

in a linear or a non-linear sequence of S-BPM activity bundles, as indicated in Fig. 1.1.

Linear development (left part of the figure) corresponds to traditional life cycle approaches to Business Process Management (BPM) (cf. Weske 2012): In order to complete a phase each activity has to be executed, and needs to be completed at least one time before entering the next life cycle (i.e., the next level in development), even when there are cyclic activities within each life cycle, such as modeling and validating models several times. The transition to the next BPM step is traditionally defined by reaching a dedicated bundle of activities, mainly running and monitoring. It allows observing running a business after modeling and embodying processes into the operation, and before analyzing the effect of implemented process changes. It corresponds to entering already the next BPM cycle, as indicated when following the bold directed link to the upper level in the figure.

In the *non-linear S-BPM approach* (right part of the figure) reaching the next step of organizational development is characterized by being able to switch to a higher stage of development (displayed as the upper layer) from each of the activities, as indicated in the figure through the bold directed arcs. The most typical example is changing individual functional behavior while keeping the interaction interface to other subjects. It allows improving the individual organization of work on the fly.

However, its effects become evident on the organizational level through monitoring the concerned subject's behavior in its operative context. Since this emergence of organizational behavior resulting from individual functional behavior modification can be driven by several subjects, the results need to be evaluated (monitoring and analyzing) on another level of organizational development than the one where the changes actually occurred. The more an execution engine is intertwined with the activities of the life cycle, the more can direct effects of changes be experienced and the more likely stakeholder changes lead to the next level of organizational development. It accelerates organizational development.

When handling the S-BPM life cycle in a non-linear way, modeling has to be considered one of the core activities, as models may serve as focal points for improvements or for changes of the communication behavior before becoming effective on the operational level. In S-BPM the organizational and subject-specific levels and their interfaces are addressed in a consistent way. An organization is represented in terms of interacting subjects specified in the S-BPM Interaction Diagram. Outcome is generated through the exchange of business objects that are processed by functions. Functions are performed by the involved subjects, and are specified in the S-BPM Behavior Diagram.

In this way, S-BPM captures all essential aspects of BPM, namely the Who, the What, the How, and the When. However, it is the communication-oriented way of specifying organizational and stakeholder behavior that ensures coherence and reducing complexity in change management. Hence, there are several ways of applying S-BPM. Field studies, such as qualitative descriptive reporting, have turned out useful for demonstrating the practicability of novel paradigms and the state of affairs in the field (cf. Senge et al. 1994). A field study is generically a story. It presents the concrete narrative detail of actual events. It has a plot, an exposition, characters, and sometimes even dialogue. Each study focuses on an essential issue, such as capturing exception handling in business through extending subject behavior diagrams with non-routine behavior, as it is not only a description, but also an analysis.

The authors of a case explain step-by-step how the story develops, and give readers context in each step for the explanation and conclusion drawn. This contextualization also relates the happenings to the concepts or theories of S-BPM, in particular how a certain framework, procedure, concept or feature can drive or drives a case. Besides capturing the processes of data collection and analysis, interventions or disruptions are listed, along with a strong attempt to make connections between the data and the analysis (conclusions) evident. Since field studies tend to be exploratory, most end with implications for further study. Here, significant variables are identified that emerged in the course of the study, and lead to suggesting S-BPM novelties. Implications for contextual factors, such as skills of project participants, are helpful for conveying a complete picture of the case.

The field studies could be clustered according to three main S-BPM themes:

- *Business Operation Support* documents approaches to the practical development of S-BPM solutions in various application domains and organizational settings.
- *Consultancy and Education Support* provides cases helping to train S-BPM modeling and knowledge acquisition for S-BPM life cycle iterations. It also

refers to architecting S-BPM solutions for application cases based on experience knowledge.

- *Technical Execution Support* comprises concepts for utilizing specific theories and technologies for executing S-BPM models. It also refers to building reference models for certain settings in the field.

In part I, *Business Operation Support*, in five field studies S-BPM support is addressed from practical cases, ranging from value-driven and strategic development to implementing subject-oriented workflows.

- Matthias Lederer et al. report on interfacing strategic management with subject-oriented processes in manufacturing. They demonstrate how strategic objectives of an organization can be put in relation to operational S-BPM models, namely using novel developed Strategy Process Matrices.
- Augl et al. demonstrate how to integrate S-BPM into organizational development, in terms of acquiring work knowledge and bringing it to operation via S-BPM models. They introduce Value Network Analysis as an intermediate representation and processing technique for effective change.
- Sprogies et al. tell the story of how an IT service provider managed to establish agile, flexible and transparent processes to meet customer needs. They address the software deployment process as part of application lifecycle management by following the various bundles of the S-BPM life cycle up to executing and monitoring S-BPM models.
- Lothar Hübner documents how employees in the business departments can be qualified to compile large and complex processes exemplifying the introduction of an IT hardware service process. Besides the technical feasibility, the economic impact of approaching such projects by S-BPM is demonstrated.
- Frank Lorbacher's narrative concerns the design of an IT information architecture while taking into account an existing customer's infrastructure. In the field study business processes could be consistently propagated to Enterprise Resource Planning (ERP) functions for contract performance. Besides increasing flexibility in process design, the time for billing cycles could be reduced, which in turn influences worker satisfaction positively.

In part II, *Consultancy and Education Support*, six field studies provide conceptual inputs to design S-BPM projects, and utilize tools supporting modeling intuitively, and thus, education on the fly.

- Harman et al. demonstrate how accurate process model elicitation can be achieved while minimizing the effort of recognizing information items and specifying processes. When walking through a 3D Virtual World relevant information is marked and tagged to become part of S-BPM models. The proof of concept has been evaluated involving S-BPM tool developers.

- Fleischmann's field study concerns the usefulness and usability of the S-BPM Buildbook. This modeling device is intended to be utilized by modeling novices due to its intuitive design—it provides 3D notational elements and 3D specification support. Once a minimal set of rules is followed, consistent models can be constructed and processed for execution. Several process surveys could be completed successfully using this device.
- Christoph Piller's case addresses the effectiveness of maintenance in production. Guided by the Total Productive Management method for unplanned maintenance tasks, he created a reference model for the corresponding business process. It is available in the S-BPM notation and can be customized for different application domains.
- Thomas Schaller et al. tackled role and right management in business process management through S-BPM. Enriching S-BPM with role and right management leads to highly contextualized process designs.
- Singer et al. combine S-BPM with modeling and implementing business rules. They enhance the agility of workflows by incorporating decision making procedures. Using such transparent representations and coupling a rule engine to S-BPM runtime tools, the transformation of a business towards a digital organization becomes more context-sensitive and straightforward.
- Udo Kannengießer describes a manufacturing scenario along a developers' dialog, when agents are used for implementing subject-oriented process models. Using computational agent technology requires specific mappings of subjects to agents, and dedicated control mechanisms when executing subject behavior.

In part III, *Technical Execution Support*, three field studies provide insights into implementation requirements, taking an execution perspective on processes while recognizing technological and/or organizational particularities.

- Harald Lerchner reminds us about the benefits of a precise semantic specification in BPM, as semantic ambiguities encoded in process models could result in unintended organizational effects throughout execution. Exploring the capabilities of Abstract State Machines, S-BPM models can be interpreted in terms of both their semantic precision and their automated execution. The developed workflow engine serves as baseline and reference implementation for further language and processing developments.
- Singer et al. report on testing Microsoft technologies and reflect on a platform for modeling and executing business processes as interaction between actors. For networking organizations the technology serves as a multi-enterprise business process platform using cloud technology.
- Max Dirndorfer's field study supports organizations which intend to execute S-BPM processes while running a standard ERP system. His story reveals not only a strategy on how to tackle the implementation of an organization's work practice in S-BPM based on ERP system features, but also reports on setting up and running the corresponding change management projects.

From a methodological perspective, most of the authors followed a non-personal style of presenting their stories, while two of them decided to present their case in a dialog format, aiming to reach even the non-technical audience with implementation-relevant S-BPM issues.

Table 1.1 reflects the richness of stories when looking at the provided narratives from different perspectives. It contains all field studies clustered according to their type of core support, thus ranging from Business Operation to Technical Execution Support. The categories in the top row of the table allow a more detailed consideration of each contribution:

- *Application Domains* reveal in what type of industry or area of work practice the field study stems from or can be applied.
- *System Architecture/Tool Chain Issues* refer to system components and their interactions that turn out to be relevant when implementing communication-oriented BPM.
- *S-BPM Life Cycle Bundles* provide insight into the scope of (S-)BPM activities that have been tackled in the field study.
- *Methodological Developments* revisit each contribution in terms of methods that fit the various cornerstones of the S-BPM methodology.
- *Organizational Relevance* indicates for practitioners the significance of each field study to organizational development and change management.

Looking at the table, several patterns can be recognized on a first glance, leading to some reading recommendations once readers prefer certain semantic access routes to the field studies:

- S-BPM has been applied successfully in the service and production industries. It seems to scale quite well for networking and bootstrapping.
- Legacy systems, such as Enterprise Resource Planning systems, can be addressed in a variety of strategic and technical ways. Hence, S-BPM is not a radical re-engineering approach. It rather can be aligned with existing infrastructures and implementation approaches.
- Only few findings exist referring to the economic impact of S-BPM, although its potential is revealed through constructive stakeholder engagement.
- The prominent role of modeling becomes evident when looking to the addressed bundles of the life cycle and the baseline serving for acquisition (analysis) and (direct) execution.
- Methodologically, pre-processing knowledge seems to be of vital interest, either approached on the strategic level or addressed in the analysis or modeling phase.

Table 1.1 (a) Business operation support, (b) consultancy and education support, (c) technical execution support

Chapter	Field of interest				
	Application domains	System architecture/ tool chain issues	S-BPM life cycle bundles	Methodological developments	Organizational relevance
(a)					
2 Lederer et al.	Customer service product development manufacturing	Organizational networking	(Strategic) optimization monitoring	Strategy process matrix	Strategic management → operation
3 Augl et al.	Health care clinics		Analysis modeling optimization	Value network analysis for elicitation and pre-processing	Value-driven process management
4 Sprogies et al.	IT service provision SW-deployment		Analysis → execution	Subject-oriented application lifecycle management	Process flexibility
5 Hübner	IT hardware service provision	ERP database integration	Modeling execution	S-BPM driven data management	Effectivity gains
6 Lorbacher	Service provision	Process layer on top of ERP system	Modeling → execution	Separating business logic from data management	Shifting from ERP- to workflow management

(continued)

Table 1.1 (continued)

Chapter	Field of interest				
	Application domains	System architecture/tool chain issues	S-BPM life cycle bundles	Methodological developments	Organizational relevance
(b)					
7 Harman et al.	Human resource management	Articulation front end to S-BPM modeling and execution tools	Integrated analysis and modeling	3D virtual world elicitation of S-BPM-relevant process information	Immediate, since walk-along/through workplace elicitation of process knowledge
8 Fleischmann	Manufacturing service industry	3D S-BPM modeling front end to execution tool	Analysis → modeling	Tangible subject-oriented structure elaboration	Easy-to-grasp (stakeholder-centered) individual work knowledge elicitation
9 Piller	Production—maintenance of equipment	Reference model	Modeling	Total productive management reference model	Lean management best practice representation
10 Schaller et al.	Service processes (HR, claims processing)	Role representation server for organizational implementation	Modeling organizational implementation	Embodying traditional organization models	Role/access rights management
11 Singer et al.	Logistics	StrICT windows reference architecture for implementation BizTalk rule engine access for subject's function states	BizTalk rule modeling → implementation	Business rule representation and S-BPM Integration	Transparency of decision making business rule management
12 Kannengießer	Manufacturing	Agent-based execution of subject behavior	Modeling → execution	Assigning agents to subjects for technical implementation	Shopfloor operation management

(continued)

Table 1.1 (continued)

Chapter	Field of interest				
	Application domains	System architecture/tool chain issues	S-BPM life cycle bundles	Methodological developments	Organizational relevance
(c)					
13 Lerchner	Manufacturing	Model interpreter execution	Model transformation for execution	Semantic specification of S-BPM models	Semantic understanding of S-BPM models
14 Singer et al.	Manufacturing	Open vendor-specific execution utilizing cloud	Modeling → execution	Multi-enterprise process platform	Cloud-based execution of processes
15 Dirndorfer	Customer request handling	ERP integration via enterprise service bus, API, web service protocol	Modeling → execution	ERP-integration strategy for business processes (mapping ERP functions to S-BPM business objects)	Implementation follows IT strategy embracing ERP connectivity

Based on these findings the following chapter lists could serve as a quick reference for readers who want to jump to stories motivated by one of the topics listed:
S-BPM Methodology:

- For starters: 4, 7, 8, Appendix
- For experienced: 2, 3, 5, 6, 9–15
- For switchers from other approaches and transformers to S-BPM: 2–8, 10, 11, 12, 14, 15

S-BPM Application:

- Process industry: 2, 8, 9, 12, 13, 14
- Service industry: 2, 3, 4, 5, 6, 7, 8, 10, 11, 15
- Hybrid industry: 2, 8
- Non-profit organizations: 3

S-BPM Education and Capacity Development:

- Study programs: 2, 3, 4, 7, 8, 9, 15
- Learning environments: 4, 7, 8, 13
- Paradigmatic and systems thinking: 2, 3, 4, 5, 6, 8, 10, 12

S-BPM Technology Highlights:

- Processing environments: 4, 5, 6, 7, 8, 10, 11, 13, 14, 15
- Conceptual and/or algorithmic breakthroughs: 6, 7, 8, 10, 11, 12

Finally, the Appendix provides all relevant aspects for grasping S-BPM modeling and applying it based on fundamental examples. Its presentation format aims to balance semantic precision and syntactic rigor. However, it should suit the needs of both novices and experienced practitioners.

References

Fleischmann A, Schmidt W, Stary C, Obermeier S, Börger E (2012) Subject-oriented business process management. Springer, Berlin
Senge P, Kleiner A, Roberts C, Ross R, Smith B (1994) The fifth discipline fieldbook. Currency, New York
Weske M (2012) Business process management. Concepts, languages, architectures, 2nd edn. Springer, Berlin

Part I
Business Operation Support

Subject-Oriented Business Processes Meet Strategic Management: Two Case Studies from the Manufacturing Industry

2

Matthias Lederer, Peter Schott and Matthias Kurz

Abstract

Successful companies use business processes for the transfer of long-term strategies in operational workflows. The modeling approach presented in this chapter shows how strategic objectives of a company can be combined with the S-BPM modeling notation. The new modeling approach is used in two case studies. First, redesign rules for the strategic optimization of workflow models are demonstrated in the case of the customer support processes of an international enterprise. A second case study introduces a company-wide monitoring system through the example of the product development process of a multinational company from Germany.

M. Lederer (✉) · P. Schott
Information Systems (Services-Processes-Intelligence), University of Erlangen-Nuremberg, Lange Gasse 20, 90403 Nuremberg, Germany
e-mail: matthias.lederer@fau.de

P. Schott
e-mail: peter.schott@fau.de

M. Kurz
QUA-LiS NRW, Paradieser Weg 64, 59494 Soest, Germany
e-mail: Matthias.kurz@qua-lis.nrw.de

© The Author(s) 2015
A. Fleischmann et al. (eds.), *S-BPM in the Wild*,
DOI 10.1007/978-3-319-17542-3_2

2.1   Motivation

"How beautiful the strategy, you should occasionally look at the results".[1]

This statement suggests that strategies need an adequate implementation and measurable results in order to become alive. Successful companies know how to operationalize sustainable strategies, which means to translate long-term goals into daily business (Wolf and Harmon 2012). Business processes are a core way for organizations to operationalize strategic objectives in workflows (Mintzberg 1994). However, studies show that process managers are struggling with making this critical transfer (Minonne and Turner 2012; Sidorova and Isik 2010).

The two companies serving as case studies in this chapter were confronted with this problem in two different stages of the BPM lifecycle. The first manufacturing company needed an approach to *redesign customer support processes strategically*. In the second case, a control system was needed that allows checking *whether innovation strategies were implemented in product development processes* modeled in S-BPM. These two situations are typical challenges of companies because strategic objectives (e.g., increasing customer satisfaction, minimization of time to market, etc.) are often not systematically taken into account during typical BPM activities (Hörschgen 2001). There are two basic aspects for incorporating strategy in business processes (Petzmann et al. 2007):

- First, strategic guidelines need to be incorporated in the *process models*. This implies that process models need to be designed so that they can implement strategic objectives when they are executed. If, for example, the strategic goal in the first case study is to increase customer satisfaction by fast issue handling, the S-BPM model should include elements (e.g., activities or documents) which are suitable to achieve this goal (e.g., forwarding scenarios and role models if a decision maker is not working fast enough).
- Second, once the models are aligned, the achievements of strategic objectives need to be managed in everyday business. That means monitoring and controlling *process instances*. This way, process owners can check if workflows follow the strategy. In the second example, a suitable control system should answer the question of whether development projects are forcing the strategic objective of increasing technology push innovations.

In this context and as well as in the two scenarios, the S-BPM approach focuses on one of the most essential factors for strategy implementation (Outram 2014): humans. Studies show that the consideration of human factors such as communication and understanding (Mair 2002), compliant leadership (Weber and Schäffer 2000) as well as motivation (Richardson 2004) for strategic long-term issues are

---

[1]Winston Churchill, British politician (1874–1965).

essential for the uptake and implementation of strategic objectives. In customer support processes, requests are processed better the more accurately employees understand the objectives behind the procedures.

The modeling approach by Lederer et al. (2014a, b) shows how strategies and S-BPM models can be integrated in a communicable diagram. This *Strategy Process Matrix* is used in this chapter as a basis (Sect. 2.2). Two approaches were developed in real-case scenarios to increase the degree of strategy orientation both in S-BPM models (Sect. 2.3) as well as in *process instances* (Sect. 2.4).

In a nutshell, this contribution complements the well-known and comprehensive approaches, methods, and IT applications which exist for S-BPM by integrating principles of strategic management in the subject-orientated thinking.

2.2 Strategy-Oriented Business Process Modeling[2]

The strategy-oriented business process modeling (SOBPM) approach provides both a method and a notation for linking process models with strategy. The approach combines strategic targets (*strategy*) with the workflow of a *business process*. The resulting *Strategy Process Matrix* realizes the essential basis for the case studies.

2.2.1 Strategy Map

The Balanced Scorecard (BSc) is a widely used (Chen and Jones 2009) standard tool in business practice (Chavan 2009). It groups an organization's strategic objectives in four perspectives. A Strategy Map (Quezada et al. 2009) depicts these objectives along with their dependencies using causal chains (Kaplan and Norton 1996). While the four perspectives of the BSc ensure a holistic view on the objectives (Quezada et al. 2009), the Strategy Map assists in interpreting the dependencies between objectives.

Section 2.3 shows how to combine Strategy Maps and S-BPM business process models using the Strategy Process Matrix. In the SOBPM approach, this combination requires two adjustments. First, the customer perspective of the BSc is generalized into the *stakeholder perspective*. That way, objectives can be assigned to all internal and external stakeholders of a business process (e.g., internal customers as well as external organizations). Second, entries in the Strategy Map need to be modeled on *unique vertical levels*. This means that each row of the Strategy Map contains only one objective.

---

[2]Substantial parts of the modeling approach documentation are taken from Lederer et al. (2014a, b).

2.2.2 Business Process Model

There are numerous possibilities for the formal as well as semi-formal representation of business processes. The SOBPM approach was originally developed by using BPMN but case studies and applications (e.g., see Sects. 2.3 and 2.4) show that both Subject Behavior (SBD) and Subject Interaction Diagrams (SID) can be used for visualizing business process in the SOBPM approach. In any case, regardless of the chosen process notation, one adjustment is necessary: To later ensure an easy-to-understand layout of the Strategy Process Matrix, each *flow object* contributing to one or more strategic objectives needs to be designed horizontally on a unique level in the model. This means that no flow node may be placed below another flow node. Flow objects are understood as nodes which have the potential to execute a strategy (e.g., activities, messages, tasks). If there are parallel sequence flows with relevant nodes, one of the flow nodes must be moved to the right.

2.2.3 Strategy Process Matrix

The graphical connection between strategic objectives and the process flow creates the *Strategy Process Matrix* (see Fig. 2.1): The matrix combines each objective of the Strategy Map (lines) with flow objects of the process flow (rows).

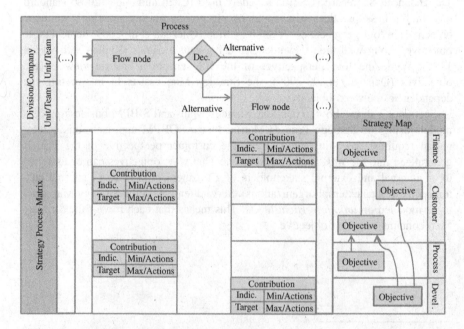

Fig. 2.1 Structure of the matrix (Lederer et al. 2015)

The Strategy Process Matrix essentially is a table. This table's columns are defined by the flow objects of the process model. Correspondingly, the table's rows are the strategic objectives of the Strategy Map. Each flow object (perhaps enriched by modeling elements like databases or documents if BPMN is used) may be assigned to one or more objectives. If multiple flow objects support the achievement of an objective, several fields of the matrix may contain information in the same row. Within each matrix field, the following four pieces of information should be documented: (1) *Contribution* (How does a flow object support strategy achievement?), (2) *indicator* (Which event, status or quantitative performance indicator can measure the contribution?), (3) *target* (What is the target value for the indicator and what deviations are acceptable?), (4) *min/max action* (What actions should be taken if the indicator cannot meet the target value?).

In the case of *Subject Behavior Diagrams* (SBD), function states of the process model are assigned to a unique horizontal place, because they contribute to the achievements of strategic targets. Since transitions present only the change of states and sending as well as receiving states are not able to execute strategic intentions of an organization, they are not modeled in unique columns. Figure 2.2 shows the illustrative and modified excerpt of a Strategy Process Matrix using an SBD from a case study from the automotive industry: The process of transferring recorded data to internal (e.g., legal department) and external (e.g., suppliers and other partners) stakeholders strives for increasing profitability which includes improved stakeholder relations. Moreover, the process has to follow external regulations, such as compliance standards which require a highly skilled process team. Also, the business process needs to increase the quality of data. The process workflow describes a data request from an external partner sent to an internal clerk from the data management team. This skilled worker receives the data request and decides,

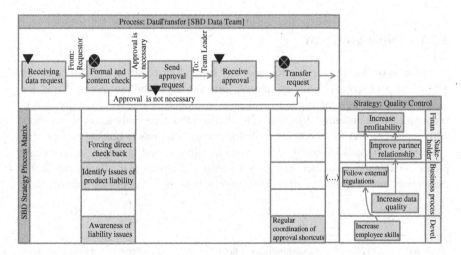

Fig. 2.2 Extract of a subject behavior matrix (Lederer et al. 2015)

based on a content check, if an approval by the team lead is necessary or if the data can directly be transferred to the external requestor.

In the Strategy Process Matrix, it becomes evident that many functions make contributions to the achievement of strategic objectives. For example, the activities of the formal examination and the granting of permits to make a special contribution to the operationalization of the strategic objectives, and in particular, to the compliance with external laws and internal process standards.

With the SBD diagram, representing process steps from the actor's point of view, contributions can be identified based on subjects. In strategic optimization projects, oftentimes, not all actors need to be examined in detail. Instead of examining or explaining the entire process, the contributions of one single subject can be used to show strategy-relevant actions. Furthermore, limiting the matrix to the SBD of a single subject yields a smaller matrix with fewer entries.

In the *Subject Interaction Diagram* (SID), each message needs to be arranged on a unique horizontal level. Since both case studies in this contribution are using the SBD-based matrix, the modeling approach using SID will not be explained. The interested reader may refer to (Lederer et al. 2014a, b), where the SID-based Strategy Process Matrix is outlined.

2.3   Case Study on Strategic Improvement of S-BPM Models

By now, the Strategy Process Matrix has been tested in different domains (e.g., product development and logistics) for analyzing, designing, and describing processes from a strategic point of view. This chapter shows a case study using this modeling approach for an intuitive redesign of S-BPM *process models* based on the rules developed by Lederer et al. (2014a, b) and Lederer and Huber (2014).

2.3.1   Initial Situation

The process owner, responsible for customer support processes in a global company located in Switzerland[3] with an annual turnover of 15 billion Euros, faced the challenge to redesign the implemented process models in one business division in accordance with business objectives. The division this case study looks at has about 200 employees and sells complex tools for energy solutions to business customers. Since some products are highly complex to install, use, and maintain, the company provides extensive customer support via phone and e-mail (e.g., clients can report complaints and warranty issues). The process models for customer support have

---

[3]For confidentiality, the name of the company is not mentioned and contents of the case study were modified, added or anonymized.

grown since they were designed some years ago. This development has been concurrent with the major problem that the process and its performance measurement no longer follow the strategy of the customer support: Although the vision of the company was to become a leader in innovation, the customer inquiries were processed in such a way that this objective was not achieved systematically. Moreover, the strategic objectives from the top management to the customer support team were to force the sales of additional products and services as well as to ensure a fast issue handling. Due to a high failure rate in the preceding years, the process team was criticized internally. Therefore, the process owner added the objective of increasing the internal reputation in addition to external customer satisfaction.

To foster these objectives, a project team consisting of the process owner, two process team members and an external consultant was established to redesign the process models.

2.3.2 As-Is Analysis

In the case study, the corporate strategy was cascaded in two workshops to the customer support. The project team used different methods (e.g., on-the-job observation and interviews) to design the actual process using several modeling notations including SBDs. Analyzing the current situation, eight fundamental processes could be identified and in all cases neither sufficient performance indicators were documented, nor were strategic objectives explicitly modeled.

The process *warranty first contact* (see left part of Fig. 2.3) as a small part of the process models is well suited to illustrate the optimization. The process starts when the clerk realizes that the customer call refers to a warranty request. The support first checks whether the warranty agreement is still valid. If so, the clerk collects the relevant contract details and determines the internal contact person in the operative department. If a warranty agreement is no longer valid, the customer has the opportunity to book an additional but more expensive warranty agreement to regulate his or her damage. This pre-sales activity is performed by the customer support team and if the client is willing to upgrade his contract, he or she is put through to the sales team.

When analyzing the resulting Strategy Process Matrix of the as-is model (see Fig. 2.3), it became evident that only two of the five given strategic objectives were supported systematically in the process. Moreover, it became obvious that two actions do not serve any strategic target at all. In a detailed analysis it also became evident that the up-selling services of the support team were rarely successful. Since only few indicators were available in the case study, the positive matrix fields in the as-is model are only marked by a color and not by an explanation.

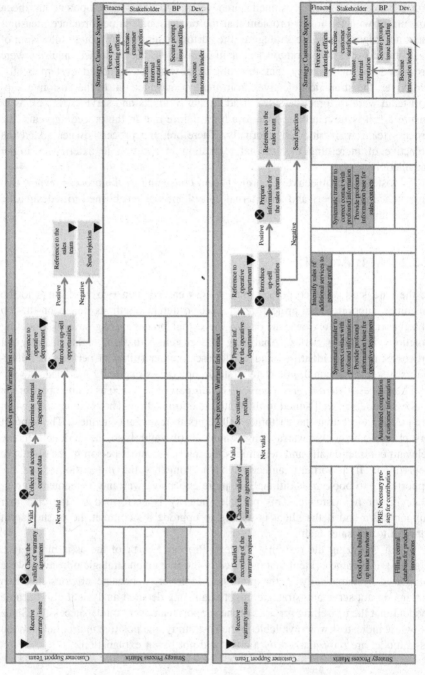

Fig. 2.3 As-is and to-be-modeling of the sample scenario (Petzmann et al. 2007; Quezada et al. 2009)

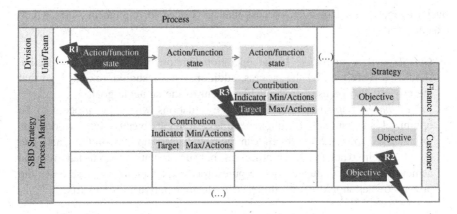

Fig. 2.4 Optimization rules for the subject behavior matrix (Von der Oelsnitz 2009)

2.3.3   Optimization Approach

Realizing these weaknesses, the project team developed three rules for an intuitive process optimization (visualized in Fig. 2.4) to adapt strategy-orientation in SBDs by following the concepts of *connectivity* (explicitly linking performed work to overarching objectives), *simplification* (questioning process models with respect to their relevance for company targets) and performance *measurement* (evaluating workflow performance) (Chen et al. 2009).

R1: "Strive for connectivity"
This rule focuses on the adaption of activities without strategy contribution. The matrix can show function states without any strategic contribution. This is indicated by an empty matrix column. In this case, two corrective actions are possible:

- *Removing state*: First is to look closely at whether the visualized function or action is necessary at all. If the action or function does not help in achieving an objective, the analyst should consider whether the activity binds resources, slows down the process time, or comes with handling costs. That way the analyst may determine whether there is sufficient reason for this activity to remain.
- *Outlining support states*: However, some function states need to be performed due to internal requirements (e.g., data backup steps), dependencies on other processes (e.g., documentation tasks in IT systems) or dependencies on other states in the same process (e.g., automated preliminary data check before interpretation). These linkages should be outlined in the matrix field.

R2: "Strive for simplification"
This rule stands for avoiding objectives which are not operationalized. If the matrix shows rows free of contributions, this can indicate a missing operationalization of

business objectives. However, process managers need to implement states which execute strategies:

- *Complement of activities*: If the operationalization of the strategic objective should be performed by the process, additional states should be added, so that the process also focuses on the achievement of the strategic goal.
- *Project-based implementation*: There are situations where the process to be optimized is not suitable for implementing a strategic objective (e.g., workshops to redesign software interfaces can help to speed up a workflow and can therefore help to achieve faster processes, but such initiatives can usually only be achieved in projects outside of the pure process execution). In these cases the process owner should clarify this fact by documentation in the matrix.

R3: "Strive for measurement"
This rule requests adjustments of matrix fields with a permanent non-achievement of contributions. In contrast to the other rules, this view does not focus on the creation or representation of strategy-orientation but addresses their actual achievement. This problem can be detected if target values in the matrix field cannot be achieved repeatedly. If the documented actions in the matrix fields have not been taken, they have to be executed first. If these actions cannot ensure that the expected indicator values are achieved, the following four corrections for changing the process model are available:

- *Correct arrangement of actions*: First, it should be examined if the defined actions are sufficient, meaning whether they are suitable to influence the performance indicator in a positive manner. Measures with an unclear effect on the indicator (and thus on the strategic objective) should be replaced by more effective actions. Moreover, large actions (e.g., one day staff training) should also be split (e.g., into the individual contents of the training) to better identify the lack of effectiveness of individual components.
- *Correct contents of actions*: Furthermore it is necessary to examine whether the actions to be taken are equipped with too few or the wrong resources. In the case of staff resources, the motivation, the competences, and the time availability need to be analyzed. IT resources (e.g., software tools and interfaces) must be examined focusing on their effectiveness.
- *Correct targets*: Usually the process owner is responsible for the design of the model including the matrix, while the objectives of the Strategy Map are given by his or her superiors or are developed together with him or her. Therefore the documented targets need also to be examined critically. Optimizing this point, the matrix offers an innovative way: From the matrix it is quickly transparent which process activities also contribute to a given objective. Sometimes less expensive, faster, or easier-to-handle actions or functions in the same row can be taken. Thus, the matrix can support a more efficient allocation of resources.

- *Correct indicator*: The indicator should also be checked for typical quality criteria. Thus, the process owner should carefully determine whether the implemented performance indicator is strategy-oriented, meaningful, actionable, and traceable. Inappropriate indicators are to be replaced.

2.3.4 To-Be Modeling

In workshops, the optimization rules have been applied step by step based on the chronological sequence of all processes. In the meetings, two employees of the support team, an external consultant, and the process owner were involved. For each state, the three rules were applied in creative meetings.

First, each status was checked according its contribution to objectives (R1). The contributions were briefly listed and later refined. Process stakeholders were mostly in the position to give a qualitative assessment on whether the objectives have been achieved (R3). Second, R2 was applied at the end of the workshop globally for the whole process.

In the case that workshop participants could not come to an adequate result, the workshop continued with the sequence of the states. Like this, the creative and motivating working atmosphere was preserved.

Critical cases where initially no solution could be found (e.g., process simplification, see R1) or in which the parties had different views (e.g., for actions following R3) were given to special small groups for further meetings. In particular, little Delphi studies turned out to be very effective: Workshop participants developed ideas separated from each other and then compared their results in a further round.

Finally, all results were summarized and cross-checked with all rules in a third step.

The resulting and optimized process can be found in the right part of Fig. 2.3: One major adjustment in the redesigned process is the introduction of a documentation step before the warranty agreement is checked. With this new documentation, the process owner is now in the position to give a detailed report on product deficiencies and desires of the customers and can thus propose ideas for innovative solutions (indicator: share of innovative solutions from the data base that lead to a proof of concept). Ad hoc requests from other internal positions, which often arise in the regulation of damages, can be answered well founded. This leads to a positive image of the customer support team (indicator: agreement rate to the statement that the customer support is a competent partner). A new IT system is able to display all relevant contract data of the customer based on the warranty agreement information. This allows faster subsequent processing. To address the poor figures of up-selling activities, comprehensive measures are planned in the accompanying documents (an excerpt can be found in Table 2.1). Moreover, new preparatory actions before transferring a customer call to other internal departments can support the work of these departments and improve the customer experience.

Table 2.1 Excerpt of the accompanying matrix documentation (Lederer et al. 2015)

Intensify sales of additional services to generate profit		
Performance indicator	I1: Percentage of customer dialogues which lead to contact with the sales team (annual review)	
	I2: Percentage of up-selling offers which result in premium after sales products (quarterly review)	
Target	I1: 17%; Falling down to 15% is acceptable.	
	I2: 5%; Falling down to 4% is acceptable.	
Actions (excerpt)	In case of falling below	▪ Building pair teams for dialogue situations (support team and sales agent at the phone)
		▪ Training on the training guide for presenting the value proposition
		▪ Fictitious test calls to ensure compliance
Running project-based implementation	▪ Annual workshop to redesign the interview guidelines together with	
	▪ Weekly work on the whiteboard with the best tips and tricks for sales talk	

2.3.5 Evaluation

The application of the optimization approach increased the strategic focus in all eight process groups. The process owner uses the matrix for monitoring the process activities. The metrics-based management of strategic objectives can be used for communicating to the top management. The process team now understands the adjustments based on the matrix as a communication tool very well and is more motivated to align actions with the underlying objectives. All stakeholders share a very positive evaluation of the approach and its impact both on everyday process execution and new optimization rounds. This is primarily attributed to the understandable, intuitive, and visual approach. The company currently considers applying the approach to other processes as well as initiating further developments such as personal scorecards and integrated incentive systems.

2.4   Case Study on Strategic Monitoring of S-BPM Instances

The previous case study from the customer support has shown how to increase strategy implementation for S-BPM *process models*. This case study transfers the third rule of strategic measurement to single *process instances* (Lederer et al. 2015) in order to realize effective strategy monitoring and measurement.

2.4.1 Initial Situation and Approach

The proposed control system was developed and simulated in the context of the product development process of a multinational manufacturing company head-quartered in Germany.[4] The company is in its branch a world-leading producer in a business-to-business value chain. The enterprise employees about 16,000 employees and realizes a turnover of about 2.5 billion euros per year. The company was facing the problem of poor profit, which resulted, among other influences, from inadequate strategic orientation of product development projects. Major reasons for that were identified in

- the missing ability to bring new products into the market in a timely way and before its competitors,
- the tendency to produce what is possible and not what is demanded by the market,
- the missing ability to run through the development process while sticking to the predefined cost goals, and
- the missing ability to develop products that satisfy the quality expectations of potential customers.

As a result, key strategic objectives for the product development process were

- the increase in efficiency in the development process by reducing overhead to bring products into the market more quickly,
- the promotion of customer integration into the development process to increase the market chances of new product development efforts, and
- the improvement of process understanding amongst product developers to enable them to cope with the quality and cost targets.

By pursuing those objectives, the company tried to maximize its market success while developing on a low-cost level and simultaneously promoting the high-quality image of the company. In this context, *middle* (e.g., business division leads) as well as *low management levels* (e.g., project leaders) faced problems justifying their actions in line with business strategy as well as motivating the *process teams* (e.g., technicians, analysts, material specialists) to work in accordance with the tactical and strategic objectives predefined by *higher management levels*. Especially in regions outside of Europe, product development projects had a low degree of compliance and therefore could not be supervised in a systematic and reproducible way on an instance level.

A project team was tasked to design and implement a monitoring system which is able to comprehensively control process instances with respect to corporate strategy. At the same time the system should control the strategic compliance in

---

[4]For confidentiality, the name of the company is not mentioned and some contents of the case study were modified or anonymized.

Fig. 2.5 Product development stage gate process (Von der Oelsnitz 2009)

product development holistically. The implementation of control indicators and the measurement of strategy achievement using the Strategy Process Matrix instead of only focusing on compliance with the budget should help the *middle managers* to monitor several projects in their range of responsibility and should also help the *lower managers* to monitor single product development instances from a balanced strategic target point of view. Short-term objectives (e.g., preventing production risks, realizing material specifications) on instance levels should be controlled and aligned with long-term business goals (e.g., time to market, turnover, etc.).

Comprehensive BPMN process descriptions (e.g., detailed workflows, procedural instructions and documents) were already available at the beginning of the case study: Fig. 2.5 illustrates the stage gate development process of the company on the highest granularity level. Given the fact that the process steps describe a commonly known and widely spread generic development process, it becomes obvious that the process needs to be modeled in a more detailed form in order to be used on operational and tactical levels. Therefore, each stage was modeled as Strategy Process Matrix using SBDs. The contents of the matrix fields were developed in interdisciplinary workshops conducted by a project team globally interviewing project managers with several years of experience in product development. An external BPM consultant assisted in this effort.

2.4.2 Architecture of the Monitoring System

As outlined, the system to be developed by the project team needed to monitor the strategy achievement for single instances (product development projects) as well as across instances (e.g., all projects in a specific business division). Therefore, beyond the top management, which defines the corporate strategy (Von der Oelnitz 2009), two responsibility levels to control operational as well as tactical objectives were involved in the system:

- *Instance level*: The final implementation of strategy is operationalizing strategy in process instances using *operational objectives*. These objectives are managed by the lower managers (e.g., team leader or project manager). In the detailed form of SBDs for a Strategy Process Matrix on instance level, the matrix does not control and optimize process models but focuses on immediate correction actions for individual process instances (e.g., ad hoc adjustments instead of generic and long-term corrective actions for later process instances).

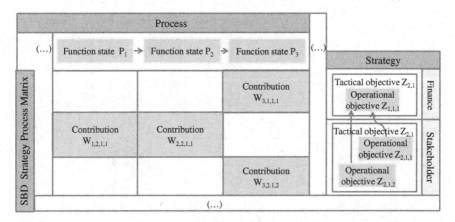

Fig. 2.6 Monitoring system architecture (Von der Oelsnitz 2009)

- *Middle management level*: On the middle management level, the *tactical objective* achievement, meaning mid-term and cross-instance, is controlled by middle managers (e.g., Business Line Directors). This level combines mid-term *tactical objectives* with SBD process models.

The project team came up with the core idea of the control system that is a *horizontal accumulation* of the contributions (e.g., indicators of $w_{1,2,1,1}$ and $w_{2,2,1,1}$) from the matrix for individual function states. By doing so, the overall objective achievement of each objective (e.g., $z_{2,1,1}$) can be calculated (see Fig. 2.6), which was one major target in the scenario. Figure 2.6 outlines that the tactical objectives from the middle level (tactical objectives) are used but may be enriched by additional operational objectives. The operational objective $z_{2,1,2}$ for example is a refinement of the existing objective structure. By a *vertical aggregation* of operational objectives (e.g., $z_{2,1,1}$ and $z_{2,1,2}$) the middle management gets the possibility to control the tactical objective achievement (e.g., $z_{2,1}$).

The matrix shows operational contributions, short-term indicators as well as ad hoc actions which need to be executed if a certain process instance seems not to be able to meet the expectations defined in the model. Since the process model and process descriptions on the middle level set up the specific requirements for all process instances following this model, the operational contributions ($w_{p,lmn}$) and targets (z_{lmn}) documented in the Strategy Map are the same as on the middle level.

Figure 2.7 visualizes the Strategy Process Matrix for the first stage of the stage gate development process for middle managers. Table 2.2 shows a small excerpt of the accompanying documents of the matrix, which were developed in several interviews and in workshops as they were introduced in the first case study.

To make the calculation of the achievement more clear for managers, the range of evaluation values for the indicator fulfillment was chosen between [0,2] according to the assessment suggestion by Benson (2007) (see Table 2.3). This

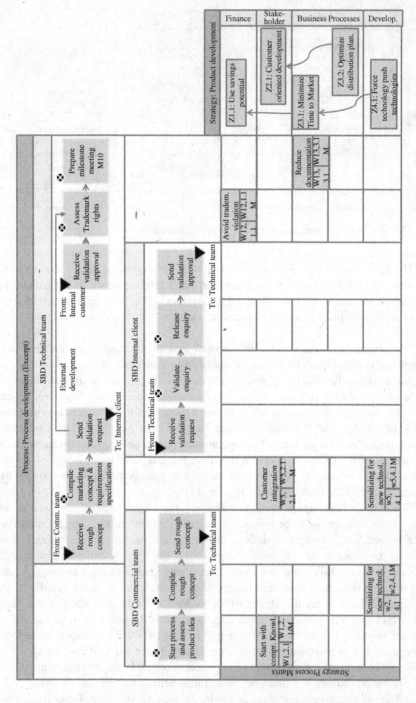

Fig. 2.7 Strategy process matrix using SBDs on middle management level

Table 2.2 Excerpt of the matrix field documentation (Von der Oelsnitz 2009)

Tactical objective	Contribution	Indicator	Actions
$Z_{2.1}$: **Customer-oriented development**	$W_{1,2.1}$: Start of development only with comprehensive knowledge of customer requirements	**(Status 1, 2.1):** Customer requirements are documented correctly and completely	Integration of lead customers before starting a development, obtaining user experiences with prototypes
	$W_{5,2.1}$: Involvement of internal and external customers in requirement specifications	**(Event 5, 2.1):** Internal and external customers are integrated in relevant workshops	Sales staff, sales force, marketing specialists and external stakeholders (customers, suppliers) participate in the preparation of the specifications as defined role
$Z_{3.1}$: **Minimize time-to-market**	$W_{8,3.1}$: Reduction of documentation requirements for milestone 20	**(Event 8, 3.1):** Evaluation workshop to short-list documents regarding their added value	Documents and concepts that are identified in the workshop with no added value will be excluded from the scope of the project documentation
	$W_{10,3.1}$: Validate the involvement of all customer requirements	**(Indicator 10, 3.1):** Number of additional identification requirements **Target value:** Permitted only in 5% of the current developments	No adoption of the specifications in the milestone panel without checking the customer integration

Table 2.3 Evaluation schema (Von der Oelsnitz 2009)

Evaluation	Indicator		
	Performance indicator (quantitative)	Event	Status
0	degree of fulfillment <30%	Full occurrence	Missed
1	30%< degree of fulfillment <90%	Occurrence in parts	Partially met
2	90%< degree of fulfillment <100%	No occurrence	Achieved

scale was adequate for the managers concerned because a sufficient variation is possible without too many details.

According to the concept of the company-wide applicable Strategy Process Matrix, the process model on the middle level set up the specific requirements for all process instances following this model. The operational targets (z_{lmn}) and contributions ($w_{p,lmn}$) described in the Strategy Map on the instance level correspond with those on the middle level. The determination of goal achievement for development projects (instance level) can be calculated by the *horizontal accumulation of operational contributions* to realize a monitoring system of the lower managers[5]:

$$z_{lmn} = \left(\frac{\sum_{p=1}^{P} w_{p,lmn}}{2a_{lmn}}\right) * 100 \quad \text{for } l \in [1,L]; \ m \in [1,M]; \ n \in [1,N]. \quad (2.1)$$

Analogously, the *horizontal aggregation on middle level* can be described as

$$z_{lm} = \left(\frac{\sum_{p=1}^{P} w_{p,lm}}{2a_{lm}}\right) * 100 \quad \text{for } l \in [1,L]; \ m \in [1,M]. \quad (2.2)$$

The *vertical aggregation* of operational objectives to aggregate operational objective achievements to tactical objective achievement can be realized as follows:

$$z_{lm} = \frac{\sum_{n=1}^{N} z_{lmn}}{N_{lm}} \quad \text{for } l \in [1,L]; \ m \in [1,M]; \ n \in [1,N]. \quad (2.3)$$

N_{lm} describes the number of operational objectives per tactical objective.

In order to extend the approach from single process instances and to measure strategy achievement for multiple instances, which is the aim of business division leads responsible for multiple development projects, the mean value is used to control the overall strategy achievement. By vertically calculating the strategy achievement for distinct process instances, the objective attainment on the middle level for tactical presets can be determined:

$$Z_{lmn} = \frac{\sum_{x=1}^{X} z_{lmn}}{X} \quad \text{for } l \in [1,L]; \ m \in [1,M]; \ n \in [1,N]. \quad (2.4)$$

X represents the quantity of process instances (e.g., product development projects) and Z_{lm} signifies the strategy achievement for tactical objectives on the middle level.

2.4.3 Sample Calculation

The monitoring system was developed to overcome the described challenges of the manufacturer to control and increase strategy implementation. The system was simulated for one large business division of the company which included 17 completed as well as running product development instances in the business year

---

[5]The extended variables are: Operational objective z_{lmn}; Running index n for operational objective; Number of operational contributions a_{lmn} per operational objective z_{lmn} (e.g., z_{111}, z_{124}); Operational contribution $w_{p,lmn}$.

Table 2.4 Simulation data (Von der Oelsnitz 2009)

Level	Contribution	Value	Contribution	Value	Contribution	Value
	$w_{7,1.1}$	1	$w_{8,3.1}$	0	$w_{5,4.1}$	1
Middle	$w_{1,2.1}$	1	$w_{3,4.1}$	0	$w_{10,3.1}$	2
	$w_{5,2.1}$	2				
	$w_{7,1.1.1}$	1	$w_{5,2.1.1}$	2	$w_{4,3.1.2}$	1
Instance	$w_{3,1.1.2}$	1	$w_{8,3.1.1}$	0	$w_{3,4.1.1}$	1
	$w_{1,2.1.1}$	1	$w_{10,3.1.1}$	2	$w_{5,4.1.1}$	0

2013. The calculation should serve to identify in which process steps as well as on which organizational level the strategy cannot be achieved. Table 2.4 shows the achievements that were evaluated using indicators, status and events.

Table 2.5 shows the calculation of objective achievement on middle and instance level based on the values of Table 2.4.

Based on the resulting values of this case, a consistent objective structure could be assumed. This means that the operational and tactical objectives were consistent in the scenario. The degrees of horizontal and vertical goal attainment on both the instance as well as the middle level coincided (e.g., the objective of cost savings [$z_{1.1}$] has been met on the two levels by 50 %).

Based on the results from this case study, the following interpretation could be made by the project team: (1) The estimation of the management that objectives on the instance level were not achieved by the instances could be shown by the calculation. The corrective ad hoc measures for the contributions which were defined in this case study in a matrix for the first time should be taken into account by the project leads to improve states with indicators not fulfilling the set target values. Special efforts should be made to force technology push innovations, since the projects observed are not able to support this objective at all. (2) The middle management objectives are also not achieved. Given the fact that the comparison between the vertical aggregation on the instance level matched the horizontal accumulation results on the middle level, the objective breach eventuated from the

Table 2.5 Calculation example based on the simulation data (Von der Oelsnitz 2009)

		Aggregation and calculation	
		Horizontal	Vertical
Level	middle	• $z_{1.1} = (w_{7,1.1})/2a_{1.1}*100 = 50\%$ • $z_{1.2} = 50\%$ (given by the available data) • $z_{2.1} = (w_{1,2.1} + w_{5,2.1})/2a_{2.1}*100 = 75\%$ • $z_{3.1} = (w_{8,3.1} + w_{10,3.1})/2a_{3.1}*100 = 50\%$ • $z_{4.1} = (w_{3,4.1} + w_{5,4.1})/2a_{4.1}*100 = 25\%$	
	instance	• $z_{1.1.1} = (w_{7,1.1.1})/2a_{1.1.1}*100 = 50\%$ • $z_{1.1.2} = (w_{3,1.1.2})/2a_{1.1.2}*100 = 50\%$ • $z_{2.1.1} = (w_{1,2.1.1} + w_{5,2.1.1})/2a_{2.1.1}*100 = 75\%$ • $z_{3.1.1} = (w_{8,3.1.1} + w_{10,3.1.1})/2a_{3.1.1}*100 = 50\%$ • $z_{3.1.2} = (w_{4,3.1.2})/2a_{3.1.2}*100 = 50\%$ • $z_{4.1.1} = (w_{3,4.1.1} + w_{5,4.1.1})/2a_{4.1.1}*100 = 25\%$	• $z_{1.1} = (z_{1.1.1} + z_{1.1.2})/N_{1.1} = 50\%$ • $z_{1.2} = 50\%$ • $z_{2.1} = (z_{2.1.1})/N_{1.1} = 75\%$ • $z_{3.1} = (z_{3.1.1} + z_{3.1.2})/N_{1.1} = 50\%$ • $z_{4.1} = (z_{4.1.1})/N_{1.1} = 25\%$

consolidated objective breach on the subjacent instance level. Whereas projects were on a good path to increase customer-oriented developments, the objectives of distribution planning and cost-cutting were only partly implemented in the given projects.

The following corrective actions to optimize the strategic and tactical goal achievement could be taken: (1) implementation or, if necessary, additional definition of ad hoc measures on the instance level, (2) conducting a root cause analysis considering the non-compliance with instance and middle contributions, (3) long-term monitoring and assessment of general measures on the middle level regarding the supportive impact for goal achievement in later process instances, and (4) critical reconsideration of target values for set objectives regarding their achievability in the company-specific organizational context.

2.4.4 Consequences

By developing and implementing the monitoring system, the business division lead is now put into the position to take corrective measures as well as to vindicate additional process resources by assigning them to the given superordinate objectives. An evident advantage of the presented system lies in the identification of possible root causes that are accountable for the non-achievement of strategic and tactical goals. It provides a systematic and reproducible procedure to identify and correct the root of strategic and/or operational drawbacks. Additionally, it allocates all relevant information and support to accomplish process instances in a strategy-oriented way. The indicators and action lists provide a reproducible line of action for how managers in charge can use the approach to show their quantifiable additional value within a company.

However, the proposed monitoring system needs to be assessed in further research by verifying quantitatively measurable improvements for a comprehensive set of case studies. In the case study, a new assessment after one year of implementation can show whether the use of the system, and in particular the implementation of corrective actions, supports the strategy achievement.

Another obstacle that has to be addressed in additional research activities is the fact that the presented approach only focuses on positive contributions that support the achievement of goals. Negative contributions that impede sufficient goal achievement and may be processed in the context of optimization projects need further assessment and consideration.

The described case study concerning the product development process of a multi-national manufacturing company already indicates that the approach tends to become quite complex and hard to comprehend for large process models and calculation schemas. Therefore, an IT-based support for creating and managing the matrix including the aggregations necessary for the control system is crucial for introducing the proposed approach in entrepreneurial practice.

2.5   Summary

S-BPM has a strong and successful foundation in the efficient elicitation and automation of business processes. This contribution brings in a new aspect by demonstrating how to link S-BPM with strategy implementation.

As a matter of fact, the S-BPM's focus on per-subject process models makes it easier to develop reasonably sized Strategy Process Matrices than process modeling notations, which do not possess this instrument of decoupling models of different process participants. Furthermore creating individual Strategy Process Matrices for individual subjects makes it easier to measure, guide, and motivate individuals taking part in the process team to think about their strategy contribution.

Two case studies show that the Strategy-oriented Business Process Modeling approach already has won merits in the business worlds. While the first case study shows how to implement strategies in process models, the second case study demonstrates that strategy implementation can also guide tactical and operational objectives of individual process instances.

From the first case study, practitioners can use the applied rules for their own optimization projects. The rules are very simple to use, yet provide good optimization results. Moreover, the presented working in teams could help in other projects and domains for coming up with creative solutions for increasing the strategy achievement. The second case study could show an approach with which process mangers can read and measure the contribution strategy close to the process. In particular, the horizontal aggregation was intuitively understood by managers. Nevertheless, they result in partly surprising outcomes that have led the company to rethink activities.

Currently, the authors are working to transform the very complex matrices in simple graphs or to equip the approaches with IT support. By doing so, in particular, the applicability of the monitoring system is to be increased, which has been implemented with simple spreadsheet or database systems so far.

References

Benson A (2007) Qualitätssteigerung in komplexen Entwicklungsprojekten durch prozessbegleitende Kennzahlensysteme. Vorgehen zur Herleitung, Einführung und Anwendung. Cuvillier, Göttingen (in German)

Chavan M (2009) The balanced scorecard: a new challenge. J Manage Dev 28:393–406

Chen CC, Jones K (2009) Are employees buying the balanced scorecard? Manage Acc Q 11:36–44

Chen H, Daugherty PJ, Roath AS (2009) Defining and operationalizing supply chain process integration. J Bus Logistics 30:63–84

Glavan LM (2011) Understanding process performance measurement systems. Bus Syst Res 2:1–56

Hörschgen H (2001) Geleitwort. In: Daniel A (ed) Implementierungsmanagement. DUV, Wiesbaden (in German)

Kaplan RS, Norton DP (1996) Linking the balanced scorecard to strategy. Calif Manage Rev 39:53–79

Lederer M, Huber S (2014) Connectivity, simplification, and performance measurement: guidelines for business process strategists in re-engineering projects. IADIS Int J Comput Sci Inf Syst 9:132–145

Lederer M, Huber S, Kocak I (2014a) Increasing strategy-achievement in business processes and information systems using an objective-based optimization approach. In: Nunes MB, Peng GC (eds) Proceedings of the international conference information systems post-implementation and change management 2014 Lisbon, International Association for Development of the Information Society

Lederer M, Kurz M, Lembcke U (2014b) Applying the strategy-oriented business process modeling to S-BPM. In: Zehbold C (ed) Communications in computer and information science (CCIS), S-BPM ONE application studies and work in progress, vol 422. Springer, Berlin

Lederer M, Schott P, Keppler A (2015) Using a strategy-oriented business process modeling notation for a transparent company-wide business control system. Int J Decis Support Syst (forthcoming)

Mair S (2002) A balanced scorecard for a small software group. IEEE Softw 19:21–27

Mintzberg H (1994) The rise and fall of strategic planning. Prentice Hall Europe, Edinburgh

Minonne C, Turner G (2012) Business process management—Are you ready for the future? Knowl Process Manage 19:111–120

Outram C (2014) Making Your Strategy Work. Pearson, Cambridge

Petzmann A, Puncochar M, Kuplich C, Orensanz D (2007) Applying MDA concepts to business process management. In: Fischer L (ed) BPM and workflow handbook: methods, concepts, case studies and standards. Future Strategies, Lighthouse Point

Quezada LE, Cordova FM, Palominos P, Godoy K, Ross J (2009) Method for identifying strategic objectives in strategy maps. Int J Prod Econ 122:492–500

Richardson S (2004) The key elements of balanced scorecard success. Ivey Bus J 69:7–9

Sidorova A, Isik O (2010) Business process research: a cross-disciplinary review. Bus Process Manage J 16:566–597

Von der Oelsnitz D (2009) Management. Geschichte, Aufgaben, Beruf. Beck, München (in German)

Weber J, Schäffer U (2000) Balanced scorecard & controlling: Implementierung-Nutzen für Manager und Controller-Erfahrungen in deutschen Unternehmen. Gabler, Wiesbaden (in German)

Wolf C, Harmon P (2012) The state of business process management. A BPTrends report

Communication- and Value-Based Organizational Development at the University Clinic for Radiotherapy-Radiation Oncology

3

Martina Augl and Christian Stary

Abstract

This field study embodies S-BPM into organizational development processes, both methodologically, exploring how to capture work knowledge, and with respect to implementation, providing accurate specifications for process support. Eliciting and acquiring knowledge of work procedures have been exploited by means of Value Network Analysis (VNA). It engages stakeholders on elaborating by scenarios of work they have experienced and supports exploring opportunities of change in terms of exchanged deliverables along actor-specific communication structures. VNA roles correspond to subjects and interactional transactions to business objects. The approach has become part of an SOP for organizational development of clinics. We exemplify the development of patient-critical treatment planning in the University Clinic for Radiotherapy-Radiation Oncology.

3.1 Introduction

The University Clinic for Radiotherapy-Radiation Oncology (ROI) is the Tyrol's only radiotherapy facility, and thus represents a major part of the regional and national infrastructure in cancer medicine. About 70 % of all cancer patients of the

M. Augl (✉)
Medical Department, Organizational Development Unit,
Tiroler Landeskrankenanstalten GmbH, (TILAK), Innsbruck, Austria
e-mail: martina.augl@tilak.at

C. Stary
Department of Business Information Systems—Communications Engineering Knowledge Management Competence Center, Johannes Kepler University of Linz, Linz, Austria
e-mail: christian.stary@JKU.at

© The Author(s) 2015
A. Fleischmann et al. (eds.), *S-BPM in the Wild*,
DOI 10.1007/978-3-319-17542-3_3

federal state hospital (Landeskrankenhaus Innsbruck) are treated at the University clinic. The complexity of planning cancer treatment is reflected through involving staff from different professions and disciplines. In addition to the medical staff, radio technologists, medical physicists, technicians, biomedical analysts, psycho-oncologists and administrative staff form the planning team for patient treatment. In recent years the number of patients has started to increase significantly, resulting in a corresponding increase of services and treatment capabilities, in terms of both technical resources and personnel.

In order to ensure the professional development of the clinic its director launched an organizational development process after holding a strategy meeting involving its multi-professional management team. Major internal organizational issues were discussed, and a mission statement of the clinic has been released. To sustain it in daily routines, an organizational development project has been started. In addition, establishing specialized tumor group treatment as part of organization's structural change should be explored. The project's management team specified two central objectives for the organizational development process:

- developing task allocation models referring to job profiles, and
- establishing regular communication patterns. In this context, motivation, job satisfaction, and professional handling of conflicts also played an important role.

The organizational development team of the umbrella organization Tiroler Landeskrankenanstalten GmbH (TILAK) set up a corresponding change project entitled "Reflect ROI" for one year. After refining the existing mission statement involving the extended leadership board, a workplace satisfaction survey was launched. All clinic staff was invited to judge the image and quality of patient management, the satisfaction with the content of work, the social relations (including management), and workplace conflict management.

Figure 3.1 shows the public and internal image including patient performance as judged by the various professional groups at ROI. While the various professional groups rated the image and performance quite highly (as indicated by the dot cloud

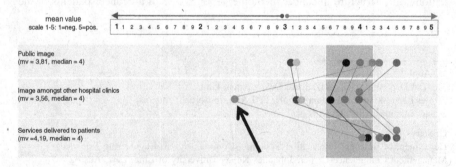

Fig. 3.1 Perceived image from outside

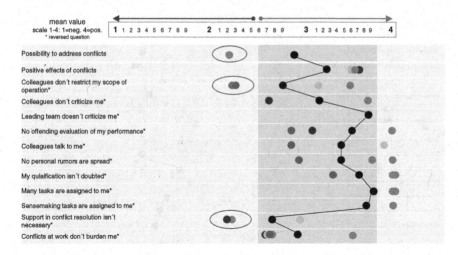

Fig. 3.2 Conflicts and their management

on the right-hand side), the internal image of physician trainees (leftmost dot) has been perceived quite ambivalently.

With respect to conflict handling, physician trainees questioned openly addressing conflicts and indicated the need for professional support for conflict management (upper and lower circled dots in Fig. 3.2).

With respect to collaboration, again physician trainees did not experience team feeling and indicated the need for improving cooperation with administration and their peers (Fig. 3.3).

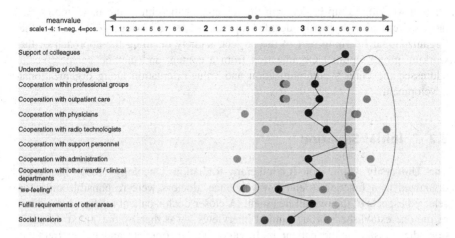

Fig. 3.3 Team work

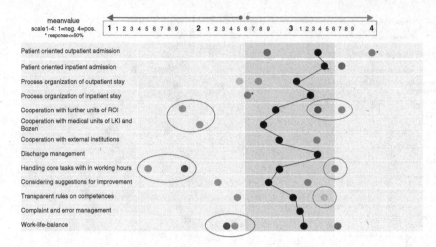

Fig. 3.4 Evaluating the organization of work

Finally, as indicated in the middle of Fig. 3.4, accomplishing core tasks when being on duty was not organized satisfactorily for physician trainees, besides the lack of cooperation of other ROI units and aligning private and occupational duties.

In a follow-up (one-day) workshop representatives from all occupational groups across hierarchical positions developed a vision of the future of the clinic. This vision should be put to operational practice by four working groups (WGs): Optimal Organization, Division of Labor, Professional Profiles, and Communication. All working groups were staffed inter-professionally by clinic members, and accompanied by the project team. The meetings had different formats: workshops, impulses, focus groups, solution development.

Concrete suggestions were discussed in a monthly meeting by the clinic's internal working group leader with the director of the clinic, and their implementations were always jointly decided upon. In the following we focus on the Organizational Learning part of the project, namely detailing the approach of the working group Optimal Organization from a content and method perspective. It addressed the clinic's communication and value-orientation along organizational development.

3.2 Initial Situation

The University Clinic for Radiotherapy-Radiation Oncology (ROI) has been organized in a function-oriented way. Hence, doctors were responsible only for selected aspects of the overall treatment. A closer doctor-patient relationship—such as the one established through initial interviews—was thereby prevented. In addition, the transfer of the patient information was incomplete and led to frequent losses of information. Compensating for these deficiencies still required lots of resources and continuously rebuilding of doctor-patient relationships.

Working along functional units as indicated above has been perceived as "assembly-line work" and created frustration albeit high patient satisfaction with the clinics' performance according to the survey (see also in Fig. 3.1). However, the need for increasing consistency in medical care has been expressed by patients over and over again.

With regard to assigning physicians and the supervising wards (including his/her own ward) the allocation of tasks and patient responsibility was not quite clear: Each patient could be in contact with four different units at the same time, according to the functional division of labor at the outpatient department, Linac team, tumor board and ward. This confusion also hindered sufficient time resources for each patient and focused academic work.

The working group had a core of two conductive senior physicians and 11 other members involving all other professions. Such cross-section of the clinic's staff enabled consensus when formulating the problem statement to be handled in the context of the organizational development project:

Is there an optimal form organizing our work, which contributes to good patient care and high employee satisfaction as well as to an efficient use of resources?

It triggered the specific mandate of the working group:

Developing a model of how the work needs to be organized, ensuring optimal patient care, while improving employee satisfaction at ROI.

This mandate has been implemented by developing different possible variants, and revealing associated advantages and disadvantages by evaluating their consequences of a corresponding implementation. The latter should serve as a basis for optimizing the organizational structure of work.

With respect to methodological and practical know-how the project participants of ROI were neither educated in Organizational Design and Business Process Management, nor familiar with Workflow Management Systems. Hence, the elicitation and representation of work (process) knowledge had to be accompanied by informing activities.

3.3 Project Implementation

The ROI members of the working group together with the TILAK organizational development team defined the following procedure to achieve the objectives of the project:

1. Documentation of current situation
2. Development of model variants
3. Analysis of the consequences of the models' implementation

In order to perform these steps subject-oriented and systemic knowledge management methods were used, which were accompanied by an external consultant.

3.3.1 Documentation of the Current Situation

For the representation of the actual situation with regard to the operational and
organizational structure of the University Clinic for Radiotherapy-Radiation
Oncology, members of the working group modeled the structures and core processes
of their clinic. In two workshops an interactive structure elaboration tabletop system
was used. It allowed visualizing work knowledge (structures, processes, and the like)
using three differently shaped elements and arbitrary relationships (see Fig. 3.5).

   After introducing the table and its functionalities, participants developed a
common understanding on modeling their work. It supported their visualizing
complex processes and structure requirements within a short period of time. A total
of 12 models, three structure and nine flow models emerged:

- Job/workspace structure
- Overview of workspaces (see Fig. 3.6)
- Structure of out-patient department
- Out-patient department process
- Planning process
- Linac process (see Fig. 3.7)
- Brachytherapy process
- Ward process
- Emergency process on weekends and during holidays
- Blood irradiation/experimental irradiation process
- Benign diseases/conventional therapy process
- Procurement process

Fig. 3.5 Interactive structure elaboration tabletop system. Adopted from Stary (2014)

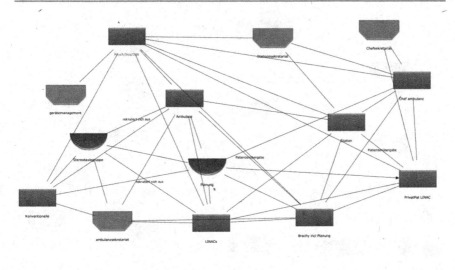

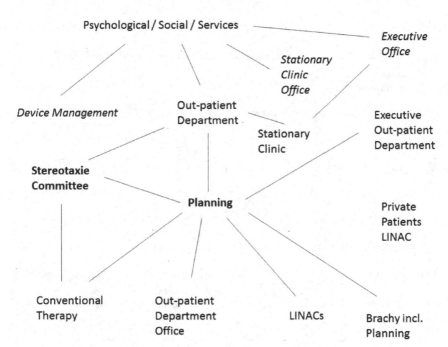

Fig. 3.6 Structure model: overview of workspaces (*upper part* original pattern, *lower part* nodes with their main relationships). Adopted from Stary (2014)

The various elements were used with different meanings. In the structure model (see Fig. 3.6, the lower part shows excerpted text items with their main relationships), rectangle elements describe workspaces with direct patient reference. Semicircular elements represent workspaces which in part are already contained in

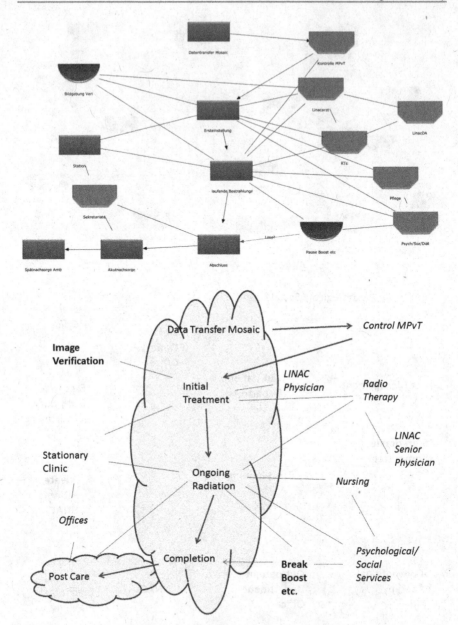

Fig. 3.7 Flow model: Linac (*upper part* original pattern, *lower part* nodes with their main relationships)—core process elements are located in the cloud (*lower part*). Adopted from Stary (2014)

the rectangle elements. They refer to planning as an essential element of radiotherapy. Hexagonal elements define workspaces without reference to patients, elaborating on the rectangle units. In this context, device management and the front office of the various work units were specified. The connections between the rectangle and hexagonal elements indicate the cooperation between the units. Once a semicircular element is connected, a 'has-part' or 'recruits from' relationship has been set. The structure model of all workspaces was used subsequently as a framework for the selection of the processes to be modeled.

In the follow-up (process) models, e.g., Fig. 3.7 (the lower part shows excerpted text items with their main relationships and the patient-relevant process in the cloud), rectangle elements define main process steps or top-level starting points triggering procedures. Semicircular elements specify major equipment or operators supplying additional information for the process. Hexagonal elements represent functions to be included in the course of patient-oriented planning, or responsible organizational units. Undirected connections represent bidirectional collaboration between groups of actors and responsibilities of persons for process steps. For instance, Linac physicians and radio technologists collaborate when being responsible for the initial setting for a patient at the Linac. Directed links enable mapping the sequence of process steps to the elaborated structure.

The application of the structure elaboration tabletop system revealed that professional groups such as physicians who are used to make decisions under time pressure in clinical practice, are highly active when the workshop participants were asked to model their work practice. The other professionals joined them once the initial elements had been identified, depending on the addressed actors and their process knowledge. The members of the working group evaluated the four processes "Linac", "out-patient department", "planning", and "performance profile" in terms of critical success factors. They identified strengths, weaknesses, ideas for solutions to open problems, questions, and potential for improvement. These results formed the basis for the development of model variants. As each of the process models in the stakeholder-genuine notation included actor- and IT system-specific information elements as well as lines of communication, the most relevant input for subject-oriented representation had been provided.

3.3.2 Development of Model Variants

In order to develop and analyze appropriate models for optimizing the organization of work regarding patient care, use of resources, and employee satisfaction, two more workshops were conducted. At the beginning of the first workshop, the working group agreed on two favorable variants:

- optimization of (existing) function-based process organization
- organizing work according to tumor groups

For analysis and refinement of the two variants the participants split into two groups, each moderated by the TILAK organizational development team and an external consultant. In a first step the necessary functions/roles, tasks and tools were documented in a network of organizational activities utilizing HoloMapping (cf. vernaallee.com). The same symbol colors were used as for the structure elaboration on the tabletop system, namely hexagonal for functions/roles, rectangle for tasks, semicircular for work equipment and committees.

In addition, solid arrows (Tangibles) visualized the information and knowledge exchange required for the fulfillment of tasks, whereas dashed arrows (Intangibles) between the individual elements visualized experience knowledge and action-guiding values. Particularly controversial or dysfunctional exchange relationships were drawn in a dedicated color like the value-creating and neutral relationships (see Figs. 3.8 and 3.9).

The collected hot spots (subscribed exchange relationships) of both forms of organization were formulated as critical success factors in each subgroup. Then, corresponding solution ideas were created and documented in tables—see, e.g., Table 3.1.

In order to further analyze the effect of the (critical) exchange relationships on sender and receiver or the entire organization, each deliverable was according to the Value Network Analysis (VNA) (cf. vernaallee.com). In addition to the already carried out Holomapping and exchange analysis (i.e. analysis of structures of the represented actor network), the VNA includes an Impact and Value Creation analysis for both, the communication-oriented reflection of the impact of values of existing exchange relations/activities, and value creation opportunities for individual participants and the overall organization of work. In the Impact Analysis, stakeholders identify which "deliverables" (=exchange/services) flow between the (critical) roles. A table is created for each role (see Table 3.2). It is listed therein which role receives inputs, from whom it receives these inputs, what activities are triggered at the respective role, and what effect on the used work equipment is experienced. In addition, corresponding intangible impacts, costs, risks and benefits are recognized.

Table 3.2 shows some data entries for the tumor board (role). The physician needs to specify for each incoming transaction of the Tumorboard (see rows of the table) the activities triggered by the input, the effort created by the input to the work flow for each actor, the immaterial (Intangible) effects on them, and the general costs and risks associated with the input. In this way, results that are not adequately achieved are questioned with respect to the usefulness of each deliverable.

The first data entry in the table exemplifies the input 'patient information' to the 'Tumor Board'. It is delivered by the Assigning physician for decision making in the Tumorboard, based on the quality of received information. Currently the Tumorboard experiences a lack of information due to missing data. Planning overhead is high since the board does not issue demands for the missing information. Consequently, the risk of incorrect decision making is high. On the contrary, the benefit of complete information would be high, since it forms the basis for further work (treatment planning).

In the Value Creation Analysis (see Table 3.3) all outgoing transactions are discussed for each role, including the receiver and the value added. It needs to be documented by what activity a possible increase in value, e.g., a possible solution for a problem when organizing work, can be achieved. As in the Impact Analysis, also costs, risks and benefits arising from the respective outputs are documented.

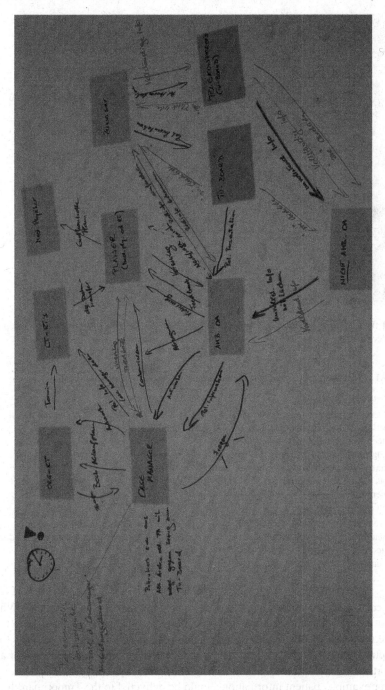

Fig. 3.8 HoloMap representing function-oriented organizational form. Adopted from Stary (2014)

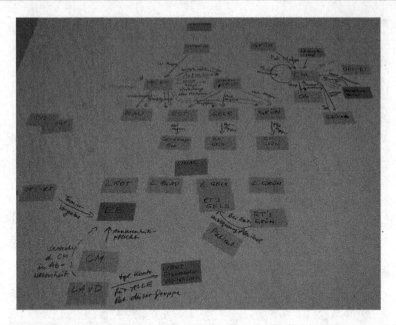

Fig. 3.9 HoloMap representing an organization of work according to tumor groups. Adopted from Stary (2014)

Table 3.1 Processing critical success factors from the hot-spot analysis (example)

Critical success factor	Idea for solution
Completeness of information: in particular, in tele-meetings of the tumor board the coherence of information between Zuweisung (assigning physician), Tumorboard, Nicht-Ambulanz-Oberarzt (stationary senior or lead physician), Ambulanz-Oberarzt (out-patient department senior or lead doctor) is not ensured (Tangible)	Checklist to evaluate completeness for all participants
Taking over through LINAC (Tangible): timing and quality of information do not seem to fit—too early handover with incomplete information	Once the plan has been released after aligning, the patients should be introduced to LINAC

For each role and output the following questions need to be answered: What intention (value) becomes visible with this output? What activities can be set to increase the value of this output from my side (enhancement from my perspective as an acting agent)? To which actor is my output delivered (as a sender)? What are the effort, risks, and benefits when creating additional value?

In our example, patient information should be delivered to the Tumorboard for a tele conference on time, based on the activities of the Assigning physician. Then therapeutic decisions could be based on complete information. The teleconference

Table 3.2 Impact analysis (example)

TU-Board (role)		Which activities are triggered by the input? (What do I need to do acting in that role?)	Which effort do I need to spend on processing the input acting in that role?	Immaterial (intangible) impact to me (acting in that role)?	Which effort is spent on processing the input in general?	Which risk needs to be taken with this input (deliverables are not adequate)?	What is the overall benefit of this input?
What do we receive (deliverable)	Sender (role)	Activity	Value impact	Immaterial impact	Effort	Risk	Benefit
Patient-presentation (patient data)	Assigning physician	Tumorboard decision	Recognition for decision making	Informed action	High, since tumorboard does not demand missing data	High, since assigning physician needs to ensure completeness of data set	High, since relevant for further process steps

Table 3.3 Value creation analysis (example)

Assigning physician (role)		Which intention (value) becomes visible with this output	What activities can be set to increase the value of this output from my side (enhancement from my perspective as an acting agent)	Effort	Risks	Benefits
My output (sender)	Output receiver	Added value of the activity	Increase in added value			
(Incomplete) patient information (presentation)	Tele-conference (Tumorboard)	Increase in information, basis for deciding on therapy	Assigning physician needs to deliver complete information. Tele-conference. would need to request complete information from assigning physician → check list from tele conference to assigning physician: reduces additional information requests; increases worker satisfaction in tele conference; speeds up process	Medium	High, since missing information might have impact to decision on therapy	High, since subsequent actors do not have to collect (additional data)

should demand full information from assigning physicians. A checklist for tele-conferencing for assigning physicians could help to reduce additional search activities when completing the patient file which in turn could result in increased employee satisfaction.

Given the tables, fundamental subject-oriented model elements become available, namely subjects and messages. For instance, the Tumorboard and Assigning physician (Zuweiser) represent subjects. All incoming messages are identified naming the tangible deliverables in the table when filling in inputs in the course of the Impact Analysis (Table 3.2). All outgoing messages are listed in the course of the Value Creation Analysis (Table 3.3). They correspond to the tangible trans-actions with other subjects.

3.3.3 Analysis of the Consequences of Model Implementations

Detailing and systemically analyzing the two suitable variants for the implementation of an optimal form of organization at the University Clinic for Radiotherapy-Radiation Oncology showed that certain patterns of work behavior had been established over time. It also became evident that these patterns could be addressed independently of whether the current situation would be kept or not. They affected:

- Organization of tumor boards
- Completeness of assignments (Assigning physician)
- Staff shortages
- Incomplete performance measurement (number of patients)
- Adherence to deadlines
- Procedure of the afternoon meeting

Although organizing the work according to tumor groups would imply switching physicians at the interface Out-patient Department/Linac from the perspective of patients (which needs to be resolved separately), this shift would bring substantial benefits for the continuity of patient care and employee satisfaction. These issues were discussed in one of the monthly coordination meetings and redirected to the working group for detailing solution proposals.

Many of the inputs have been already elicited in the course of the Value Network Analysis or resulted from processing critical success factors of the HoloMap. In order to clarify medical staffing, the current staff allocation and the process of planning, including the highly debated service exchange, were again modeled on the structure elaboration tabletop system. Required changes could be derived from this session. In general, it was found that physicians have to be on-site for successful task accomplishment, in particular when the work is organized according to tumor groups.

In addition to the organization-independent optimization issues, the change to focused work areas (tumor groups) promised the following advantages:

- Strengthening doctor-patient relationships
- Clarification of ROI profile due to designated work areas
- Provision of dedicated contact persons for patients, stationary units, and assigning physicians
- Improvement of training
- Simplification of planning absences, primarily when self-organizing them in each group
- Clarification of responsibilities for tumor board representatives, case manager, and their substitutes
- Promotion of special skills of individual employees
- Improvements in recruiting patients for studies
- Development of scientific priorities
- Continuity of support and documentation of study patients
- Increasing efficiency when introducing innovations
- Increased continuity in caretaking of patients with combined tele-brachytherapy or combined photon-neutron therapy
- Better integration and representation of part-time employees in a group.

3.4   Going Live

The trigger for implementing changes was the director asking the group leaders and the TILAK organizational development team to develop a business plan containing all necessary implementation steps. They critically reviewed the developments in healthcare with respect to

- the structure of the task force according to tumor types
- the composition of the focused working units
- the required functions and tasks for each group
- classifying medical staff
- a planning procedure concerning the absence of doctors
- clarifying organizational details and context, such as planning Linac slots, room layout, and late night services
- providing contact persons for all occupational groups
- training rotations

The implementation concept (being part of the business plan) included changes in physician staffing and patient assignment. Implementation should be supported by focus groups and specific case managers for each tumor group. The implementation also required some IT adaptations.

The business plan was presented to the management team of the University Clinic for Radiotherapy-Radiation Oncology. It agreed on a certain date for switching to the implementation of the novel concept. As a result, a further project, namely implementation support of the focus groups, was set up by the organizational development team of TILAK. This project comprised both all communication-related and all

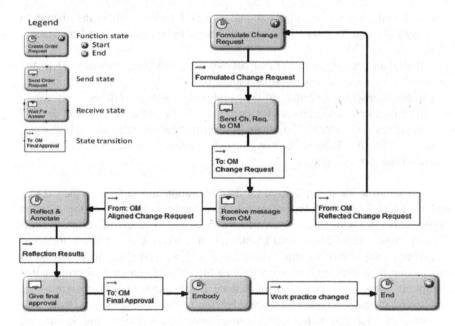

Fig. 3.10 Sample subject behavior diagram: change request by Physicians to Operation Manager. Adopted from Stary (2014)

technical-organizational preparations for implementation. It also established the monthly reflection of the implementation status involving the focus group leaders and the management team of the clinic, allowing re-re-planning when required.

In the course of the implementation support project a short survey involving all staff members of the clinic was conducted. It focused on their expectations and barriers concerning the implementation. It is planned to repeat this survey one year after introducing the focus groups and establishing the tumor groups.

As an effective means of documentation and interaction with the IT department, subject-oriented models have been prepared, as exemplified by change requests by physicians to the operation manager in Fig. 3.10. The (re-)engineering process of the interactive application is done in collaboration with staff users and the TILAK organizational development team.

3.5 Conclusive Summary

From guiding the change processes several lessons became evident:

- Rather than starting with a modeling session to analyze a situation of an organization or to capture stakeholder needs a goal setting procedure should be established. It gives an organizational unit and their members the chance to consolidate and formulate objectives that need to be graspable and transparent throughout a change project.

- Rather than applying a predefined notation for articulating mental models and stakeholder needs an open format should be used allowing all stakeholders to - express themselves according to their preferences and capabilities.
- Rather than optimizing process for a group let the involved stakeholders develop alternatives and variants. Help them to identify relevant measures and schemes, such as success factors, as they have the relevant experience and domain knowledge for evaluation.

With regard to the methods used for the elaboration and analysis of the existing and envisioned situation, the interactive and haptic instrument of the tabletop system enabled a wide and active participation of the members of various professional groups without any special knowledge of work process modeling methods. In addition, the choice of this setting facilitated incorporating all occupational groups and their perspectives, regardless of hierarchy or position in professional groups. It allowed for profound, immediate involvement of different groups of employees. Despite lack of prior knowledge, the parties rapidly came to work with the structure elaboration technique, and developed a coherent and sustainable modeling logic.

The subsequent analysis of the models using VNA (Value Network Analysis) opened up reflecting on causal relationships of certain problems from the perspective of communication. In some cases, they could move to the center far-reaching effects of local problems on the entire organization as well as the effects of values guiding activities. The participants were able to visualize in this way what patterns are effective in their organization for functional activities or when difficulties occur. Thus, the identified hot spots could be processed step by step using the tabletop system and solutions could be developed in terms of added value for the clinic. Here, too, it turned out, in particular by observing four workshops, that the members of the working group could become familiar with the selected method very quickly. However, it should be noted that a moderation of the group is required, both in the use of structural elaboration tabletop system and when processing a HoloMap, i.e., performing value network analyses. It helps on the one hand keeping the focus on the content and the method, and on the other hand triggering questions for reflection, in order to direct participants towards problem solving.

The developed critical success factors provided a well-defined framework for quality assurance in the context of implementing a new organization of work at the clinic. Overall, the organization could profit from its knowledge about their accuracy and meet existing and emerging challenges successfully. It occurred in a way that the decision for selecting a specific organizational form could be based on relevant patterns of communication and underlying values, in addition to factual arguments. Hereby, subject-orientation provides focusing on acting parties and their interaction in terms of work-relevant deliverables. Besides a high-level view, role-specific behaviors can be specified accurately through S-BPM models.

References

Stary Ch (2014) Non-disruptive knowledge and business processing in knowledge life cycles—aligning value network analysis to process management. J Knowl Manage 18(4):651–686

Introducing S-BPM at an IT Service Providers

4

Marc Sprogies and Werner Schmidt

Abstract

IT Service consumers have a clear idea of agile, flexible and transparent service processes to quickly get their needs satisfied. For an IT service provider like WK EDV GmbH this arises the challenge of designing its procedures adequately. For that reason WK decided to consolidate and optimize their service processes. It ran a pilot project to analyze, redesign and newly implement the software deployment process which is part of their overall Application Lifecycle Management (ALM) process. The project team applied Subject-oriented Business Process Management (S-BPM) as methodology and the Metasonic Suite as the respective software toolset in order to gain insights into and experience with the S-BPM environment. This contribution reports on the course of the project, the results and the learnings.

4.1 Project Background and Initial Situation

WK EDV GmbH (short: WK) is a well-established medium-sized IT Service Provider based in the Ingolstadt area. With about 130 employees it offers managed IT services, consulting, software development and client engineering to a variety of international customers in many different industries, from automotive to retail.

M. Sprogies (✉)
WK EDV GmbH, Ingolstadt, Germany
e-mail: marc.sprogies@t-online.de

W. Schmidt
Technische Hochschule Ingolstadt Business School, Ingolstadt, Germany
e-mail: Werner.schmidt@thi.de

© The Author(s) 2015
A. Fleischmann et al. (eds.), *S-BPM in the Wild*,
DOI 10.1007/978-3-319-17542-3_4

With a flat and agile structure, the organization is strictly oriented towards the needs and projects of its customers, offering flexible and scalable services. Each organizational unit is responsible for managing the services it provides and the related processes. As service consumers often specify their own requirements and influence the service process, WK's process landscape contains many variants and alternatives. Managing them turns out to be a major challenge for the organization, which was striving for increasing transparency and better control of all managed services and processes. Consequently the managing directors of the company aim for implementing a Business Process Management (BPM) environment which supports standardization with unique definitions of process cores and roles while keeping the flexibility to manage customer-specific process variations. This environment to develop should also include software support by a Business Process Management System (BPMS).

As a first step, management started a project for harmonizing and optimizing service processes of the business unit 'Managed IT Services', which are ordered in WK's overall Application Lifecycle Management framework (ALM). As Fig. 4.1 shows, the processes span the entire application lifecycle, embodying the typical plan/build/run scheme.

The first sub-project described here focused on the software deployment process within ALM (see Fig. 4.1). This process is one of the core competencies of the Managed IT Services branch of WK EDV GmbH. It serves to deliver software (applications) onto its customers' client computers on different operating system platforms. The process is pretty complex and instances can follow many different patterns depending on what customers specify in their order. In regular vendor evaluations customers stated their overall satisfaction, but also articulated potential for further improvement, because services and their delivery sometimes deviated contentwise and temporally from what was negotiated. The service owners on the provider side not only became aware of these facts as addressees of the questionnaires but also by their own perception. As a matter of fact they could not really monitor and control the process because of missing check and measuring points. Deployments resembled individual projects rather than instances of a standardized procedure. The service owners identified the following major reasons:

- The work procedure was roughly specified in a flow diagram, but process participants did not sufficiently follow this specification. The reason was missing IT support to force following the defined steps including communication both within WK and towards the customer.
- As a consequence it was not guaranteed that all necessary steps are performed, which negatively affected the quality of the process output. The resulting

Fig. 4.1 Application lifecycle management (ALM) at WK EDV GmbH

instances also have been intransparent and heterogeneous and could not be systematically monitored with process performance indicators (PPIs), making proper management of the process difficult. As an example, cycle time of a deployment could significantly exceed because of one pending step, a fact which might not have been recognized for quite a while.

In order to realize improvements the objective was to analyze, model and pro- totypically implement the process as an IT-based workflow applying S-BPM methodology and technology. Workflow execution in the resulting environment should allow achieving to-be values of PPIs, like reaching more than 85 % of all client computers in a deployment or more 98 % successful deployments on reached clients (see also Tables 4.2 and 4.5). The decision for S-BPM was not based on a comprehensive evaluation of methodology and tools, but on its assumed suitability for communication-intensive processes like the one in focus. Besides resolving the mentioned weaknesses the sub-project should improve process documentation, transparency and acceptance. It should also allow all participants to learn about how the subject-oriented approach could support the way to establishing and sustaining the pursued BPM concept in the organization. The lessons learned were intended to help get valuable experience for succeeding steps in organizational development.

4.2 Course of the Project

4.2.1 Retrospective Overview

Due to high workload of all employees no regular staff member could take responsibility for the pilot project. Therefore WK management assigned it to a student, one of the authors, as a task for his bachelor's thesis (Sprogies 2014). Limited time of staff to contribute to the project by giving information input was the major constraint, paired with little explicit knowledge of BPM methodology and BPMS. The student at least had some basic skills gained in a university class, but no experience in Subject-oriented BPM. This was the 'playground' on which he started and drove the project as project leader (PL).

Figure 4.2 shows the course of the project with S-BPM lifecycle activities, results, involved S-BPM roles and software tools being assigned to different phases, which are then presented in detail.

4.2.2 Preparation Phase

After having been assigned the project order, the PL started some preparation steps in order to set the stage for action. The activities included

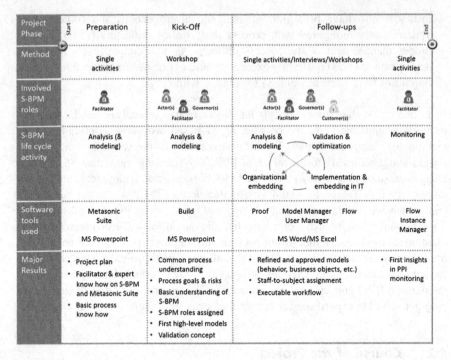

Fig. 4.2 Project overview

- Roughly planning the course of action, including the phases depicted in Fig. 4.2
- Familiarizing himself with S-BPM using the textbook by Fleischmann et al. (2012)
- Installing and familiarizing himself with the Metasonic Suite using the user manuals and the case study book *S-BPM Illustrated* (Fleischmann et al. 2013)
- Learning about the process by studying the existing flowchart (three pages) and making his own observations

Based on the knowledge he had gained the PL was ready to organize the kick-off meeting.

4.2.3 Initial Workshop

4.2.3.1 Workshop Preparation
In preparing for the kick-off workshop, the PL first defined the objectives and the time frame. The half-day meeting would serve to develop a common understanding of the process and to define the overall project frame. The PL identified and invited the participants (see Table 4.1). As input he prepared a presentation and handout for introducing S-BPM (overall approach, notation, S-BPM lifecycle, etc.) to the audience. A Word document was structured like jBook forms for subject-oriented

Table 4.1 S-BPM roles taken by WK employees (numbers in brackets)

S-BPM role (No.)	WK role taker
Governors (3)	Managing director Business unit manager 'Managed IT Services' Team manager 'Client Services'
Actors (3)	WK roles (5) in software deployment process (actors usually take more than one role): • Deployment requestor • Client management engineer • Quality verifier • Deployment coordinator • Deployment agent
Facilitators (2)	Team manager 'Client Services' Student (PL)
Experts (1)	Student (PL)

analysis in order to store online the workshop results as well as the outcome of the follow-up activities. In addition, the Metasonic Build was prepared for documenting results on the fly, in particular for creating process models.

4.2.3.2 Workshop Meeting and Results

From the S-BPM lifecycle perspective the meeting included analysis and modeling activities. The seven workshop participants spent approximately 2 h on the introduction of the S-BPM approach and on developing a common understanding of the process. They discussed for roughly another 2 h how to set the overall project frame. A fifth hour was used for separating sub-processes, identifying subjects and agreeing on future steps.

Many of the results reported below did not have to be developed from scratch. They were in parts formulated in advance by the PL based on his prior analysis and only needed to be discussed, elaborated and agreed upon in the meeting. This way the following results were achieved and mostly documented in the Word file and/or in model diagrams, with additional specifications in the Metasonic Build. *Methodology-related results*:

- All participants had a basic understanding of S-BPM and the S-BPM lifecycle
- S-BPM roles had been assigned to WK representatives (see Table 4.1)
- Middle-out analysis and modeling by construction were considered to be the appropriate ways of (further) analysis and modeling
- Validation concept (detailed in Sect. 4.2.4.2)

Process-related results:

- Process goals (see Table 4.2)
- Process risks (see Table 4.3)

Table 4.2 Goals and metrics of software deployment process

Major goals	Metrics
Improved output quality through standardized process	>85 % of all client computers (deployment targets) are reached
Improved output quality through enforcing performance of all steps, particularly in quality assurance	>98 % successful deployments (on reached target systems)
Increased transparency	Stakeholders can access instance status information at any time and in real time
Reduced cycle time	<2 weeks (for standard deployments)
Minor goals	Metrics
Automated and detailed documentation of instances (logging)	Availability of detailed event logs
Improve response time in problem handling	Meet defined time constraints for (emergency) changes

Table 4.3 Process risks and counter measures

Risk level	Risk description	Counter measure
High	Faulty deployment scopes may endanger client function → roll-outs are critical and set dependent service user projects at risk	Documentation of scope development
		Early and intensive communication in case of scope deviation
		Early alerts and communication in case of error situations
Medium	Service user misinterpret modeled process	Early and intensive service user participation in process design
Low	Poor process performance caused by service user	Careful monitoring and quick action at execution time

- IT support of process tasks/activities

  The participants identified two IT systems supporting the process activities. LanDesk Client Management is a client engineering and software deployment system with functions for creating images or administrating the client landscape. MS Word, MS Excel and MS Powerpoint were selected to be used for activity check lists, protocols and reporting.
- Process network

  For a top-down view on the software deployment process and its positioning in the overall process landscape the participants created process network diagrams (PND). First they derived a PND from the ALM process chain in Fig. 4.1, by adding calls between processes in the form of input and output relations (see Fig. 4.3, upper part). Then they split the software deployment process into related sub-processes as shown in the lower part of Fig. 4.3.

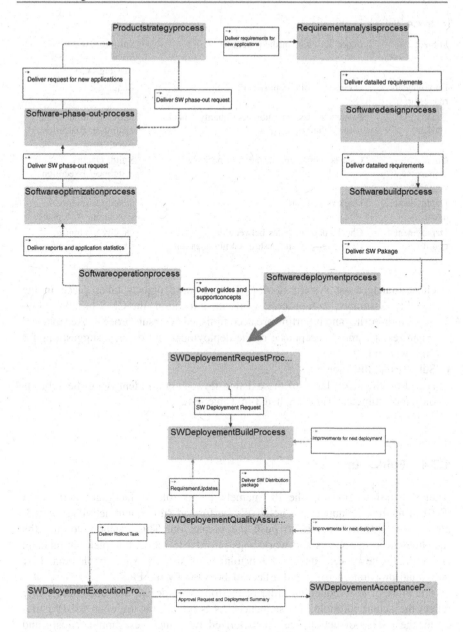

Fig. 4.3 Process network diagrams 'Application Lifecycle Management' and 'Software Deployment Process'

Software Deployment starts with the 'Request' sub-process, where a requestor defines the requirements for a deployment. 'Build' includes the creation and configuration of distribution packages and deployment tasks as objects in the

Table 4.4 Subject identification

Subject	Major activities in the process	Sub-process involvement (see Fig. 4.3)
Deployment requestor	Orders software deployment	Request
Quality verifier	Assures software deployment quality (checks scope definition etc.)	Request, Build, Quality assurance, Execution, Acceptance
Client management engineer	Creates scopes and installation packages	Build, Quality assurance, Execution
Deployment agent	Deploys software	Quality assurance, Execution, Acceptance
Deployment coordinator	Checks dependencies between deployments, checks reports and assures communication	Quality assurance, Execution, Acceptance

client management system (CMS). Testing these objects takes place in the 'Quality Assurance' sub-process, while in 'Execution' the CMS-based deployment, monitoring and reporting are accomplished. The sub-process 'Acceptance' organizes structured acceptance of the deployment and collects suggestions for improvement.
- Subject identification
  Based on the swim lanes of the existing flow diagram identifying the subjects only took minutes. They are listed in Table 4.4.

4.2.4 Follow-ups

After the initial workshop the PL, namely in his role as facilitator and expert (S-BPM method), planned and iteratively performed subsequent activities according to the S-BPM lifecycle to push the project on. This meant involving the stakeholders in interviews and workshops in order to refine, complete, implement and validate the process design. Such joint work usually was complemented by individual preparation work and a later elaboration by the PL.

The more or less sequential order of the following description does not exactly reflect the actual chronological sequence. As is typical for the open S-BPM lifecycle, the course of action was characterized by sometimes simultaneously and iteratively performed activities.

4.2.4.1 Analysis and Modeling
At first the PL interviewed the identified representatives (actors) of each subject about their work procedures in the sub-processes. The information gathered was first documented in the Word file as in Table 4.4, but more detailed, and per sub-

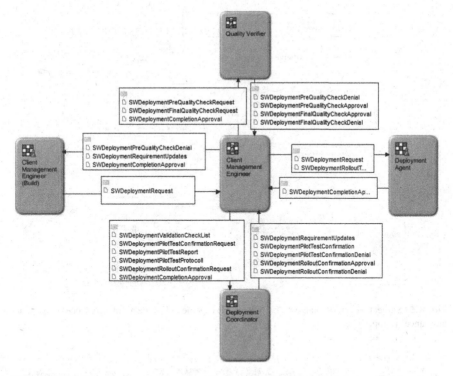

Fig. 4.4 Subject interaction diagram for sub-process 'Quality assurance'

process. It was used to clearly separate steps between subjects and to identify interaction points.

The latter formed the basis for modeling the communication structure in the Metasonic Build, for each sub-process revealing the message exchange between subjects and their linking via interface subjects. In small workshops the PL discussed and validated (see Sect. 4.2.4.2) each of the five resulting subject interaction diagrams (SID) with the concerned actors and governor (here: team manager 'client services'), ending up with 37 message types. Figure 4.4 depicts the SID for the 'Quality assurance' sub-process as an example.

Together with the existing flowchart the verbal description of subject activities also served as input for modeling the subject behavior in the Metasonic Build by the PL. In order to refine the models he also observed and participated in the processing of real·software deployment instances, taking the roles of the different subjects (apprenticing). The drafted subject behavior diagrams (SBD) were used for discussions with the actors in order to correct and complete the behavior specification (see Sect. 4.2.4.2). Figure 4.5 depicts a part of the SBD for the 'Client Management Engineer' in the 'Quality assurance' sub-process.

While observing real instances the PL could also identify business objects transferred with the exchanged messages (e.g., forms, documents, checklists),

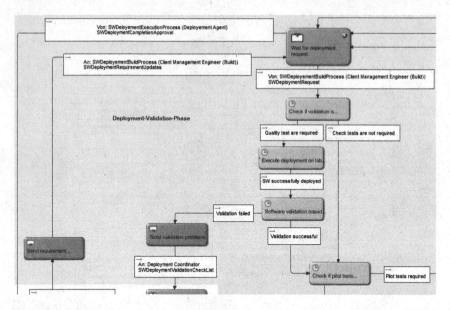

Fig. 4.5 Subject behavior diagram for 'Client Management Engineer' in sub-process 'Quality assurance' (clipped)

BO name	SWDeployment Request		
Data element	Type	Mandatory	Remark
Deployment Requestor	String	Yes	
Title	String	Yes	Rollout Title
OS	Enumeration	Yes	Options: • Windows • MAC OSX
Due Date rollout	Date	No	
Pilot phase needed	Boolean	No	

Fig. 4.6 Data structure of the business object 'Software deployment request' (clipped)

including their data structures. Again, the information obtained was documented both in the Word file (see Fig. 4.6 for a data structure) and in the Metasonic Build and then evaluated in workshops with the actors. Modeling in Build also included the specification of layouts for and views on business objects (see Fig. 4.7), later at runtime controlling the access (e.g., read, write) to data elements of business objects in any behavior state and the presentation on the screen. In order to create the business objects, views and layouts available at runtime they were assigned to the subject behavior states where necessary.

View "SWDeploymentBuildProcess_CreateModifyWrapper_view"

Elemente für View auswählen:

Element	Typ	Min	Max	Inaktiv	Versteckt	Suchfeld	Übersichtssp...
SWDeploymentBuildProcess_C							
Deployment requestor	String	0	1	✓			
Title	String	0	1	✓			
OS	Enumeration	0	1	✓			
Due date rollout	Datum	0	1	✓			
Pilot phase needed	Boolean	0	1	✓			
Pilot users	Enumeration	0	3	✓			
Additional pilot users	String	0	1	✓			
Testing needed	Boolean	0	1	✓			
Scope definition	Enumeration	0	1	✓			
Scope	Enumeration	0	1	✓			
Delivery method	Enumeration	0	1	✓			
Silent roll out	Boolean	0	1	✓			
Additional scope requireme	Text	0	1	✓			
Installation Wrapper neede	Boolean	0	1	✓			
Deployment reporting	Enumeration	0	1	✓			
Quality approved	Boolean	0	1	✓			
PreQualityCheck_State	Enumeration	0	1	✓			
Installation Wrapper	view (SWInstallationWrapper_CreateSource_view)	0	1				
Wrapper Title	String	0	1	✓			
Wrapper dialog text	String	0	1	✓			
Next logon delay	Boolean	0	1	✓			
Installation Delay allowe	Boolean	0	1	✓			
Delay dialog text	String	0	1	✓			
Maximum delay count	Integer	0	1	✓			
Fullscreen Blend needed	Boolean	0	1	✓			
Fullscreen text	String	0	1	✓			
Wrapper Video needed	Boolean	0	1	✓			
Wrapper Video source	Anhang	0	1				
Internet required	Boolean	0	1	✓			
VPN internal network req	Boolean	0	1	✓			
Prerequisites	Enumeration	0	1	✓			
Source Files	Anhang	1	1				
Installation Package	view (SWInstallationPackageView)	0	1	✓			
Distribution Task	view (SWDistributionTaskView)	0	1	✓			
DistributionPackage	view (SWDistributionPackage_Create_View)	0	1	✓			
Validation Checklist	view (SWValidationCheckList_view)	0	1	✓			

Fig. 4.7 Definition of the 'CreateModifyWrapper' view on the business object 'Software deployment request' (clipped)

4.2.4.2 Validation and Optimization

In line with the major goals in Table 4.2 the focus for validating and optimizing was on increasing the effectiveness in terms of output quality. Improving single steps came second. This primarily led to the modeling of the complete and consistent as-is procedure and to making sure that all activities are being performed. With respect to efficiency the cycle time was of interest. It will be addressed in Sect. 4.2.4.5.

The WK governors considered integrative validation and optimization already accompanying analysis and modeling to be very beneficial. For that reason they developed a respective concept in the initial workshop, jointly with the other participants. It envisages stepwise, bottom-up validation and approval of process artifacts, mainly models, on different levels, respectively involving the responsible governors besides actors and facilitators (see Fig. 4.8). In the course of the project the application of the concept was supported by the Proof and the Flow component of the Metasonic Suite with the created models having been uploaded before.

The first level refers to the subject behavior. Here the Web interface of the Metasonic Proof was used on a single computer to validate the (business) logic of the subject behavior without data and without concrete people being assigned to the

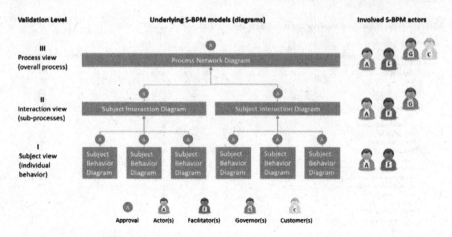

Fig. 4.8 Validation concept

subjects. Supported by the facilitator real actors of the software deployment process as subject representatives could quickly check completeness and the order of steps without the overhead of putting in concrete information. In this way they easily detected faults or missing actions. Corrections and suggested improvements were integrated on the fly and validated again.

After the behavior logic was found to be appropriate, the Metasonic Flow came into play in order to validate the behavior, including business objects and views and layouts. As the Flow component is a workflow engine for running process instances in real-world operations, the facilitator needed to assign people as concrete users to the subjects in the models before (see Sect. 4.2.4.3). After that the actors could log on as individual users to the system.

The facilitator then guided them through the workflow application, which not only controlled the interaction and single behavior steps of all users, but also presented and managed electronic forms based on the specified business objects, views and layouts. This way the users could test the behavior of 'their' subject, this time putting in valid but fictitious data and thus getting the feeling of the real workflow application. Now they could additionally recognize deficiencies with respect to business objects in the process designed so far, like missing or unnecessary data elements or inappropriate settings for change permission and the display of data. Again, modifications could be made and tested on-the-fly until an actor formally approved the correctness of his or her part of the workflow.

On approval of all subject behaviors of a sub-process, the communication as it was modeled in the subject interaction diagram was validated. On this second level the actors and the facilitator again initially used the Metasonic Proof in a server setting with distributed computers in order to iteratively test and improve the interaction in the sub-process from their point of view. The actors could 'play' their subject at their individual workplaces and report on the need for changes to the facilitator by e-mail. After they were satisfied also the team manager 'Client

Services' was involved as governor to identify potential deviations from the process interaction as he expected it. Therefore, the facilitator used the 'Recorder' function of the Proof software to meticulously show him the course of communication during processing instances (see Fig. 4.9).

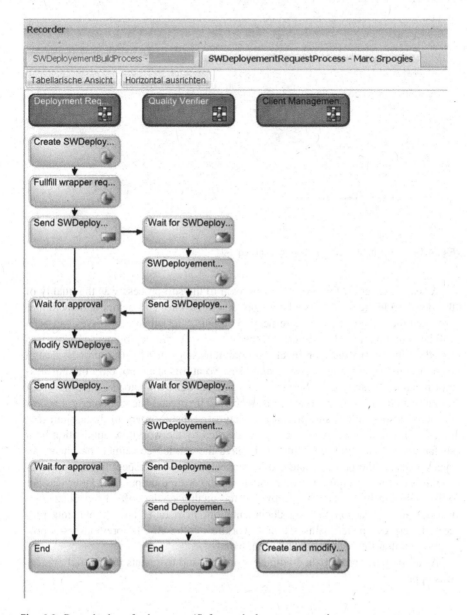

Fig. 4.9 Recorder log of sub-process 'Software deployment request'

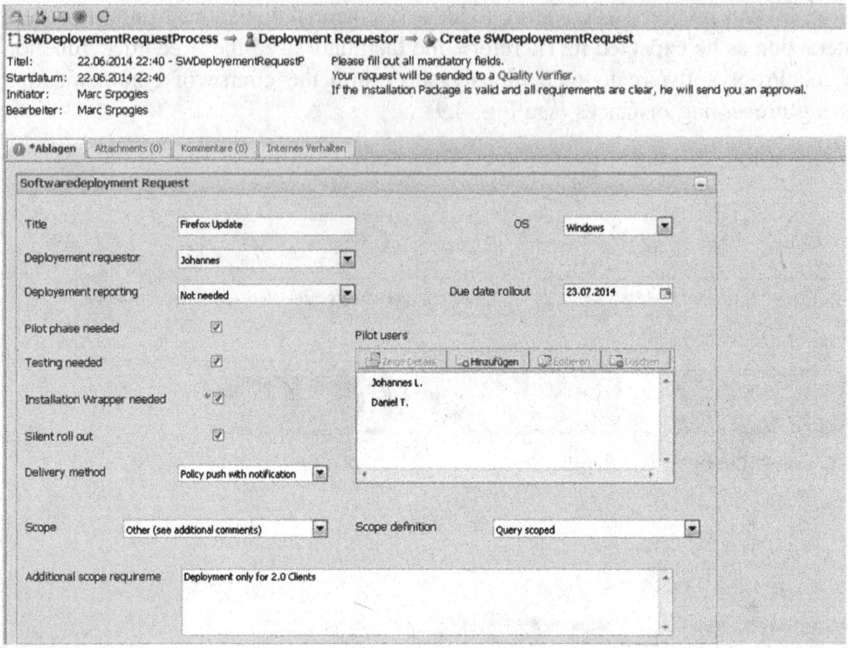

Fig. 4.10 Initiating a 'Software deployment request'

A second criterion for giving his approval to the sub-process was the quality of the deliverables (e.g., an installation package). To check it, actors and facilitator provided the governor with the respective output. After all sub-processes had been validated and approved as described, the overall software deployment process was tested on the third validation level. The previous steps had led to a process design without logic or content-related weaknesses. So at this stage not only the business unit manager 'Managed IT Services' and the managing director as governors, but also a real customer as a service consumer were involved. The customer got access to the Metasonic Flow and placed a variety of realistic orders in the system (see Fig. 4.10), which were then processed supported by the workflow application built so far without any programming. This gave the service consumer the chance to check whether the process matched his expectations with respect to the course of communication with the service provider and the desired output. The latter was not only evaluated by isolated inspecting of the quality of the software package, the roll-out and the accompanying documentation. In parallel all deployments processed were completed using the new workflow following the previous as-is procedure, so that the results could be compared.

As all parties were satisfied with new process and its results the overall process was approved.

4.2.4.3 Organizational Embedding

In S-BPM organizational embedding means relating process models to the actual organization, in particular assigning concrete human actors to the abstract subjects, allowing the workflow engine at runtime to involve the people as specified by the organizational design. For the software deployment process this only took minutes applying the User Manager component of the Metasonic Suite. The relevant information was already obtained during analysis and modeling. The facilitator just needed to represent it by defining the few users and, via groups and roles, finally assigning them to the subjects modeled in the SIDs in Build.

4.2.4.4 Implementation and Embedding in IT

Thanks to the nature of the S-BPM notation and the Metasonic Suite, bringing the designed process to execution as an IT-based workflow only required uploading the models to the Model Manager component. It became available for interpretation by Flow to process real-world instances. IT implementation of electronic forms included in the workflow at runtime had already been accomplished by modeling them in Build as business objects with data structures, views, layouts and specifications for their use in behavior states.

The PL also used the Metasonic Build functionality to define so-called dynamic process rules in order to automate state transitions at runtime based on business object content. This helped automatically route to the right process branch without user intervention. Such a rule, e.g., was used to control the behavior of the Client Management Engineer depending on the value of the data element 'silent roll-out' (true or false) in the business object 'deployment request'. In the 'True' case the workflow engine would perform the state transition to the respective activity thread and otherwise follow the transition to the alternative path.

The integration of other IT applications was realized by so-called refinements in the respective states, e.g., invoking MS Excel and opening a spreadsheet in the behavior specification of the subject 'Client Management Engineer' in the sub-process 'Software Deployment Build'. Integrating LAN Desk via refinements, where appropriate, was taken under consideration, but postponed to a follow-up project.

4.2.4.5 Monitoring

Monitoring aspects were considered in the project in a twofold manner. The first was providing real-time information about the current status of process instances at runtime. This transparency could be realized using the 'Recorder' function already described in the validation and optimization section (see Fig. 4.9) and also available in the Metasonic Flow.

With respect to the goal of reducing cycle time this PPI needs to be measured and controlled. For that reason the target value of two weeks (=10 days $\times$ 24 $\times$ 60 = 14,400 min) was specified in Build as a maximum on (sub) process level (see Fig. 4.11).

Fig. 4.11 Setting of maximum cycle time

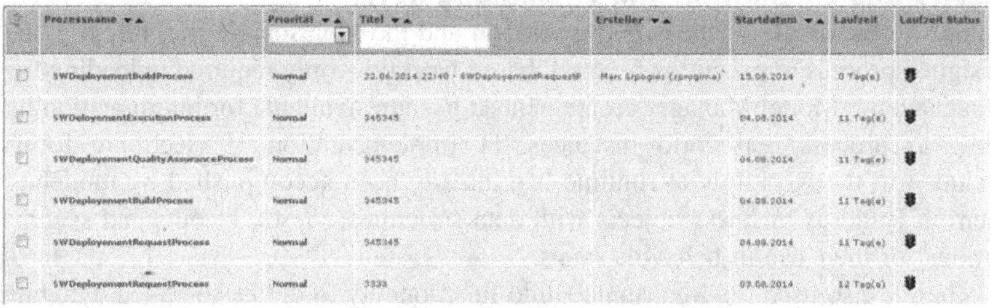

Fig. 4.12 Monitoring running process instances

At runtime the Instance manager component of the Metasonic Suite allows monitoring the running instances by displaying the elapsed processing time and traffic lights indicating the status with regard to the given maximum of cycle time (see Fig. 4.12).

As the Metasonic Flow process engine logs all sorts of events during execution (e.g., timestamps for state transitions), many valuable pieces of information are available for middle and long term analysis and reporting. Limited time in the project at hand prevented the stakeholders from getting deeper into that. Defining sense-making PPIs and further exploiting the capabilities Metasonic Suite offers for monitoring and reporting are candidates for future steps.

4.3 Results

Results of the work described in the previous sections can be distinguished in achievements and findings in the domain of software deployment, and in experiences related to S-BPM.

4.3.1 Goal Achievement in the Software Deployment Domain

Table 4.5 summarizes the achievements of the project in terms of improving the software deployment process, referring to the goals and metrics in Table 4.2.

Table 4.5 Goals, metrics and achievements

Major goals	Metrics	Achievements
Improved output quality through standardized process	>85 % of all client computers (deployment targets) are reached	Approved standardized process design implemented as IT-supported workflow automats decisions and can guarantee completeness of process steps
Improved output quality through enforcing performance of all steps, particularly in quality assurance	>98 % successful deployments (on reached target systems)	
Increased transparency	Stakeholders can access instance status information at any time and in real time	Subject-oriented process models and the 'Recorder' function allow one-stop info about status of instances being processed by distributed contributors
Reduced cycle time	<2 weeks (for standard deployments)	Cycle time is modeled as a constraint, can be monitored and thus be managed
Minor goals	Metrics	Achievements
Automated and detailed documentation of instances (logging)	Availability of detailed event logs	Given by process design and log file capabilities of the workflow engine
Improve response time in problem handling	Meet defined time limits for (emergency) changes	See above

Some more findings not directly related to the aspects in the table were:

- Intensive stakeholder discussion about process goals helped to identify process quality factors like client reachability, installation success and cycle time, which had not been completely understood before.
- During analysis, modeling and validation, stakeholders gained deep insight into how specifications (decisions) in the deployment order have impact on the steps and the course of a deployment and thus also influence cycle time. For instance, the customers can decide whether they want their package being tested only in a laboratory setting or during a pilot phase. Choosing the first option apparently leads to a different procedure and different consequences compared to the second one. The stakeholders explicitly understood that the customer thus takes a decision like "time before quality" or the other way round.
- Based on these insights the participants could clearly structure the process in several parts, in future allowing intermediate evaluation of (sub) process results (quality gates) and measurement of elapsed time in order to intervene early in case of deviations from to-be settings.

The proof of concept was given throughout the extensive validation and optimization sessions. The positive impact on the quantitative metrics still needs to be evaluated in daily operation after going live.

4.3.2 Experience with S-BPM Methodology and Software

The student started working on the project early in April and finished by the end of June 2014. He spent half of his working capacity on the project, which means the effort from his side was 40 man-days. Table 4.6 summarizes the experience gathered in the course of the project.

Table 4.6 Experience with S-BPM

What worked well? (positive aspects)	What needs to be considered? (Trade-offs, issues)
Analysis and Modeling	
Middle-out approach worked well	
Top-down structuring in process networks reduced complexity	Increasing modeling effort because of many external subjects
Independent bottom-up behavior modeling 'picks up' the individual actors and lets the process emerge	Missing end-to-end view (compared to flowchart) caused some irritation on management (governor) level
Active modeling by stakeholders increases their attention and concentration and accelerates elicitation of process information	Although the Metasonic Build user interface was perceived quite intuitive S-BPM modeling without substantial training turned out to be not as easy as expected
Direct modeling in the Metasonic Build is more efficient than using jBook forms initially	
Existing flowchart with swim lanes allowed behavior modeling in advance what significantly saved time of the actors	Flowchart was not very detailed
Apprenticing by the PL also helped preparing and refining behavior models, business objects and added to actors' time savings	
Interviews and small dedicated modeling workshops were very efficient (compared to workshops with many participants as experienced in other projects)	
Intensive stakeholder inclusion eliciting a lot of implicit process knowledge like communication patterns and information exchanged which were documented so far	

(continued)

Table 4.6 (continued)

What worked well? (positive aspects)	What needs to be considered? (Trade-offs, issues)
Stepwise validation concept	
Misunderstandings and logical errors were early and quickly identified and resolved both on individual behavior and on interaction level	Validation sessions are time-consuming and collide with daily operation. The facilitator needs to carefully coordinate them for balancing time savings through clearing faults with respect to the work capacity invested in validation
Stepwise procedure saved time of governors as they were only involved on an advanced maturity level (after approval of all actors)	
Time to (overall) approval was felt to be pretty short	Individual behavior validation can be performed with subject representatives of each subject at their workplace. The facilitator comes with a portable computer running a single instance of the Metasonic Proof. At the latest when the Metasonic Flow is used to test the process with real users and business objects a server installation is necessary to do it in a distributed environment. Otherwise the stakeholders need to leave their workplaces and meet in a single location which costs them additional time
Contentwise intensive but resourcewise moderate participation of all stakeholders until their approval fostered high acceptance of the resulting process design	
Involving a service consumer as customer can help increasing customer satisfaction	
Business objects	
Definition of business objects in general is easy	
Validation steps help quickly defining and verifying business objects	
Views and layouts allow sophisticated specification of behavior at runtime without programming	Defining high numbers of views and layouts is rather time-consuming
Organizational embedding	
Easy and quick assignment of concrete users with the Metasonic User Manager	
Changes of user data and roles do not require deployment to be effective in the runtime environment	
Implementation and embedding in IT	
Deployment of models and business objects is easy and does not require expert know how	
Refinements offer good opportunities to integrate software applications like LanDesk Client Management	For autodidacts like the student the available version of the Metasonic Suite documentation was not sufficient in the area of particular functionalities, such as refinements, process performance indicators, reporting

4.4   Conclusion and Outlook

The project results presented in the previous section indicate that the S-BPM methodology supported by suitable software tools actually can unfold many of the benefits claimed by its proponents.

The experience gained in this to a certain extent typical application setting provides valuable findings, even though the developed solution has not gone live yet. Whether and when this will happen is a matter of management decision, not only in terms of the overall future of BPM in the company, but also with regard to the underlying methodology and tool environment.

During the project a single cycle of organizational development was walked through completely, however without putting the result to operation. After going live, continuous organizational development could start, following and occasionally adjusting the presented pattern. As mentioned above, pushing forward PPI-based monitoring and seamless integration of LanDesk Client Management could be among the activities to further develop the designed business process as well as the S-BPM process.

References

Fleischmann A, Schmidt W, Stary C, Obermeier S, Börger E (2012) Subject-oriented business process management. Springer, Berlin
Fleischmann A, Raß S, Singer R (2013) S-BPM illustrated. Springer, Berlin (Open Access)
Sprogies M (2014) Prototypische Implementierung eines nach der subjektorientierten Methode entwickelten Geschäftsprozesses bei einem IT-Dienstleistungsunternehmen. Bachelor Thesis, Technische Hochschule Ingolstadt (in German)

A Service Hardware Application Case Fiducia

5

Lothar Hübner

Abstract

The various perspectives on how requirements for a process-developing IT application are described have led to the long-standing challenge of business IT alignment. For BPM (Business Process Management) modeling at Fiducia for many years, employees in the business departments have been able to compile large, complex processes by involving experts. Such models are not focused on the point of view of each individual employee involved but on the process as a whole. Consequently, the specification is coarse-grained to such an extent that an identification of the employees with a model and how they effectively work along a process cannot be achieved. Moreover, the superficial examination does not allow deriving guidelines for implementing an IT solution based on coarse-grained models. Introducing S-BPM brings the point of view of the individual employee to the center of describing processes. It thereby enables describing how processes actually run from his/her point of view. We have used this capability to empower the employees of the business departments to carry out this description task (modeling) themselves. Based on a sample project, which also includes integrating SAP as a database, I shall describe the difference between the "traditional" approaches to BPM and S-BPM. Since both approaches were used in this project, the benefits can be described precisely. The savings in Euro and time (earlier availability) represent an important factor here besides the quality of the description. By considering the details of the process, the quality of the description is significantly increased, and, last but not least, the identification of the employees in the business departments with their models, who finally were able to create applications by themselves.

L. Hübner (✉)
Rossbergstraße 54, 72336 Balingen, Germany
e-mail: lothar.huebner@lhci.de

© The Author(s) 2015
A. Fleischmann et al. (eds.), *S-BPM in the Wild*,
DOI 10.1007/978-3-319-17542-3_5

5.1   Background

As early as in the mid-1980s I had been considering possibilities of enabling employees of the departments to run data-processing operations by themselves. In those days this was known as end-user computing or fourth-generation language processing. The possibilities for letting employees from the department access information were still very limited at that time.

Despite this, the needs of the departments to generate information, regardless of IT (according mainly to their subjective viewpoint), was already very large at that time.

5.1.1   History of PCs

With the more widespread introduction of PCs into companies in the early 1990s the departments became increasingly independent of 'centralized' IT and thus started developing their own, 'shadow' IT departments. Tools such as Excel, Access and even Lotus Notes gave department users new flexibility to perform their individual processes and information gathering with IT support. In this way, an IT structure developed that was local to and controlled by the department.

5.1.2   History of the 'Mainframe Mind Set'

The IT departments in companies were still acting largely within the culture that had evolved with application development for mainframes since the early 1960s. In the early phase of the development process, quality was assured by long specification phases. This was necessary since changes to the programming languages used could only be made with difficulty, due to the complexity of the code. The departments were used to the fact that implementing IT applications costs a lot of time and money and that, therefore, demands for new IT applications, or modifications of existing applications, could not be implemented quickly or spontaneously.

5.1.3   The Change Brought by Globalization

The effects of globalization and the resultant changes in the market have led to a demand for continuously shorter and more frequent product development cycles. The interconnectedness brought by the Internet provides customers with ever more information to let them compare the offers of competing suppliers, which significantly affects product development in the companies. The agility required as a result directly influences the processes and the associated IT systems.

There is often a need for changing the original concept as early as in the specification phase of an IT application development process. After the subsequent development phase before the 'going-live' deadline there are always a number of requests for changing the 'finished' application by the involved department. Consequently, the expectations of the departments concerning a new IT application are not met by the time the application is launched.

5.1.4   Effects in the Companies

In the companies as well, the agility of the market is resulting in changes of methods with respect to collaborative work. Collaboration (close networking) among the people involved in the process results in better adaptations to the rapidly changing challenges. This is also causing changes in roles and creating new workflows that then must be modified quickly. This much narrower, frequently changing interplay increases the complexity and traceability of the overall workflows IT is required to support. Each department knows 'its' roles and workflows. In the past it was the role of the IT department to bring together these different viewpoints, ensuring a well-targeted application landscape for the company based on an economically viable IT architecture. The IT department was thus the link between all IT applications in the company.

5.1.5   Departmental Expectations Are Changing

Due to the increasing number of new opportunities available to the departments and their 'shadow' IT, the use of apps and actual cloud solutions, the expectations of the departments to respect with the IT solutions in the company are changing. Now they want to exert influence on the 'development' of IT applications—quickly, flexibly, and without the 'hurdles' that IT development requires when delivering high-quality applications.

The now familiar way of working with IT applications—resulting from the spread of apps—creates the expectation that company IT applications will also allow greater ease of use (usability) through a reduction in complexity from the user's point of view.

Forecasts by analysts that IT budgets will in future be shifted increasingly to the individual departments underline the trend that sees departments increasingly seeking opportunities for IT support for their processes independently of their own IT experts.

At the same time, due to the increasing complexity and more frequent changes in workflows and roles, it is becoming increasingly difficult for IT to function effectively as a central coordinator for the different roles/views (developing an authorization concept). The expert-driven consideration which IT applications are required in which situation (and which are not) is becoming ever more difficult to sustain.

5.1.6   An Ideal Scenario

In an ideal situation the experts of each department would be able to create and modify IT solutions directly in their own 'language'. In this case the description of which workflows are performed with what information by each individual (subject) from his/her own viewpoint would be most suitable, since it allows describing exactly what an employee of a department actually understands. He or she is the expert on what can be done with what information. If it were possible for him/her to describe this simply and create an IT application out of it, the solution would be to have IT applications created (for different types of application) by the department directly. This would have to be achieved within the technical framework conditions of the IT department, which is also responsible for providing the information.

At the same time, IT development would be relieved of the many and growing demands by the departments for applications, driven by the need for agility. The backlog of requests that is caused by capacity limits in the application development section would be significantly reduced. The IT department could then concentrate on important aspects such as standardizing the IT architecture and, above all, on ensuring data availability. The IT department would thus gain strength as a business enabler, while the department would be used as an 'extended workbench' for application development.

5.2   Needs at Fiducia

5.2.1   The Introduction of S-BPM

Over the last 15 years Fiducia has documented its business processes using a BPM (business process management) modelling tool (ADONIS by BOC). The modelers trained in company organization for this purpose have adapted their modelling environment so as to be able to use it highly efficiently. Realizing that this way of modelling operates on a very abstract level, it turned out not suitable for the required level of detail when modelling actual IT-supported workflows. Hence, I decided to introduce an entirely different and unique methodological approach: Subject-orientated Business Process Management (S-BPM), based on the Metasonic S-BPM suite.

The aim of this shift was to be able to describe business processes from the viewpoint of the 'subjects', i.e., the roles involved in the departments. The level of detail would have to be so precise that each employee could describe all the steps and information required to perform each process. Since the employee performs these processes himself, it is easy for him/her to formulate his knowledge in a descriptive way. Since workflows need only to be described from individual perspectives, the description should also be simple. An employee describes what he/she obtains as an input to a process and where it comes from, what actions he/she performs and what outcomes he/she passes to other subjects (employees, systems, etc.).

Such as description results in a defined process for each subject, created by the role-holder.

The interplay between individual subject-based models is then described in terms of the communication between these models. Through this separation of individual processes assigned to each subject and the description of the interfaces between individual processes there emerges a modular process system that develops in its own components independently of other components, and that, if nothing changes at the interfaces, can also be modify each component independently.

The Metasonic S-BPM suite can then generate workflows directly from these process models, making the processes testable or even allowing generating a complete IT application directly.

To introduce these new methods along with the tool it was necessary to persuade two groups of staff of the need for this change: the 'experienced process modelers' and the IT specialists.

5.2.2   The Process Modelers

The new method was easy for the young process modelers to accept. They had no resistance to using and learning new methods or procedures. They adapted straight away to the new methodology and quickly realized that it offers many advantages. The specialists in the departments were also able to describe their subjective knowledge of workflows and the information they require for processing. The descriptions were developed in their own 'language' and thus their identification with the outcome was very strong.

Acceptance by the experienced modelers was different, however. They did not adapt to the new method at first. They expected that the subject-oriented business process management method would not be capable of describing complex processes. They felt this way in particular because the modelling was done with only five modelling symbols. The greatest hurdle, therefore, was to gain the acceptance of these modelling experts. The first attempts to demonstrate the new method would not be usable focused on very large complex processes. Again and again, workshops were held whose objective was to implement complex processes.

Yet by considering these complex processes from separate viewpoints, namely from each individual subject involved, even the most complex process lost its perceived complexity. The scope of each process was of course retained, yet the individual process steps, isolated for each subject, were not at all complex. Linking these individual process elements via the communications interfaces brought the whole process back together. It was thus possible to represent any process, however large or complex, simply and clearly in terms of each subject.

Once this procedure had gained acceptance, another point of resistance was being encountered. Having separated processes and thereby simplified the understanding of what was still a large and complex process, there was now the demand to view the entire process in a single overarching representation. Using S-BPM this also is naturally possible. The individual subjects addressed on the communication level give a complete overview. The interaction between the subjects becomes clear. In this way it is possible to fully understand the entire process. What the individual subjects are then required to do with the incoming and also the outgoing information is described by the behavior model of each subject separately. For a complete overview of the project, however, this representation is not necessary. The 'subject jigsaw pieces' and their communication via interfaces create an overall picture, while the links between these jigsaw pieces provide a detailed communication description.

Now that S-BPM and the Metasonic suite had been introduced not only as a modelling tool, their benefits to generate applications became evident. From the description using the S-BPM method in Metasonic, the process workflow is directly generated as an executable IT application. This ultimately demanded a high level of precision in the description, but in turn resulted in much higher quality. Finally, the model does not have the character of something that is used once and stowed in a drawer; on the contrary, it forms the direct programming for the future IT application.

5.2.3 The IT Experts

Recognizing the automated execution is exactly what provoked the resistance of the IT experts. Being forced to generate IT applications from subject-orientated business management representations initially created disbelief, and then fears of having to surrender competence. The applications developers sensed a threat that the departments would chip away at their sovereignty as experts with entrenched traditions. The current handling of the technical IT architecture was targeting several aspects: scalability to the appropriate number of users, security, performance, interfaces to the operational databases, and much more. Once all these points had been tested to the highest satisfaction they had met the demands of Fiducia, with its 4000 workstations. However, these technical reservations could be dropped now.

The discussion of IT applications being developed solely by the IT department persisted. The idea of enabling the departments to create small, simple workflow applications by themselves was perceived as a loss of competence for the IT department. The IT department rather accepted being the bottleneck when the development section was simply unable to implement many of these demands due to bottlenecks in capacity. The applications developers could in fact give highest priority to the ongoing development of the core applications. Normally, this by itself results in a very good level of utilization. On the other hand, flexible IT applications demanded by the departments on short notice that are also not intelligibly described can be implemented only when conditions allow that. This results in either frequent refusals or realization dates that are far too late to be of use for the departments.

This fact, compromising the image of the IT department as a business enabler, was ignored, in addition to the increasing orientation of the specialist department towards its 'own' solutions without involving the IT department. This ignorance was precisely one of the motives for introducing a change. Introducing the S-BPM method via the S-BPM Metasonic suite was intended to offer a flexible, agile solution to the department by IT. The interfaces with the operational systems, the data and the infrastructure would be delivered by IT; the department itself, meanwhile, would provide the business logic in its own language. The two sides would meet in the Metasoniç S-BPM, suite to create complete applications. The IT department retains 'control' over the applications created on a uniform IT platform, while the department can implement its requirements as flexibly as IT applications.

The fact that the need for this change existed could demonstrated by over 7000 Notes databases that have increasingly multiplied; the IT department was no longer the owner of these applications, while the department had also lost control over them. It was therefore urgently necessary that a solution supported by the IT department could be made available to the department.

5.3 A Sample Project: Managed Service Hardware (IT-Supported Process Introduction)

The hardware for over 4000 workstations at Fiducia was procured centrally for the 17 departments. This hardware was supplied centrally by the internal IT department (company organization), which was also responsible for ensuring that these workstation devices were working (incident process). Fiducia decided to bundle the procurement and the allocation process within the in-house IT department. One of the company's subsidiaries had already provided this service for a major client. Hence, the internal IT department commissioned the subsidiary as provider to implement the managed service hardware. The result was a project, 'The Introduction of Managed Service Hardware', that will be described in this case study, in particular in conjunction with the description of the benefits of S-BPM.

5.3.1 The Need to Introduce Managed Service Hardware

Standard practice for each department was to define their budgets for PC hardware needs for their workstations themselves. The result was that while the PC hardware was normally purchased in accordance with the standard company procedures, the choice of what hardware was purchased/replaced, and at what time, was the responsibility of the department. This led to three problem areas:

1. PCs that were technically outdated were being retained; it was the departments that decided when a PC should be replaced.
2. New PCs were always purchased for new employees, despite useable machines being available by departing employees of other departments.
3. It was not always possible to verify which PC was being used where.

5.3.2   Managed Service Hardware as a Solution

'Managed service hardware' was intended to supply PCs to the departments on a
month-by-month billing basis. Procurement of the PC hardware would be done
centrally and up-to-date equipment would be supplied to the departments from a
storage facility. The decision to replace a PC would be the responsibility of the
internal IT department. The device types were to correspond to the employee role.
A high degree of standardization means diversity is restricted to seven groups
(roles), including laptops and tablet devices. Software is also bundled on the basis
of role. In case of fault occurrence, an appropriate replacement (PC) with the proper
software could then be supplied, and the faulty unit could be taken for repair. Fault
analysis would be carried out in the repair center subsequently, which would
significantly reduce the out-of-service time of PCs due to faults.

5.3.3   Project Start: Initial Information-Gathering Process

In order to introduce this service, initial discussions were started with the subsidiary. An already established process at one of this subsidiary's clients, which has
a similar number of workstations, was selected to form the basis for the new
process. The analysis began by using the descriptions available from the client's
project on how the service is provided for that client.

Since it has been possible to base the required IT solution on what seems, at
least, to be a similar business logic used for an external client, the possibility of
letting the department develop it with S-BPM and Metasonic was not considered.
Instead, the project was carried out in the 'classic' manner, with some BPM
modelling, (which was no longer to be used) and implementation effort carried by
an application developer—in this case, SAP customizing experts.

These descriptions, including how they can be adapted to Fiducia, were discussed in a series of workshops. The following five process elements (abbreviated
to IMACR) were examined:

- Install
- Move
- Add
- Change
- Remove

All staff nominated as responsible for the workshops contributed its experiences
to the corresponding process. These were the responsible roles nominated:

- Persons responsible for interfacing with the process to be outsourced
- Persons responsible for hardware specifications
- Responsible persons representing the subsidiary
- The dispatcher (task distributor)

Since the process had already been used for a client of the subsidiary, and the process was thus known in detail, these four roles were identified as those primarily involved in the process.

However, as it became clear later on, many more roles were relevant for the process. They had not become evident in the course of modelling, as in the beginning the focus was not on the subjects involved but rather on the workflow of each partial process. Most of the relevant information was thus discussed at a highly abstract level, in terms of workflows, their sequences and the interfaces.

5.3.4   Framework Conditions

To allow information about the status of the PCs to be punctually updated by the service technicians, it was necessary that the service technicians collect data directly on site and send them using smartphones. This would be achieved via an IT interface. Since the inventory data is managed in the SAP system as assets, a solution within the SAP system was assessed to be the naturally most suitable one. Here, each asset would be stored including its status, in a way that the current status for each PC would be known. The following parameters were defined as status properties:

- In use at a workstation
- In storage
- Undergoing repair
- Scrapped

To make this process more transparent it was modelled in the 'classic' manner (BPM) using the Adonis modelling tool. The modelling was done by internal modelling experts together with the departmental role-holders. The latter were asked in focus groups how the workflows run according to their view, and their responses were transferred to a BPM model (Adonis).

It was soon apparent that transferring the individual steps of the individual roles from the department into a model (to be created for each of the five process sections) was getting increasingly difficult. Although, e.g., an 'install' process is entirely straightforward at first sight, the different viewpoints of the different roles cause the modelling of each process step and thus tend to become ever more difficult to follow for the persons responsible in the respective roles. They do not see their individual roles as being central, but rather the workflows that have been documented across all roles.

The experienced process modelers nevertheless succeeded in modelling a process that is inherently consistent. They could achieve their objective, and validation was obtained at this very abstract level. What actually takes place in detail in the process is, however, remains open on this modelling level. It requires observing the actual role behavior, thus bringing the role to the center. As long as it is not the aim to create executable IT applications with BPM, much information can be dispensed with, which can in fact be of great importance if one models the process as it actually occurs.

The role-holders, who themselves have no experience in process modelling, were only able to test the process model under certain conditions. They could only identify themselves to a certain extent, since the modelling was performed by 'experts'. It was thus not 'their' process model. In the dialogue between the process modelling experts and the specialist role-holders from the departments, no common level for understanding could be achieved. While the modelers were constantly focusing on the overall process, the role-holders had in mind their individual areas of responsibility in detail. This was, however, not emphasized by the modelers, who necessarily held on to their overall view of the process.

After seven workshops, a comprehensive process model was established for each of the five partial processes (IMACR). These process models, together with the descriptions of the scope of each individual task (SLA), were adopted as the basis for implementing the managed service-hardware scheme, including its technical realization.

Since the task descriptions were related to the subsidiary's client company, they only needed to be adapted to the present situation. The actual outlay of over 50 person-days to that point had been necessary for modelling the five partial processes. All persons involved were satisfied with the outcome, and work started with creating a specification for the technical support. Based on the outcomes of the modelling process, the service-level agreements with their requirements and the necessary extensions in the system assets in the SAP system, a specification was created. Initially, a solution was drafted that could gather the data using a Lotus Notes-based workflow; this data should then be used as the basis for updating the SAP data stock once a day.

This mechanism, however, had to be rejected. Out of a total of some 4000 PCs, roughly 20 are in use (IMACR) each day. To allow the service technicians and the other roles to find the current state of affairs in a timely fashion in the database, the changes need to be made directly in the SAP database as the leading system.

The solution scenario was now defined in such a way that all participants were provided with dialogues within the SAP system. It supported them with the necessary information to search for and/or update information. The necessary process logic could be implemented accordingly with SAP tools (service manager), enabling the accurate execution of the required workflows. The SAP dialogues could be implemented on the intranet platform, as had been done previously for other SAP solutions, and could also be invoked from there. The interface to the smartphones could be enabled when purchasing new software.

5.3.5 First Rough Estimate: 150 Person-Days

Once the specification was created, an initial rough estimate was made for implementing the concept. An optimistic scenario projected at least 150 person-days for customizing SAP and for modifying the SAP database.

5.3.6   Weaknesses Recognized

After a first inspection of the specification and its estimation for implementation, various issues became evident.

5.3.6.1 Lack of Detail

The actual tasks required for implementing an IT application, which were known to the role-holders, had not been modelled. The role-holders were not aware of that; they knew the details after all, and were already overloaded when representing the total model on the level of detail used in the process model. Despite the lack of required detail, it was too complex for them, since it was not their viewpoint that had been modelled, but rather an overall system perspective.

5.3.6.2 Redundancies in Partial Processes

Due to the focus on the partial processes (Install, Move, Add, Change and Remove), in the development of the process model the employees who are actually involved in the process were only 'assigned' to these partial processes. They were not central to the process design. Hence, redundancies appeared in the individual partial process steps. Considered from the viewpoint of the subject (role) such phenomenon would have been clear, since the role-holders would have defined their tasks from their viewpoint, their area of responsibility. Yet, in this way, each partial process was described independently of the other processes. In addition, 'merely assigning' the employees did not make evident which further roles were seen and needed by these employees in their partial processes. This knowledge was not collected by an exclusive observation of the overall process. In other words, the process has been put to the foreground rather than workflows of individual roles.

5.3.6.3 Modelling Outcomes Are not Sufficiently Detailed

Another problem concerned the quality of the modelling outcomes. The departmental specialists were mainly knowledgeable in their own areas of responsibility, being part of a large overall system. By looking at the overall process in the course of the modelling, their awareness of its complexity increased. The discussion about workflows involving many other roles was considered overloaded by the 'role specialists'. They also kept giving a coarse-grained representation of their partial processes, trying not to increase the perceived complexity.

5.3.6.4 Low Level of Identification with the Outcome

As the departmental staff members are not skilled modelers, they need to accept the developments of the modelling experts. Similarly, the modelling experts are not specialists in the non-IT topics and struggle sometimes to understand what they are modelling. Accordingly, two cultures (the process modelers and the departmental specialist roles), each with different objectives, a different understanding and a different language, have come together in a dialogue that demonstrates the typical difficulties of translation between the business areas of the company and IT. For the departmental employees the outcome of the modelling process was not 'their' solution they had created by themselves.

5.3.6.5 Lack of Confidence in Making Mistakes

The role-holders from the departments are still not used to making statements on a higher level of abstraction of a process than their viewpoint. Due to their experience, if such statements are made, they will have to be interpreted for implementation. And, in case the statement is not absolutely correct, a change request will have to be made, which

(a) drives up costs,
(b) delays the planned implementation date, and *
(c) results in an even more difficult collaboration of the department with the IT section.

Overall, due to lack of detail, needless redundancies and ambiguities stemming from different viewpoints, the quality of process models is too poor to obtain practically useable inputs for implementing them.

5.3.7 Project Restart from Scratch

With a minimum of 150 person-days planned for implementation, modelling of insufficient quality and, finally, too many open questions about how to implementation the processes, I decided to rethink the project from the beginning. The new approach was based on the already introduced subject-orientated business management (S-BPM), although it was not popular with the 'experienced' process modelers.

5.3.8 Workshops with the Role-Holders

Together with a new team from the company organization, the persons in the responsible roles for the 'managed service hardware' process were invited to a relaunch workshop. This time, with S-BPM, the role-holders were the focal point. In the first workshop the departmental specialists were informed about the 'methodology' of how their knowledge would be collected and used to develop an IT application. Hereby, three different actions were represented in different colors.

• Green for 'I'm receiving something',
• Yellow for 'I'm doing something with it',
• Red for 'I'm delivering an outcome'.

Using this simple structure, discussions began about the 'Install' process. The content of the different tasks and the framing conditions were already known. What needed to be questioned, just as in the earlier project, were solely the necessary workflows and the roles involved.

Three different media were provided to enable the employees to 'capture' this information.

- Direct capture on the PC with an easy-to-use interface in Metasonic.
- Direct modelling on a 'modelling table' that at this time was still at an early stage of development (today this would be by far the best medium in my view).
- The 'flip chart' to which magnetic cards are attached in three colors and which can be connected in the sense of an S-BPM model. The model can then be captured directly via the PC interface.

In the project, the latter method ·was adopted, since no technical hurdles (working on PCs with management) should arise, and the attention would be on the methodology rather than on tools from the beginning.

5.3.9 S-BPM Supports the Departments' Way of Thinking

It became clear from the first workshop that the departmental employees could work with this method while maintaining a strong sense of identity. Using these three questions, each could describe the workflow known to him/her. The important details were also addressed immediately, in particular what information is required and who else also needs to be linked to this element of the workflow. It was thus the world the individual subjects perceived that was described. For each involved role (subject), a workflow with the necessary interfaces and content elements could be developed in this way. Shortly after being introduced to the methodology the role-holders took over the modelling themselves.

At the end of the first workshop the workflow models were entered directly into the Metasonic S-BPM suite. The data capture was complete in barely an hour and an initial workflow could already be visualized and simulated as a prototype. It became clear very quickly that more roles were required than those that had been originally defined. They are given in the following for Fiducia and the subsidiary.

Fiducia:

The departmental employee
The employee's manager
The person responsible for the hardware specifications
The person responsible for the interface to the outsourced process
The person responsible for the commercial stock

These five roles were represented by two employees.

Subsidiary:

The responsible person of the subsidiary
The dispatcher (task distributor)
The technician

Head of repair center
Head of software loading

These five roles were represented by three employees.

5.3.10 Methodology Can also Be Used by the Department in Connection with a Tool

These role-holders were thus also incorporated into the modelling process. In two further workshops (one day each) all the partial processes of the managed service hardware process were modelled with all participants based on the S-BPM method. Since the outcomes of this modelling could also be run directly on the PC, it was decided at the second workshop to use the PC directly for the modelling. The hurdle of using a tool had been overcome; the method had gained acceptance. At the point in time when a finished workflow emerged from the modelling and could be verified by simulation on the PC, many details emerged that required clarification. Since, however, the model could be modified straight away, the departmental specialists continuously gained confidence bringing their experience and understanding to bear. They could make no mistakes that would be difficult to rectify. They could make changes at any time and these would take effect straight away.

5.3.11 Full Identification with the Outcome

A further interesting effect could also be observed. Since the subjects (here, departmental experts) were at the center stage and were themselves 'modelled', the demand for certain special requests also changed. However, now the departmental experts themselves had to describe them, rather than passing them as development requests to the application development team without being aware how much effort was involved. The result of this approach was that functions that were not strictly necessary were left out, while the departmental experts identified entirely with the completed outcome. They had, after all, developed it by themselves. This accounts for a significant potential for savings in development costs, since only the genuinely necessary functionality is developed and no 'frictional loss' occurs between the department with its demands and the IT department with its limited resources. And since changes can often be made 'on the fly' by departmental staff themselves, they are motivated to remain involved with the IT application even after it has been created.

5.3.12 IT Application Could Be Completed at an Early Stage

After three workshops with five attendees each (15 person-days), modelling was completed—and already in an executable version. Now work could begin on the IT application itself.

The depth of detail was now sufficient to execute the workflows immediately, including all their content-related requirements. There were therefore no longer redundancies in the partial processes, as these had become apparent using the subject-centered approach and the prototypical execution. A very important insight was that the subsidiary could not provide this level of detail for the processes, although they would also have been conducted in a similar way for the external client.

However, the attempt to represent the processes using traditional BPM methods, as at the start of the project, did not result in a model representing the actual process in full detail, containing the actual workflows. Despite a very high outlay on modelling with BPM, the outcome did not represent the real-life situation. Using S-BPM, on the other hand, the workflows as actually being performed became evident. It resulted in many significant improvements with respect to standardization and clarification of interfaces, and thus in optimized work practice.

Additionally, the degree of completeness of the description of the workflows increased during these three workshops. For the first time, not only the standard processes, i.e., 'when everything works according to plan', were examined, but also the many exceptions that arise in practice. For the latter there had not been specific descriptions so far. Somehow it had always worked out, however, leading to unnecessary excess costs due to unclear definitions. Now, this excess outlay was no longer necessary.

The role-holders involved in the process still collaborated yet each from his/her own perspective or position to describe the workflows in such detail that the specification and technical concept were to a large degree already complete at this stage. To implement the IT application, data storage in SAP was still required. The SAP system was therefore considered as a subject in itself when modelling. Here again the same logic was used: what information SAP receive, what should be processed using that information, and what information should be passed on. In this respect, what a 'subject' represents is of no consequence to the method. This simplification also proved immensely helpful in facilitating the discussion when creating the model and the 'technical' interfaces.

Following this initial gathering phase of the descriptions of the current processes from each subject's viewpoint during the three workshops, the process models were further refined and complemented with additional detail. Since the IT application thus obtained needed to be available to all employees on the intranet, the design of the input dialogues was specified in greater detail. When a managed service request was made, the interface to SAP was implemented to create a ticket automatically, and to adapt the relevant status message in SAP to this asset.

The Metasonic S-BPM suite has its own solution for including the dialogues on smartphones. It was integrated along with the interface to the SAP system. The service technicians can thus use their smartphones to store information about a ticket directly in the database of SAP and can also directly view new orders or changes of orders. The complete implementation of the outcomes (from the three workshops and a few subsequent specialist discussions), i.e., the executable IT applications required about 30 person-days development effort. Compared to the previously (optimistically) estimated 150 person-days this difference represented a significant cost saving.

Another factor was owed to the limited capacities of the SAP customizing personnel implementation had earlier been planned to take some nine months. Yet using the S-BPM approach provided by the Metasonic suite, the application was running in production in just two months. Due to this much earlier availability, the benefits of the solution could come into effect seven months earlier than planned.

5.4   Summary of Experiences Gained in This Project

The former standard procedure, in which process modelers (as the developers of the model) and departmental staff (as the process experts) sit opposite each other and try to map the workflows from their own viewpoints to create an IT application, has significant disadvantages.

The modelers are not experts in the departmental fields (non-IT); rather they need to represent in a model what the departmental staff tries to explain to them.

The departmental staff members, meanwhile, have their focus on those parts of the process that they deal with themselves, while the process modelers are concerned with the overall business process or work procedure. The roles involved are thus only assigned to parts of the overall process they are not the focus in reaching an outcome. Using a different approach, namely following the S-BPM method, the departmental specialists have now begun to describe, in their 'own language', the part of overall processes that they individually handle. Now the process modeler is mainly a moderator who provides support for how the method is used. The departmental staff members soon came to understand the method and are now capable of doing the modelling themselves.

Since there was no longer a media gap between the specialists and the modelers, the quality of the created model was substantially higher. The departmental specialists created the model themselves. No modelling expert was required to interpret what the specialists had told them in order to then integrate this information into a model. Since the outcome was immediately executable, it could be validated straight away, and deficiencies could be quickly spotted and corrected.

The difference between the process models created with the traditional BPM method and S-BPM could be revealed clearly, as it became clear how limited the level of detail is that can actually be portrayed with traditional BPM modelling techniques. Although this situation can certainly be improved with further expenditure, the underlying deficiencies, due to the focus on the overall process and its workflows rather than on those of the subjects, always remain.

The departmental employees identified themselves fully with the solutions they had produced. They were able to avoid excessive demands on themselves, while fully understanding in a verifiable way their workflows and actions, including exceptions in the process.

This statement also holds for the final documentation, as it captures how the workflows are actually used. Any change of the IT application is based on S-BPM models. Consequently, the documentation is always up to date. The employees' understanding of the workflows, including exceptions, was deepened, which in turn increased their cooperation in terms of efficiency and the quality for the customer due to the achieved transparency of work procedures.

The standards for database interfaces in the Metasonic S-BPM suite enabled the integration of SAP as data storage system in a simple and comprehensive way. Since the user interfaces for the workflows were generated via the intranet or smartphones directly (without additional programming), the IT expenditure was significantly lower than in the solution originally conceived. The expenditure for the project was significantly below the planned effort for the original approach.

Expenditure with BPM (approx. 260 person-days):
BPM modelling (approx. 40 person-days), creation of specification and technical concept for implementation in SAP (approx. 50 person-days), SAP implementation by Customizing dept., including testing, documentation and productive release (approx. 150 person-days). Acquisition and technical implementation of a smartphone support system (approx. 20 person-days). Implementation was to be expected in one year.

Expenditure with S-BPM (approx. 70 person-days):
Modelling with the S-BPM method including documentation of IT application (approx. 30 person-days), implementing interface into SAP system and adapting database for the required parameters (approx. 30 person-days). Tests and pilot runs (approx. 10 person-days). Final implementation could be done in 3 months.

5.4.1 Outcomes and Recognized Effects of the Actions Taken

The introduction of S-BPM into a company is initially met with various forms of resistance. They vary according to the extent of the culture of readiness to change in a given organization. Changes are often perceived as threats. Hence, once a change requires fundamental rethinking, it is necessary first to get those on board who tend to hold onto the old approach. Modelers who have used BPM for years are likely to continue working according to the logic familiar to them; they will regard any change as nothing more than an augmentation or modification of BPM. They cannot (or will not) admit the possibility of a subject-focused approach. It is certainly hard for such groups to accept this new approach when they are not keen to recognize any undermining of the dependency of the departments on the modelling experts for IT application development. Further developments in traditional BPM, such as BPMN 2.0, are generally easier to accept. Comprising at least 50 notation elements, each having different characteristics, this modelling notation is sufficiently complex to be left in the hands of modelling experts. The benefits of S-BPM in enabling the departments to develop their models themselves can never be achieved with BPMN 2.0.

Application developers do not want, on one hand, to deal with the demand of the departments for small, agile IT applications. They simply have neither the time for meeting them, nor perceive the importance of such applications to the business areas. On the other hand, they do not want to give up their 'unique selling point' of being the only group capable of creating IT applications; this has always been the case, after all, for 50 years. In general the IT department's confidence that departments can create their own applications is extremely low, and thus they tend to reject new approaches, such as S-BPM, in the beginning.

The departmental employees, the business experts, are also not immediately convinced that this S-BPM method, created specifically for their way of thinking, will provide them with a solution overcoming the IT application bottleneck. The practice that has been in place for the last 50 years and plays a major part is such that the interaction between the departments and the IT section is seen only to work in the way as experienced in the past. Nevertheless, the business experts are the group that has the highest willingness to engage in implementing new approaches. Due to the pressure of the market to provide new, agile IT applications that can respond quickly to changes in customer expectations, this willingness has increased. This development could be triggered by the need for shorter product development times, better, more flexible services, or a different sales approach.

The former 'shadow IT' in the departments suffers from the fact that it is not being supplied with the actual data of the company. Attempts had been made to make all information available to the departments by developing sophisticated data warehouse solutions; yet the workflows and actions had to be somehow supported with mails or Notes databases, in case it was not possible to wait for solutions from the IT department. And this shadow IT no longer meets today's demands of IT applications. Its functionality is far too limited, it is isolated, as few groups in the department are able to use this tool, and it is impossible, finally, to integrate databases or to link such solutions with an operative core system.

From the viewpoint of the continuously increasing compliance requirements, there are now provisions that cannot be satisfied by shadow IT, too. Consequently, all three groups—department, process modeler, and IT department—need to be persuaded when S-BPM should be accepted. Gaining the approval of the departments is relatively straightforward due to the simple and straightforward development procedure. An early implementation meeting a typical need of one of the departments can help increase the acceptance of a novel methodology. A highlight in the project described was a change request that occurred 15 min before the application was due to go live. An employee had another good idea for improving the process at a certain point. When we offered him the possibility of implementing this modification, he could not believe us. Yet we made the change, and the application went live with this modification in place ten minutes later. This was a typical positive multiplier effect.

For process modelers it needs to be clear that they will continue playing an important role in the future, however, from a different perspective. Lengthy print-outs stemming from modelling large processes are no longer acceptable. Rather, by viewing an overall process from separate viewpoints according to individual subjects, intelligible processes are created. In most cases the departments will be glad for the continuing facilitation by the modeler. After all, even with the S-BPM approach it is possible to define optimal or rather suboptimal workflows. The future role of the modeler will focus on such aspects, and lead to optimized process models that support the continuous improvement process through their flexibility for adaptation and their representation close to the perceived reality.

Application developers need to realize that their importance as business enablers will be recognized by the department only, once the changed requirements can be satisfied from the business areas, such as agile IT applications that can be both created and modified quickly. By using S-BPM and the Metasonic S-BPM suite, such an approach is enabled. The application developers and the overall IT department remain the owners of the platform and the interfaces. As such, they are also responsible for the most important element in the entire data-processing operation—information. This new role creates space for large and central application systems that cannot be created by the departments themselves. At the same time, however, the business areas are supported by the IT department in such a way that they can respond to the quickly changing demands of the market.

5.4.2 Several Benefits Have Been Achieved by Introducing S-BPM

Significantly less expenditure when implementing an S-BPM model created in cooperation with the department reduces the production costs. By separating processes by means of individual subjects, the complexity can be significantly reduced. This in turn considerably simplifies working with the role-holders in the departments, as they understand these 'isolated' viewpoints. By describing the individual communication to the other 'isolated' viewpoints of the other role-holders, the overall process and thus also the entire IT application emerge.

Achieving such a level of understanding facilitated working with the department when modelling processes. A form of 'language', S-BPM, was used for describing and implementing the IT application. This resulted in significantly better quality of outcome (no media gap), and the acceptance of the created solution in the departments was considerably higher. They had created the solutions by themselves.

Due to separating into subjects it was also much easier to make changes within complex processes. When beginning to describe a process, not all details are always present, yet with the S-BPM method it is possible to begin straight away. Changes often affect only individual, subject-related solutions. Using S-BPM they can then be modified independently of the others. Precision can thus be increased step by step.

Due to the significantly shorter production times for IT applications when using S-BPM, the benefit of a solution can become effective much earlier. Its flexibility allows meeting the need for adaptation arising from its use in production far sooner, leading to competitive advantages through application systems that can be used earlier and better adapted. Similarly, IT solutions that have not yet been thought through in detail can be made available at a very early stage. The stimuli for optimization popping up when using these applications can be implemented straightaway, dispensing with a long analysis phase that attempts to predict such optimization. It can be recognized when analyzing typical change request procedures after an application has gone live that this traditional way of development does not lead to the expected benefits. Obtaining experience directly from practical operations and then implementing work support quickly amounts to a paradigm shift in application development.

Documenting the IT applications and the associated processes and maintaining this documentation in its most up-to-date status, reflecting actual practice, offers a new level of transparency. Documentation no longer needs to be something laboriously assembled after release: it is now a component of the application itself and fully integrated. Information about the actual execution of the process steps, including content and time, is logged and can be automatically generated using a uniform procedure in S-BPM and the Metasonic suite. Such information also forms a significant element of process cost optimization, since only information actually obtained can be used to drive improvements. Often the benefit of such exact logging of process tasks is overlooked in IT applications.

Using a process interface that is uniform for all workflows, the different user interfaces of different IT applications can be aligned. Thus, e.g., in case of authorization management for data access, a single IT application was created using S-BPM to manage the various different authorization systems due to the variety of databases and systems and their specific tools. This uniform application provides the employees with a single user interface.

5.5   Closing Remarks

In conclusion I can only stress that S-BPM offers an entirely new approach to defining processes and their direct implementation utilizing IT applications. The underlying development principle is to decompose processes, however complex they are, into the individual subjects that are involved in the process execution. Apparent complexity is thus broken down and at the same time the quality of requirements of an IT application is ensured in such a way that an application can be derived from the specification directly.

This decomposition leads to an understanding by the departmental employees of how they can describe a process from their own viewpoint. They are ultimately the experts who are best able to describe their work. The fact that executable IT applications can then be created immediately enables the specialists to verify and to change workflows straightaway. They are thus enabled to engage actively and to take responsibility for the outcome, while identifying themselves with the results.

Using the standard Metasonic platform provided by the IT department, IT applications automatically generated from the modelling can be put into operation straightaway, still under the supervision of the IT department. The interfaces to data and systems are provided centrally by the IT department and can be selected by the departments. Changes in the course of modelling, and even during execution of an application already in use, are often very easy to achieve owing to the isolating subject view. On the basis of my experience, the adoption of this change process for this kind of IT application development is a must for agile organizations. S-BPM enables such significant benefits for the IT support to the business areas that considerable savings and, above all, quality improvements can be achieved only after completing few projects. Using a corresponding tool, agility can also be achieved professionally with IT applications.

Designing an Agile Process Layer for Competitive Differentiation

6

Frank Lorbacher

Abstract

The services offered by the management consultancy Detecon International GmbH include the support of its clients during digital transformation. One of the major pillars in the design of digital transformation is process digitalization, i.e., the consistent and complete automation and integration of processes. The author reports here on a fictitious client project which he has created on the basis of his experience from a large range of similar, real projects. The objective of the client project is the subject-oriented design of a core process digitalized completely and consistently on this basis. The necessity of digital transformation gave rise to our client's requirement for a consistent design and complete digitalization of the process for contract performance. At the same time, the contract performance implemented in a large ERP system was to be made more flexible. Despite that, the process was to be implemented in such a way that it relieved work pressures on personnel and reduced the time for billing cycles. The requirement was realized by separating the process logic from the ERP system and putting it in a dedicated process layer. Simultaneously, the ERP system was established as a data-carrying layer. The two were connected via an integration layer in which the Web services were located. The process layer was designed by the workers involved in the process on a subject-oriented basis so that the processes were broadly accepted by the business side.

F. Lorbacher (✉)
Detecon International GmbH, Sternengasse 14–16, 50676 Cologne, Germany
e-mail: frank.lorbacher@detecon.com

© The Author(s) 2015
A. Fleischmann et al. (eds.), *S-BPM in the Wild*,
DOI 10.1007/978-3-319-17542-3_6

6.1   The Challenge

During our initial meeting with our client, the later project manager described to us the challenges confronting his company because of the severe competition on the market and the growing demands of its customers:

"We see ourselves as a broker between our customers and the service providers. Our customers expect us to coordinate the contract execution completely, but they also want us to be faster and more flexible in our service performance. Even if the contract award and execution become highly dynamic through flexible design, we cannot really allow ourselves any mistakes in the billing, and the billing cannot become too complicated from the customers' standpoint. If we do not meet our customers' expectations, they can also go straight to our service providers to make their purchases".

"Our customers can place their orders on a customer portal, on the phone, or by email. For example, we receive orders from new customers via email or by phone when we have a contract with them, but their account has not yet been created for administration on the portal. We utilize a large ERP system to coordinate the orders. We have attached a service portal to the ERP system and use it to pass the orders on to our service providers. Billing of customers on behalf of the service providers is handled by the ERP system. A file for internal offset of services and reconciliation of balances is generated from this system. Customers can see the progress of the orders on the customer portal, but not completely. The service providers can report progress for order execution via their service performance portal, but not completely. The progress reports from the service providers are synchronized only in part with the progress reports we place on the customer portal".

"We always have a problem when a customer wants to make changes after placing an order and the order has already been sent to our service providers. Things really become complicated when our service provider bills a customer for a change in services agreed upon with the customer, but we don't know anything about it. We cannot make the changes directly in the order in either of these cases. We must take the long way around of working with cancellations, new orders, and unstructured order references. There are similar complications when something changes in the customer's master data during the performance and billing of the service and the master data are not maintained properly."

This was how our client expressed its requirements for a consistent and complete digitalization of its service performance and billing process. Taking the description of requirements, we distilled the following approaches as the starting points for optimization and concentrated especially on finding solutions to them during the course of the complete and consistent process digitalization:

- The data about the customer, contract, service provider, and invoice are located in separate systems.
- The lifecycle of an order is not consistently defined and implemented from the customer order to the contracting of the service provider to the accomplishment and billing.

- The central IT system for service performance and billing is the ERP system.
- The ERP system supports a standardized process for service performance and billing which does not completely cover the client's requirements. When there are changes in the order, the rigidity of the standardized process causes additional expenditures of time and effort in processing.
- Information used for service performance and billing is not available when it is needed.

6.2   The Solution

During the first two steps, we did some work on the architecture aimed at complete and consistent digitalization of the process and the exploitation of optimization potential. The first step was to analyze the processes from an end-to-end (E-t-E) view; afterwards, we designed a three-layer architecture for the implementation. We did not commence design, automation, and integration of the process until the work on the architecture had been completed. For the process work, we used subject-oriented business process management (S-BPM) and a suite of tools which supports S-BPM in modeling and implementing processes.

End-to-end (E-t-E) view in the process To begin with, we incorporated the end-to-end view into our client's architecture as a means of structuring and reducing process complexity. This enabled us to decompose a process monolith into six separate processes. The functional scope was defined for each process and clearly distinguished from the others. The E-t-E view is moreover an approach for the complete and consistent identification of the required business objects and their lifecycles. Using the E-t-E view provides a dedicated trigger for the launch of each process. At the same time, the E-t-E view is used to identify the business object which is the necessary input for the process. It also identifies the business object which is handled within the process and which becomes available as the output when the process has been executed. From the E-t-E view, it is possible at a later time to derive important business statuses for the specification of the lifecycle of a business object and consequently to identify flag stops for process measurement and process management. The E-t-E view of the process results in the following clear structure (Fig. 6.1).

The E-t-E view of the process revealed the following business objects (along with others), including the appropriate, relevant business definitions.

The **service order** is received on the customer portal, by email, by fax, or on the phone.

A **service provider order** to a suitable and available service provider is generated for every **service order item**.

The service providers enter a **service report** for every **service order item (service provider order)**.

Process Architecture

The end-to-end view of the processes is oriented to the input/output objects. This decomposes the service order processing into six processes.

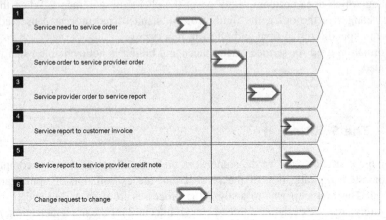

Fig. 6.1 E-t-E process view

The **customer invoice** showing all of the reported service order items for a time period for a specific customer is issued.

The **service provider credit note** showing all of the reported service order items for a time period for a specific service provider is issued.

The **change** is related to one service order and can affect one or more service order items and consequently one or more service provider orders.

Architecture structure for process digitalization In the next step, we supplemented the process architecture by the addition of another layer based on the clearly structured E-t-E view. The result was an architecture comprising three layers. The process logic was capsulated in its own layer for the consistent and complete process digitalization. This approach made it possible to decouple the process for the complete and consistent process digitalization from the restrictions imposed by existing interfaces in the legacy systems.

The process with the business process functions and process logic is located in the **process layer**. The process is characterized by its subject-oriented nature. This means that the business process functions are executed as the internal behavior of a subject (process worker), and the subjects are synchronized during process execution via their communication relationship, the exchange of messages. The process logic is implemented in a workflow engine. Each process function is implemented either as a manual activity or automatically by a Web service call or automatically by a number of Web service calls within a business context. So the services required for a complete and consistent digitalization are orchestrated according to business procedures along the process logic and brought together with the manual activities in the process layer.

The services for the automation of the process and integration of the data-carrying systems and legacy systems are located in the **integration layer**. The services are integrated into the process by means of service calls from the process layer. The file structure of the services is aligned with the business capabilities required to execute the process or to be able to carry out our client's business. We defined these business capabilities in consultation with the client independently of the IT system landscape currently in operation and the implemented processes. The file structure aligned with business capabilities is what makes it possible to differentiate clearly, retrieve, and thereby achieve the greatest possible reusability of the services. Figure 6.2 shows a part of the service repository created in this way. We decided against the integration of an enterprise service bus (ESB) for the realization of the integration layer because the highly standardized services available from the ESB do not, from the business perspective, satisfy the process requirements.

The data objects are located in the **data layer**. The data objects are differentiated along business lines and allocated without overlap to the business capabilities required to execute the process or to carry out our client's business. Simultaneously with the differentiation along business lines of the data objects and the allocation without any overlap, a system which takes over create, update, and delete functions for the data object was allocated to every data object. This approach clearly defined responsibility for data maintenance without any overlap. In this way, the redundant maintenance of the data and the required validation and consolidation of the data within the framework of process execution could be reduced to a minimum. The ERP system was retained as the central data-carrying system, a step which

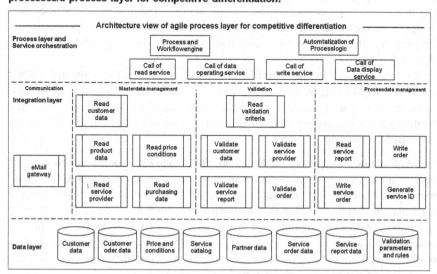

Fig. 6.2 Architecture structure for process digitalization

secured the investments in the ERP system. In the future, a far greater share of the necessary changes can be covered using the standards in the ERP system. It became possible to reduce significantly the expenditures for any client-specific changes in the ERP system because their implementation had been shifted to the process layer.

Subject-oriented design of the processes We used the S-BPM approach for modeling the processes in the process layer and a workflow engine which made it possible to generate 1-to-1 the process application for implementation of the process logic from the process models. I would like to emphasize this especially: no more programming is required for the implementation of the process logic because the application is generated from the models. This means that changes in our client's process logic now lead solely to modeling expenditures. Changes in the process involve development expenditures only if and when the Web services for process automation and process integration must be modified, supplemented, or newly developed. Thanks to the creation of a process layer characterized by subject orientation, our client is able to reduce significantly the change cycles and change expenditures. This process layer gave our client the ability to implement changes in the process flexibly and quickly. Even before the project was completed, our client had discovered that it now had at its disposal an instrument for the design of agile processes which could be used for differentiation from the competition.

The question still remains whether the business users, the process agents, are capable of working with these flexible and quick changes and of adapting their daily work to them.

Our client was able to answer this question with a clear YES. The justification for this YES was just as simple as the method we used for the design of the processes in the process layer. The business users designed and modeled their processes and any necessary changes themselves. The process logic they had designed themselves and the collaboration in the process could be experienced and tangibly handled immediately after being modeled in a process application (Fig. 6.3).

It is not necessary for me to give a comprehensive explanation of the method in a book on S-BPM in the Wild. My co-authors have certainly done a fine job of this. At this point, I want to address only a couple of critical success factors for process digitalization which we were able to influence to the benefit of our client by using the S-BPM approach.

Utilization and acceptance of the modeling language among business users Five symbols in combination with natural language generate unambiguous statements. The business users immediately grasped how the modeling works. It was a particular moment of revelation for us when the business users realized that the description of process functions and their explanations could be seen 1-to-1 in their process applications as well and not only in the models. In this way, the process models served not only to describe the process, but were also usable as operating procedures in the process application.

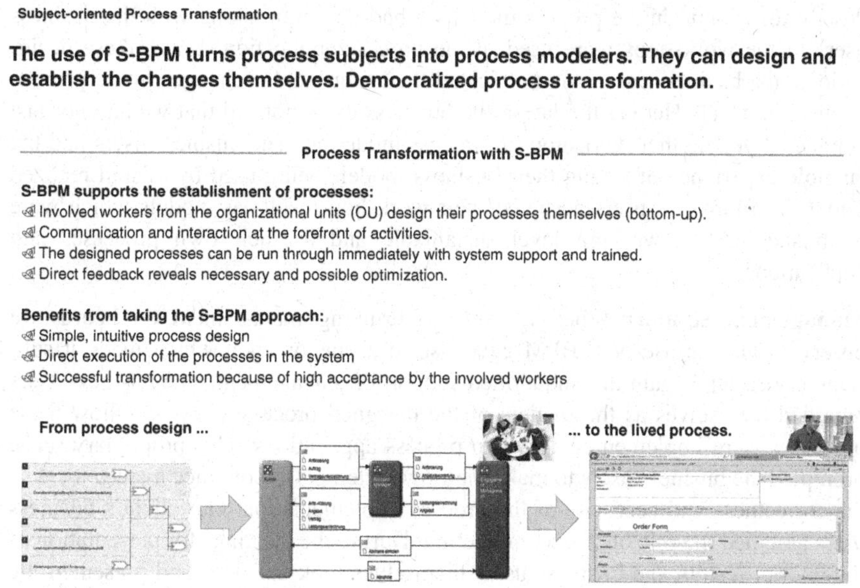

Subject-oriented Process Transformation

The use of S-BPM turns process subjects into process modelers. They can design and establish the changes themselves. Democratized process transformation.

-- Process Transformation with S-BPM ----------------------

S-BPM supports the establishment of processes:
- Involved workers from the organizational units (OU) design their processes themselves (bottom-up).
- Communication and interaction at the forefront of activities.
- The designed processes can be run through immediately with system support and trained.
- Direct feedback reveals necessary and possible optimization.

Benefits from taking the S-BPM approach:
- Simple, intuitive process design
- Direct execution of the processes in the system
- Successful transformation because of high acceptance by the involved workers

From process design ...   ... to the lived process.

Fig. 6.3 Democratization of the process transformation

Willingness of the business users to contribute during the modeling workshops

During the first workshop, we spoke "only" about the communication relationship among the process subjects and determined what information would have to be shared. This led straight to addressing critical points in the collaboration model among the process subjects. The business users found out in the very first workshop that tasks were in reality not distributed in the way provided for in the company's governance model. We did not sweep these critical points under the rug. We conducted an exhaustive discussion of these topics so that we could achieve an improved, yet feasible, process sequence in our client's organization. The constructive criticism from this head-on confrontation with current issues and the easily understandable presentation of a solution using only two symbols (the subject and the message) caused any initial reservations on the part of the business users to evaporate.

Lasting acceptance of the workshop results and interaction with IT
Right from the beginning, we had representatives from the IT department sitting alongside the representatives from the business side in the workshops. This was initially only of symbolic importance. We wanted to demonstrate that the business side and IT sit down together and collaborate on a model. During a later project phase, when Web services for the automation and integration were implemented for the refinement of the process, we showed that we did not intend this to be a purely symbolic gesture. We were able to prove that business users and IT speak one language and are talking about the same model. As mentioned above, the same designations and

descriptions found in the process model we had drawn up along with the business users in the workshops were used in the process application. Using these designations, the business users communicated their requests for changes in the process application to IT. Here at the latest, the business users noticed that we had not just conducted yet another workshop on process modeling. The business users had the tangible experience of seeing their business models being used by IT and realized 1-to-1. The business users accepted their workshop results as models which were established at the working level sustainable and as their own processes and applications.

Management support When it came to bringing management on board, we observed that the use of S-BPM gave rise to a phenomenon which made it substantially easier to gain the unqualified support of management. The business users regarded themselves as the owners of the designed processes and saw how these processes were implemented 1-to-1 in process applications. This proprietary sense prompted the business users to make their own attempts to convince management of the correctness and necessity of the process implementation. Our client's business users assumed the role of project marketing. During the meetings for presentation of the interim results, the business users themselves took the floor and presented the process application and its benefits. Management's response was only logical: If our own employees are convinced of the value and have been given a lever for achieving our goals in the form of the process application, then we will give our support. At the first presentation of interim results, the project was no longer our project that we, the consultants, were conducting for our client. The project was now our client's project and belonged to the employees from the business side and IT; we, the consultants, were merely guides.

6.3 The Project Work

We organized the project on the basis of the Scrum rhythm so that we could get a handle on the complexity. Our basis for the conduct of the modeling workshops was a participation-acceptance model which would maintain the highest possible level of motivation among the workshop participants throughout all of the workshops in the series. We proactively designed the communication of the project results to match the rise in the business users' understanding of their process.

6.3.1 Agile Procedure in Scrum Rhythm

We aligned the process releases to the E-t-E processes and differentiated them in accordance with the growing process automation and integration. At the end of every sprint, a process application was presented as a process increment in the sprint review. The process application became more refined with each successive sprint, i.e., the degree of automation and integration grew from one sprint to the

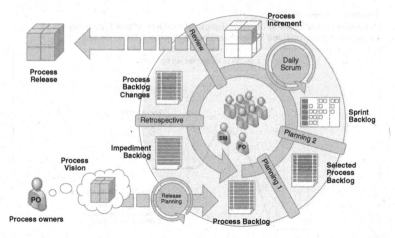

Fig. 6.4 Adaptation of Scrum for subject-oriented process digitalization

next. In discussing the process backlog items, we spoke about communications model, internal behavior, business object specification, business object mapping, rules, forms, interfaces, and Web services. The chart outlines how all of the process backlog items always contributed to the creation and modification of a process application as a process increment (Fig. 6.4).

6.3.2 Participation-Acceptance Model (PAM)

The conduct of a workshop, and the conduct of an entire series of workshops in particular, demands tremendous concentration, discipline, and stamina from facilitator and participants. The paradigm of a subject-oriented approach for process digitalization which shifts the focus of the approach to the process subjects can be transferred to the design and conduct of workshops as well by using the PAM. Speaking concretely, this means putting yourself in the shoes of the workshop participants and orienting the workshop to their fundamental motivation and willingness to participate actively. We have observed that the participants' motivation to participate in and contribute actively to the workshop results in changes over the course of a workshop or of a series of workshops. By becoming aware of these changes, facilitators can adjust and adapt the style of the workshops to take advantage of these differences (Fig. 6.5).

Motivation Phase (1) Skepticism At the beginning, most of the workshop participants were skeptical and did not yet know what the project's goal would be or how it would be achieved. The motivation level was not especially high.

We attempted to keep this phase of skepticism as short as possible. We began by asking participants about their expectations and writing their responses on a flip

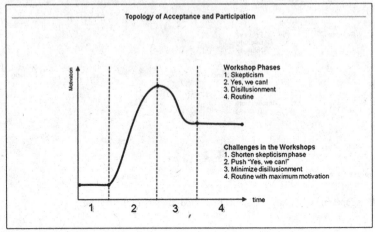

P-A-M Participant-Acceptance Model

Motivation for participation in the workshops for subject-oriented modeling varies among the participants and is dependent on their acceptance of the project.

Fig. 6.5 Participation-acceptance model (PAM)

chart. This was followed by our concretization of the workshop's objectives so that all of the participants entered into the discussions on an equal footing.

Motivation Phase (2) Yes, we can! During the second motivation phase of "Yes, we can!", there was a significant rise in the motivation level. It was important that we were able to point to the most concrete results possible at the end of every workshop so that the "Yes, we can!" phase was established as firmly as possible in the participants' minds.

During this phase, we were able to lay the groundwork which would prevent the collapse of motivation during the phase of disillusionment from becoming too great.

Motivation Phase (3) Disillusionment The motivation curve took a downward dip during the phase of disillusionment in this project as well. We were unable to make any precise predictions about this phase because we could not foresee when the light would go on for which participants. Disillusionment may occur, for instance, from a change in the conference room used for workshops if the general conditions in the new conference room are not as optimal. But disillusionment may also result from major insights gained by a workshop participant from the business side about his/her process, the processed data, and his/her workplace. During the section "spectrum of process transformation", possible insights are described and our workshop facilitators are sensitized to them, making it possible to deal proactively with the issues.

We sought to minimize the drop in motivation levels right from the previous "Yes, we can!" phase. At the end of each workshop, we made the results transparent and asked a workshop participant to present them.

Motivation Phase (4) Routine The group dynamics which had been generated ran their course during the routine phase of this project as well. Now it was important to do the practical work conscientiously. We communicated all of the results, we spoke frankly about impediments, and we collaborated in the drafting of strategies to remove impediments. During the routine phase, we regularly recalled the project objectives and communicated the progress that had been made in reaching these objectives.

Here is another highly practical tip for fostering motivation. We went to the creative laboratory for the modeling during the first sprints. This is a room with a sofa, various chairs—some comfortable, some uncomfortable—toys and, above all, large-area walls offering plenty of space for modeling—writing down ideas and suggestions, then erasing them again. This unusual environment surprised the workshop participants and opened a door to their collaboration during the workshop.

6.3.3 Spectrum of Process Transformation

Management of expectations is especially significant during projects for subject-oriented process digitalization. As a consequence of the subject-oriented process digitalization, there may be substantial changes in the working environment of the process workers, who have expectations concerning these changes. It was important to become highly aware of these expectations and to channel them in communication with the business users and management for two reasons: one, to avoid disappointment of these expectations, and second, to prevent the changes from overwhelming the process subjects. Over the course of our projects, we have identified six major areas for change. These areas should be actively guided in the communication with the client so that the success of the project is not jeopardized.

Another aspect of these changes is that every change is related to insights about the process gained by the business users. Every change is related to a project result and can lead to a fundamental reassessment of the process and the collaboration in the business department. This fundamental reassessment can precipitate a crisis in the project if it changes people's understanding of the way work is done in the business and IT departments. But mastering the crisis also leads to change in behavior, lasting improvement, and even innovations. Findings can also lead to revamping of communications, internal behavior, and distribution of tasks. In such a case, it is highly valuable to have a system for concretization of the changes available for execution at any time so that the changes can be made tangible (Fig. 6.6).

Spectrum of Process Design

During the process design, the process subjects recognize not only their process but also opportunities to create transparency and starting points for optimization.

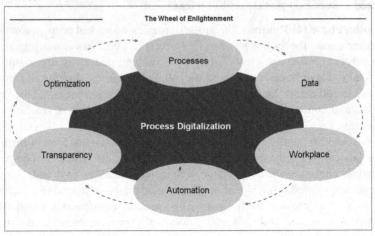

Fig. 6.6 Spectrum of process transformation

Processes The participating project members see and recognize who is involved in the process, how communication proceeds (content), and what tasks must be completed at every step of the process.

The starting prerequisites for the process and the process objectives are clear to all of the involved parties.

Data The required data (input and output) are modeled. There is an exact definition of what data in the process are processed/required by what subject at what point in time and who will make these data available.

Workplace The computer workplace is designed. The great revelation: "This is how I work?! This is how tasks are shared?!" A "new" workplace is created for the employees on the business side. It is important to point out to them the advantages of the new workplace and to guide them into the new processes.

The project employees recognize that the type of process and data modeling leads directly to a certain way of working at the computer monitor.

Automation By this time at the latest, the project employees accept the present, process-oriented IT application.

The project employees recognize that the quality and user friendliness at the workplace can be substantially improved through various steps of automation. Process acceleration and improvements are also realized here.

The automation of statuses simplifies the users' workplaces.

Transparency Information in the form of data which can be assessed using IT is now available for every step of the process and can be taken as a basis for analysis and improvement of the process.

Even if supervisors do not play an active role in the process, the enhanced transparency results in the recognition and demand for new management mechanisms/management processes.

This serves as a basis for the generation of qualified KPIs for evaluating, planning, and managing the process in real time.

Optimization Cross-department opportunities for optimization are recognized. Operating procedures for the users are derived from the process description. The clarity of the operating procedures is reviewed.

At this point, all of the users from the business side join in as input sources and contribute what they have noticed and experienced as improvements.

6.4   Summary and Outlook

Subject-oriented digitalization of processes will do more than promote the establishment of BPM as a management discipline in companies. The design, implementation, and practicability of processes are raised to a previously unknown level of quality. We will see this happening when we have a full-area market for tools which can generate 1-to-1 the process applications for executing the process logic

Overview

> **At a Glance**
> **Agile Processes and Stability of the IT Landscape**
>
> **1** Many companies have **established** large **standard systems** in their IT landscape and **spent a lot of money** for their installation and operation. Moreover, **changes** in these systems for the implementation of key requirements from the business side are possible only **at great time expense** and **put a significant burden on IT budgets**.
>
> **2** Securing the investments in these central systems of the IT landscape and reducing the burden placed on IT budgets by changes **can be realized through an agile process layer** for process automation and process integration.
>
> **3** An agile process layer for support of competitive differentiation of a company **demands flexibility and speed on the business side** during the instigation and implementation of changes. This is why a method for drawing up a concept, the design, and the implementation of the processes must **support the transformation for the establishment of the changes on the business side**.

Fig. 6.7 Process digitalization with S-BPM at a glance

from the business models and simultaneously utilize these business models to orchestrate the IT functions for process automation and integration. Like us, many others will also discover the advantages which arise when the business side and IT really speak one and the same language and navigate through the process in the same model (Fig. 6.7).

I am looking forward to working on more projects for complete and consistent process digitalization using S-BPM, and I would like to see the market for the appropriate tools grow over the coming years and the method become the standard. When this happens, BPM will finally be able to keep all of its promises from recent years.

Part II
Consultancy and Education Support

Model as You Do: Engaging an S-BPM Vendor on Process Modelling in 3D Virtual Worlds

7

Joel Harman, Ross Brown, Udo Kannengiesser,
Nils Meyer and Thomas Rothschädl

Abstract

Accurate process model elicitation continues to be a time-consuming task, requiring skill on the part of the interviewer to extract explicit and tacit process information from the interviewee. Many errors occur in this elicitation stage that would be avoided by better activity recall, more consistent specification methods and greater engagement in the elicitation process by interviewees. Metasonic GmbH has developed a process elicitation tool for their process suite. As part of a research engagement with Metasonic, staff from QUT, Australia have developed a 3D virtual world approach to the same problem, viz. eliciting

J. Harman (✉)
Science and Engineering Faculty, Queensland University of Technology,
2 George St., Brisbane, QLD 4000, Australia
e-mail: joel.harman@connect.qut.edu.au

R. Brown
Information Systems School, Science and Engineering Faculty, Queensland University
of Technology, 2 George St., Brisbane, QLD 4000, Australia
e-mail: r.brown@qut.edu.au

U. Kannengiesser
Metasonic GmbH, Münchner Straße 29, 85276 Pfaffenhofen, Germany
e-mail: udo.kannengiesser@metasonic.de

N. Meyer
Research Development, Metasonic GmbH, Münchner Straße 29,
85276 Pfaffenhofen, Germany
e-mail: nils.meyer@metasonic.de

T. Rothschädl
Ruxit, Blütenstraße 14, 4040 Linz, Austria
e-mail: Thomas.rothschaedl@ruxit.com

© The Author(s) 2015
A. Fleischmann et al. (eds.), *S-BPM in the Wild*,
DOI 10.1007/978-3-319-17542-3_7

113

process models from stakeholders in an intuitive manner. This book chapter tells the story of how QUT staff developed a 3D Virtual World tool for process elicitation and took the outcomes of their research project to Metasonic for evaluation, and of Metasonic's response to the initial proof of concept.

7.1   Metasonic Engages QUT June 2013

Metasonic GmbH, a German business process management vendor, has implemented a complete process management suite called Metasonic Suite and a process elicitation tool called Metasonic Touch, developed from a previous university research project (Oppl and Stary 2011). Metasonic sought to engage with researchers at QUT to explore new areas of innovation around the effectiveness of their software tools. After a brief phone call with Dr. Albert Fleischmann, director and co-founder of Metasonic, Dr. Ross Brown pitched the idea of using virtual worlds in the task of process elicitation. Metasonic accepted this proposal, a scholarship was offered to QUT by the company, and an IT Honours student, Joel Harman, was taken on in December 2013 to begin the twelve-month-long research project.

Process model elicitation still poses a huge challenge with respect to the quality of the resulting process models, independently of whether the information was gathered from interviews (Kabicher and Rinderle-Ma 2011), by exploiting existing data sources (Dunkl 2013), or by process mining (Bose et al. 2013). Subject-oriented BPM (S-BPM) seeks to assist this process by providing a methodology that presents process models in a manner analogous to natural language features, namely, subject, object and predicate constructs from the stakeholder's perspective (Fleischmann et al. 2012). This enables users to be engaged more effectively via a simple and intuitive process representation and via the implementation of user-centred elicitation hardware and software.

The goal of the proposed research was to use 3D virtual worlds as a means of extracting process information from stakeholders in line with S-BPM concepts. Rather than use traditional modelling elicitation techniques which heavily tax the analyst (such as interviews), or using an abstract representation and interface, such as the Metasonic touch (Oppl and Stary 2011), QUT wished to explore the idea of using 3D virtual world models of workplaces as elicitation environments. Such an approach was designed with the intention to reduce the training time and complexity of modelling by providing a more natural modelling interface. To achieve this goal, a 3D virtual world was constructed which closely matched a typical office environment. Users were then able to interact with objects in this virtual world to complete tasks as they normally would in reality. As users perform actions within the virtual world, a process model begins to develop automatically, thus the term *model as you do*. Once the process is completed, the model can be exported and given to analysts without stakeholders ever needing to understand the underlying grammar of the model. An overview diagram of this concept is shown in Fig. 7.1.

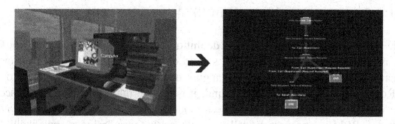

Fig. 7.1 Image of the overall approach. The virtual world on the *left* is used to specify processes that emerge as S-BPM grammars on the *right*

If this virtual world can be easily learnt, it should allow for much faster creation of processes. In addition to this, situated cognition theory suggests that the generated models should potentially have greater accuracy than what could normally be achieved with common interview techniques. Reducing the strain on external analysts would also enable many more people to be consulted about processes. Rather than have process interviews become a bottleneck for elicitation, this tool could be deployed online to allow for hundreds of people to all build process components simultaneously.

Having an easy to learn, and deployable, elicitation tool would also enable businesses to have a platform for engaging with customers during process specification. Rather than business estimating customer viewpoints, customers could directly specify exactly how they want to perform their tasks within a process. This may result in developed processes more closely matching customer expectations.

The rest of this chapter details the research, implementation and usability testing that was performed with Metasonic to meet the previously specified research goals. Section 7.1 covers the underlying reasons and processes that led to the development of the tool, including meetings with Metasonic. Section 7.2 details the actual tool developed. Section 7.3 details a trip from Brisbane to Pfaffenhofen to visit Metasonic, where QUT staff tested the tool with Metasonic staff. The chapter concludes with a discussion around Metasonic staff responses, and provides recommendations for other companies seeking to use virtual worlds for similar projects in process modelling.

7.2 Theoretical Inspirations from Readings Dec. 2013 to Jan. 2014

As part of the preparation process for developing the new approach, a literature review of the field was performed by the student, Joel Harman, to provide a theoretical context for the development processes, in particular, enhancing customer involvement with the development of business processes.

7.2.1 Customer Involvement in BPM

While there is debate over the exact definition of BPM and its associated goals, there is a strong consensus that BPM should enable companies to adjust business processes rapidly to meet the ever changing demands of customers (Vom Brocke and Rosemann 2010). With this in mind, it is critical that the customers be accurately considered when building process models (Margaria et al. 2012). Towards this end, S-BPM is a process modelling language that was designed specifically for use with process stakeholders. The goal of this language is to simplify the grammar to a level that could easily be taught (Fleischmann et al. 2012). With this simplicity, it is surmised that businesses could involve a larger portion of their staff in the modelling process and rely much less on external analysts for support. S-BPM was designed specifically for process stakeholders, and rather than focus on completeness, it instead aims for simplicity. Processes are modelled by connecting only three types of commands: internal actions, sends and receives (Fleischmann et al. 2012). S-BPM is based on the principle of view-based modelling. Rather than build a complete model, several smaller models are constructed from the individual views of those involved in the process. The goal of this approach is to align the construction of the process much more closely with how those involved perceive it to operate (Kabicher and Rinderle-Ma 2011).

7.2.2 Tacit Knowledge for Process Modelling

Tacit Knowledge is the concept that not all knowledge can be easily codified. Polanyi first introduced the term with the assertion that people can know more than they can tell (Polanyi 1967). The field of knowledge elicitation ties in closely and deals with trying to work with tacit knowledge either transferring this knowledge between individuals, or converting it into encodable, explicit knowledge. There are four common methods for performing this task: interviewing experts, learning by being told, learning by seeing (Parsaye and Chignell 1988) and learning by doing (Herrgard 2000).

Interview methods are usually the most common in process modelling when working with experts. This methodology allows for the trained analyst to gather information about the process from all of the people involved in its execution and verify the process quality with respect to all parties involved. Due to the distributed nature of this approach, it has attracted significant use when working with view-based process models (Kabicher and Rinderle-Ma 2011).

The issue with interviews is that they rely heavily on the stakeholder to provide accurate information to the analyst. In an interview setting, however, this is not always possible especially if the interviewer is unfamiliar with the field (Parsaye and Chignell 1988). Many experts forget tasks they assume to be widely known, or have difficulties explaining what they do without actually doing it (Grosskopf et al. 2010). This block on memory is commonly associated with situated cognition, the concept that knowledge is inseparable from doing (Nunberg 1978).

7.2.3 Situated Cognition via Virtual Worlds

Traditional accounts of memory often focus heavily on the concept of passive storage of information. Much formal learning involves wrote-learning of information or testing of knowledge without context (Glenberg 1997). The theory of situated cognition is an alternate view on cognition which suggests that all knowledge is, to some extent, tied to the situations in which it was gained (Brown et al. 1989). This was originally considered within the context of teaching. Until this point, many believed that schools or other educational facilities were neutral environments that allowed for knowledge to be easily applied to other areas. Miller and Gildea (1987) later verified that this assumption was not true with respect to learning vocabulary. The suggested reason for this is that knowledge can only be applied to the context in which it was learned (Nunberg 1978). In language, a word is not a contained concept; words can change meaning when placed in different sentences or verbalised with different tones (Barwise and Perry 1981). The problem with this contextual information is that it cannot be encoded with standard data. While an expert may be able to explain what they do, they are unable to easily provide context to the information (Brown et al. 1989). It is suggested that the only way to accurately teach this information is to first provide this context, a practice commonly used during apprenticeships (Lave 1990). From this, theories of explicit memory (sometimes referred to as tacit knowledge) have emerged as knowledge which cannot easily be conveyed to other people. To retrieve this information, it is easiest to use a simulation-based approach for memory recall (Rubin 2006).

Jestice and Kahai (2010) back up this claim by suggesting that the reason virtual worlds prove so effective in remote learning is that they provide a level of situated cognition which cannot be achieved when operating under standard remote learning techniques. This allows for both a much more structured learning experience and the ability to learn by visiting real-life locations within the world. Leidl and Roessling (2007) have also shown that in addition to this, these worlds also improve user embodiment and experience when compared with regular external learning methods. Such research shows that we can expect greater engagement from stakeholders when using 3D virtual worlds, as we are using a visual representation that is aligned with their direct experience of work (Guo et al 2013; Brown et al. 2014).

7.2.4 Brisbane Design Workshop Jan. 2014

After exploring the relevant literature surrounding this project, a design workshop was carried out with staff from Metasonic (Thomas Rothschädl and Udo Kannengiesser), who visited Brisbane in Feb. 2014. The goal was to establish a potential virtual world modeller design and to identify future goals for the research work. The workshops included presentations by Thomas and Udo on their technology implementations and the theoretical bases underlying S-BPM. During the workshops, design concepts and prototype implementations were presented by Joel Harman and Ross Brown, and critiqued by Thomas and Udo. Those ideas were:

1. Use the Metasonic Touch to control a virtual world representation of the process model.
2. Use a stationary top-down world as an alternate interface to provide an overview of the business while using integrated S-BPM objects.
3. Execute a virtual world scenario based on an S-BPM model previously developed using the Metasonic Suite.
4. Use a first-person camera view to act out parts of a process and automatically construct a model to be exported to the Metasonic Suite.

Thomas and Udo thought that having an avatar represented in the scene was important, as it put the focus on specifying individual subject-oriented behavior, rather than a single overall model, so we decided to eliminate number two. Both QUT and Metasonic staff agreed that building the virtual world on top of the Touch device would limit its usability as a desktop PC virtual world could be handed to anyone, but touch tables would be rare, so number one was discarded. After further discussion, it was decided that the final option, number four, of using a first person camera view to act out the model would be the most rewarding choice of the four presented.

7.3   Designing an Integrated 3D Virtual World S-BPM Approach Feb. 2014

From the previous focus group and literature readings, we developed an approach to integrating S-BPM process elicitation into a 3D virtual world. The evidence from literature suggested that this virtual world approach would be an optimal candidate, and so a design concept was developed to be presented to the Metasonic partners at a later date in 2014.

The implementation is designed to exploit virtual world functionalities for modelling real work environments, and to enable the specification of S-BPM activities within such a world. In short, the intention is to structure the interactions with the virtual world in a similar manner to S-BPM, which has a natural language structure as the basis of its approach. We have used this interaction approach in other work (Brown et al. 2014), due to its application to a subject-oriented viewpoint in a virtual world.

3D virtual worlds often incorporate an immersive first-person view (Weller 2007) in order to enable deep engagement with the content in question; viz. the actions taken by the viewer are from his or her own perspective. This insight has driven the research into using virtual worlds with S-BPM, as the visual metaphor facilitates a direct engagement with the fundamental concepts inherent in S-BPM, that of specifying processes from a subjective point of view (Fleischmann et al. 2012).

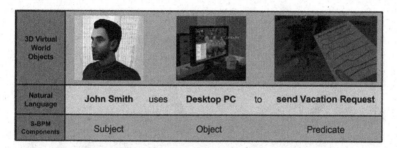

Fig. 7.2 Diagram mapping natural language constructs utilised in S-BPM onto 3D virtual world objects

This means that the concept of subject, object and predicate specifications that are the foundation of S-BPM map directly to 3D subjective virtual world interfaces. We illustrate this with a diagram showing the general S-BPM language constructs (Fleischmann et al. 2012), applied to virtual world 3D content; see Fig. 7.2.

Using a virtual world, the stakeholders can have their memory activated regarding work details and then execute their work in the environment, modelling as they do. We now show how these concepts were encapsulated and operationalised within the virtual world tool to provide an engaging interface to process modelling stakeholders.

Off-the-shelf 3D virtual world technology is used to provide the interactive environment to support process elicitation tasks. Such technology is ubiquitous, due to the rise of advanced graphics technology enabling virtual world and games systems to run on standard desktops. Such game engines are developed to hide (encapsulate) away underlying aspects of a game, enabling reuse of code. For example, scripts used in the environment can be uploaded into other scenes using the same engine. They also facilitate porting code to other hardware platforms, as hardware-specific factors are hidden in the central engine modules. Our implementation is created using a common proprietary game engine known as Unity3D.[1] It is a completely integrated environment for the development of games which has become very popular due to its favourable licensing arrangements and its superior development technology. The major components used in the development of this application include its level design system and scripting language, Mono C#.[2]

The game level design system is shown in Fig. 7.3. This environment enables the uploading of 3D content and placement of items into the scene to be created. Once content is entered, the world can be configured by attaching scripts to the world objects, which enacts any interactions and world simulation activities. Our example application uses C#, but other languages can be used, such as JavaScript. For our example, these scripts enable the user to move around the environment, touch objects and type text describing the tasks they have done.

---

[1]Unity3D Game Engine: www.unity3d.com, accessed August 2014.

[2]Unity3D Game Engine: www.mono-project.com, accessed August 2014.

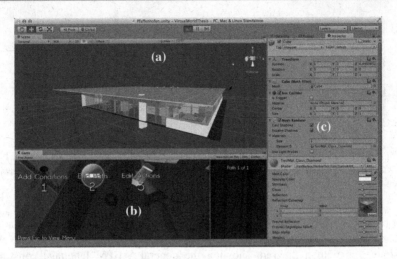

Fig. 7.3 Image of Unity3D development environment, with **a** level editor, **b** execution window and **c** asset management area

Using a floor plan and imported artefacts, the general layout of key areas can be quickly modelled for use in an interview scenario. For our Metasonic study, we analysed typical workspaces to determine the key objects in the rooms (e.g., chairs, tables and phones) in order to select corresponding virtual world artefacts. We argue, logically, that the objects of most relevant use should be presented at the highest level of detail as they have the most influence on the cognition of the user with respect to their process activities. We also argue that the rest of the scene may be left in lower levels of detail, with a lowered effect on the tasks being elicited. We used office artefacts gained from the Unity 3D Asset Store,[3] thus minimal modelling was required for the office example tested at Metasonic. Bespoke content can also be modelled when required using typical tools such as 3DS Max.[4]

Once the virtual world is built, the interactions for the environment need to be scripted. Such programming is a typical part of developing 3D worlds, in a manner analogous to that of 2D widgets on standard windowed interfaces. These interaction functions support the modelling tasks undertaken within an S-BPM application. Thus, the interactions fall into two categories, human subjects and non-human objects. As per the other subject-oriented elicitation systems that have been built on the S-BPM platform (Oppl and Stary 2011), the main components that can be specified are sequences of actions, messages to other subjects and choices.

As this project is, at its essence, a process elicitation project, the 3D view is from a worker perspective, being an avatar-based first-person view (Burdea and Coiffet 2003). This world view provides a setting that is cognitively subjective, facilitating a personal viewpoint when eliciting to-do lists from interviewees. Objects in the virtual

---

[3]Unity3D Asset Store: https://www.assetstore.unity3d.com/en/, accessed: August 2014.
[4]3DS Max: http://www.autodesk.com.au/products/3ds-max/overview, accessed: August 2014.

world are scripted to reveal their functionality via a menu upon being clicked. The direct manipulation interface provides a natural mnemonic approach for interacting directly with the objects having most affordance for the activity (Galitz 2007; Stone et al. 2005). A further benefit of the usage of direct manipulation interfaces—also called WYSIWYG interface (what you see is what you get)—is that the objects are visible and hence the interviewees do not need to remember complex syntax (Stone et al. 2005; Hutchins et al. 1985). In this way, novices can also learn object functionalities quickly. For virtual worlds, direct manipulation principles are very helpful in providing the feeling of direct involvement with the simulation (Stone et al. 2005; Shneiderman and Plaisant 1998; Hutchins et al. 1985). Such involvement results in a more consistently defined set of activities, due to the priming interaction with a visually familiar representation of subjects and objects.

Object and subject interactions are enacted by the provision of a set of options for the object or subject being used in the action or message respectively. The actual document or artefact being exchanged between subjects is free-form text to provide the user with the flexibility to specify objects and messages. Specific steps in carrying out these interactions will now be detailed.

7.3.1 Activity Specification

For activity specification, the method involves the clicking on an object of interest to the execution of the action; the interface provides a mnemonic for the S-BPM approach; see Fig. 7.4.

For each object, the information recorded is drawn from embedded virtual world data, e.g., its instance name, such as "Desktop PC." A single script is used for each object, which packages the subject, object and document specification from the user,

Fig. 7.4 Clicking on an object lists the actions that can be done with the object in question. In this case a desktop PC can write, print, send and receive a document, or examine, upload and retrieve data from a service

saving it to disk. An object to be used, for example the PC shown in Fig. 7.4, has this single script attached to it via a menu interface. From then on, it is able to provide process elicitation information as text descriptions typed in by the user. This can be done for every object in the world that is relevant to the process being elicited.

S-BPM also has a message-passing construct for specifying if a person sends a message to a subject in the environment. We provide a subject overview of the environment to enable the user to identify people present in other areas of the environment. This overview prevents the person getting lost inside the environment, even if it is familiar to the user; see Fig. 7.5.

In addition, the user may specify messages sent to subjects directly in the world by traversing the environment in the first person; see Fig. 7.6.

Fig. 7.5 Example using the tool to specify messages to subjects via an overview of the workplace

Fig. 7.6 Example using the tool to specify messages by navigating the world directly and clicking on the human subject

7.3.2 Choice Specification

In addition to the specification of activities with objects and messages to subjects, we have developed a method for the specification of choice using the virtual world. This involves the use of a stepwise editor in the virtual world to go back and form a break point at the initiation of choice in the past, and then to execute the task along the new fork, as shown in the following Figs. 7.7, 7.8 and 7.9.

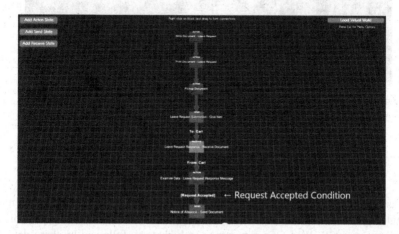

Fig. 7.7 Using the tool to specify choice in the world, showing the original S-BPM diagram, annotated to show choice insertion point

Fig. 7.8 Traversing the virtual world actions to a branch point, where the new choice is to be defined

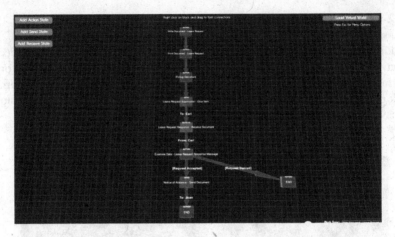

Fig. 7.9 Snapshot showing the final S-BPM diagram with a newly integrated choice after the previous interactions are performed

7.4 Evaluation at Metasonic Headquarters April 2014

It was agreed in April to organise a flight from Brisbane to Pfaffenhofen to strengthen the working relationship between QUT and Metasonic. The trip involved attendance at the S-BPM One conference in Eichstaett, followed by three days in Pfaffenhofen working with Metasonic. The goals for the visit were twofold. Firstly, the intention was to ascertain user acceptance of such a modelling tool with S-BPM practitioners, such as Metasonic. Secondly, is was to educate the Metasonic staff and leadership about the theoretical background to our research and provide a practical workshop in the use of the Unity 3D games engine so that Metasonic would be given a primer on strategies for using this technology in future projects. We now detail the execution of these two goals in turn.

7.4.1 3D Virtual World Tool Evaluation Approach

The virtual world tool was evaluated using an experiment, garnering preliminary quantitative and qualitative data from Metasonic via a four step approach:

1. a short screening questionnaire, to ascertain virtual world experience levels;
2. a training video showing how to specify activities, messages and choices within the virtual world tool;
3. a test modelling scenario based upon a travel application process within a generic business;
4. a follow-up questionnaire and semi-structured interview on the usability of the virtual world tool.

The response from Metasonic staff was encouraging, with nine people taken through the preliminary test, producing a rich set of qualitative results from participant replies. This cohort included the CEO, Herbert Kindermann, and Dr. Albert Fleischmann, a director of the company, along with software developers, sales representatives and administration staff. Overall, the response was positive to the tool, especially regarding the concept of using the virtual world to elicit process model information from the stakeholder. However, there were specific issues with the tool that were highlighted by their staff, as we now show.

7.4.2 Quantitative Results

Each post-test questionnaire contained 18 questions covering a number of usability factors about the virtual world tool. The questions were scored on likert scales of between one and seven, with 3.5 being the middle score. The screening test showed participants had low exposure to 3D virtual worlds at 1.4, but had high modelling exposure at 5.10. Therefore, experiment participant responses are from virtual world novices, who are experienced in business process modelling. The average value for every question from the users was 5.30. This indicated a positive response, as it is above the middle value of 3.5. However, drilling down on first the negative and then the positive responses in detail provides a more nuanced story of the reception of the new tool:

- participants had major issues with recovery from mistakes, scoring 3.20, and the completeness of the functionality of the system, 3.90.
- highest scores revolved around the interface of the system, with participants enjoying using the system, 5.60, and finding the interface pleasant, 5.40.

In summary, while the quantitative results are only preliminary in a scientific sense, the tool and approach have been marked as promising by participants. Some key issues were found in dealing with errors and a perceived lack of completeness to the functions in the system. We now list some of the more important observations by Ross and Joel as experimenters, and the comments of participants during the post-test interview.

7.4.3 Experiment Observations

- After thinking about a task, sometimes participants would forget which tasks they had already entered. This was commonly caused by participants being unable to remember all of the scenario at once.
- Many participants tried to complete actions from other subjects. After one person in the office sent a document, they wanted to specify actions for how the receiver should analyse it.

- A lot of the participants spent a great deal of time looking around and exploring the scene.
- Participants would sometimes get lost in a scene and would be unable to find what they were looking for, potentially symptomatic of using a generic office for the testing.
- Participants couldn't recover easily from mistakes. When they would perform an incorrect action, many would usually continue through the scenario regardless.
- A number of participants took the "lazy" path and did all of their messaging and work from a computer. The implication here is that many business processes may be enacted completely from a computer, so such an approach is valid.

7.4.4 Participant Comments

- Almost all the participants commented that the tool was enjoyable to use. Some even went on to say that it did not feel like they were modelling at all.
- Many of those who used the tool noted that process stakeholders and others who were unfamiliar with modelling grammar would probably enjoy the tool, as the concept was easy to grasp.
- A lot of participants commented they had issues splitting paths correctly. This was largely a tool user interface problem.
- A lot of participants wanted the scene to be a lot more interactive than it was. This was especially noted with regards to sending of messages. Users wanted responses sent back automatically by the scene.
- Some participants were uncertain which commands they should be performing (e.g., 'Give Document' vs. 'Give Information'). They were unsure if these options would have different effects.
- People were unsure if different computers would provide the same results.
- Some participants wanted an 'Inventory' or something equivalent to know what they had/could use.
- One of the few interactive items in the scene was the piece of paper. Many participants printed out the piece of paper and manually handed it to the supervisor commenting that it gave them a sense that they were performing the process.
- Many participants commented that the UI had too many buttons and they couldn't always easily do what they wanted.
- A lot of participants wanted to be able to see the model created in realtime. In particular, a lot of them wanted to be able to see the model they were constructing. This could be due to their heavy modelling experience.
- Many wanted additional feedback when they had successfully completed a task. In particular, they wanted the world to change in some way.
- Some participants liked being able to have the choice to do the same thing in different ways (e.g., message on a computer, make a phone call, talk in person).

- Many thought that it was very interesting to use, but some thought that it may be a novelty that quickly becomes monotonous when used repeatedly.
- Participants commented this would be especially helpful for spatially separated tasks, but less useful in largely online tasks.

7.4.5 Games Engine Workshop

After the previous experimental assessment of the system by Metasonic staff, the QUT researchers presented a workshop day on both the research background, presented in Sect. 7.2, and the Unity 3D technology used to generate the elicitation tool. A large number of Metasonic staff, approximately 30, attended the workshop.

The morning presentation consisted of descriptions of the theory behind this work, and an elucidation of two projects being run by Ross Brown in this research domain, including one with the University of Vienna (Brown et al. 2014).

In the afternoon, both Ross and Joel presented an introduction to games engine technology, and their instantiation in Unity3D. Ross presented a small introductory primer on game engine theory and technology, introducing some of the major features of Unity3D, especially with reference to how it is used to create interactive 3D worlds. Joel then presented a workshop session in the afternoon on how to use the level design tools and the scripting interface to generate the functionality inherent in the demo described in Sect. 7.3.

To further emphasise the ease of developing such virtual worlds using modern tools, Joel developed a model of the Metasonic headquarters (see Fig. 7.10). A convincing model was created quickly, the morning after visiting the business, in roughly three hours. This answered the often asked question regarding virtual worlds, viz. the effort required to model such environments. This was surprising and informative to the staff of Metasonic, as they realised that such tools were within the bounds of budget resources for process modelling projects due to their ability to speedily model a business.

7.4.6 Metasonic Staff Reflections

Metasonic staff members now note their reflections on the process of designing the tool and learning about the potential of such game engine technologies.

Nils Meyer, Metasonic CTO Business objectives are typically achieved by a close collaboration of different individuals. Taking this as a basis, the ideas of a subject- or communication-oriented view on business process models have been developed. Taking this on from a model perspective to a tool perspective is a consequent next step that fits nicely with the 3D virtual world approach.

Many practitioners today know 3D virtual worlds from gaming and very often as well from multi-player gaming. Objectives in a multi-player game can often be achieved by the close collaboration of different individuals being similar to the achievement of real-world objectives. From that perspective a 3D virtual world

Fig. 7.10 Images taken from the Metasonic modelling exercise, built in a morning's work from photos and a floor plan. Image **a** is the reception area, **b** the meeting room and **c** is an overview of the entire building. In real life, the Metasonic headquarters is 536 m^2 in floor area, housing 35 employees

approach for subject-oriented process model elicitation seemed to be and turned out to be a nice match.

The work carried out so far illustrated already some potential, especially for people not being trained in using an abstraction of real life represented by business process models. Further developments can make this way of modelling even more collaborative, easing some things being experienced now as difficult in the tool. If different individuals really could work in the same virtual world 'online' at the same time, meeting each other and observing each other, no questions on 'how should I proceed after I send the information to my colleague X' would occur, as I could see that he's still working on my answer. I could just wait and as soon as he's coming back to me, continue working.

Udo Kannengiesser, Metasonic R&D Department One of the strengths of the 3D elicitation tool is that it closes the gap between abstract business processes and more concrete work contexts. The richness of the 3D representation cues more detailed memories of how the work is performed, thus leading to more accurate process models. Another advantage of having such a broad range of contextual information available in the 3D world is that it helps identify opportunities for process improvement. This is more difficult to achieve when all you have is an abstract process model. It would be interesting to apply this elicitation tool to domains where interactions are more physical than in typical office settings, where you interact mostly with computers and printers. This would include shop floor and logistics processes, where people operate machines, unload trucks, move boxes, drive vehicles, etc. I expect there would be an even greater impact of the tool in these domains.

The tool is built in a way that nicely integrates with key ideas of S-BPM. In subject-oriented modelling, process participants need to model only their own subject behaviour, while the behaviour of other subjects remains opaque. This is well supported by the first-person, "subjective" view of the avatars, which lets you model only the behaviour of your own avatar (i.e., your subject), and no one else's. The third-person view that is implemented in the tool lets you visualise interactions between subjects, but does not allow modelling subject behaviours from an "omniscient" perspective, as would be the case in other modelling approaches such as BPMN.

Another distinguishing concept of S-BPM that is indirectly supported by the tool is the notion of process validation. In S-BPM, processes are validated by subjects that "play" through their work steps and their interactions in a "try-out" environment before executing them in the real world. The virtual environment provides a stage for this role play, and the avatars provide the characters. The only difference is that validation is no longer performed after, but during, process modelling. So the tool realises not just "model as you do" but also "validate as you model."

Thomas Rothschädl, Metasonic R&D Department During the development of a first version of the tool, regular video conferences helped to create a common picture of the tool. As the first results looked very promising, it was necessary to involve a broader branch of different stakeholders such as S-BPM consultants, software developers and sales representatives to obtain feedback on how the first version is perceived and where future improvements should be focused. This also enabled a deeper knowledge exchange between Metasonic employees and QUT researchers according to the S-BPM methodology and 3D virtual world creation.

The evaluation and first tryouts of the tool brought very valuable results. Participants all saw great potential, and also enjoyed, the revolutionary new way of creating a business process model through performing them in a virtual world. Most of them saw this work at this early stage already as extraordinarily valuable. Nevertheless, some modelling experts missed a visual overview of the created process (in the S-BPM modelling language). Surprisingly, people who are not experienced business process modellers also claimed that an overview of already performed tasks and message exchange would be valuable for them.

Most of the practitioners (including me) had the biggest problems with defining different branches (choices) in the way to act within a process. For example, a person asks the manager if it is okay to take a vacation, and already knows that the manager can say yes or no. Users also want to define this choice after asking the manager, although only one path can be defined in one instance. Additionally, in my view, it would be beneficial to extend the tool to enable multiple users to interact within the virtual world.

The second day of the games engine workshop showed that, with some practice and experience in programming, the mapping of a real world into a virtual world model, based on a floor map and some photos, can be done in a very fast manner with current tools like Unity3D. From my view, this is one important requirement for showing that 3D virtual world modelling can be quickly used to define processes which happen in the real world.

Altogether, the productive "real-world" presentations, meetings and discussions in Pfaffenhofen enabled future improvement to the prototype and helped Metasonic and QUT to continue to pursue their close work on this topic.

7.4.7 Notable Program Changes

Upon returning to Australia, the QUT research team analysed the above responses from Metasonic and have implemented the following changes.

- A start-up screen has been added informing users they are only working from their point of view, to avoid any confusion on modelling other subjects' work.
- A list of actions has now been added in a side viewport, to prevent users from forgetting the previous work they have defined.
- Some participants were unsure what to do when they finished a branch. An "end" action has been added to give the user the ability to end the branch intuitively.
- A lot of participants had problems with conditions and branching. Many participants wanted to add all their conditions at once. This has now been allowed.
- Many users were waiting after they sent a message. They were expecting the recipient to send them a message back, as in a process simulation. This problem has temporarily been solved by asking the user if they want a message immediately sent back via an explicit dialogue.

7.5 Conclusions

Overall, the process of engagement between QUT and Metasonic over this new technology can be considered a success. Despite the risk of such an engagement not working, due to the innovative nature of the technology being used, there were significant benefits in both technological innovation, business relationships and development of insights into new research fields for Metasonic.

Research-wise, the design, implementation and evaluation of the new 3D tool provided useful research outcomes for both QUT and Metasonic. The tool proved usable and engaging, with a positive sentiment from the Metasonic staff during evaluation. Much useful development information was derived from the usability experiments, providing us with pointers to the list of improvements we have made to the tool.

Relationship-wise, the visits by staff from Brisbane and Pfaffenhofen had the benefit of forming a strong working relationship between a university and a company widely geographically separated. Joel and Ross were able to engage with a company performing S-BPM projects for companies as significant as Hitachi, Japan. Metasonic was able to obtain insight into novel approaches to modelling, and to have an understanding of the latest games engine development technology to assist with the future use of such 3D virtual world tools in their innovation plans.

7.6   Implications

A number of key implications for researchers and practitioners of BPM can be derived from analysis of the previous descriptions of the project experience.

Such an engagement benefits from early interactions on design and research direction factors. While this has often been mentioned in other research, it can be stated here that the close working relationship enabled a company to more easily focus the work on relevant topics, and to enhance trust that QUT staff would deliver a good research outcome.

More specifically, with such leading edge projects it is important to give companies an early insight into the possible solutions. QUT has a depth of talent in the area of 3D game development, and so was able to provide a very early prototype. This early prototype facilitated buy-in by Metasonic. A key insight is therefore to prototype early and often. Present game engine tools like Unity3D allow this to occur, facilitating easier insights into future innovation possibilities.

Such relationships can provide many insights into new technologies and research for companies. Metasonic had little experience in the area of 3D games and virtual worlds. This project has given them an assessment of its practical usefulness for their business, and importantly, how hard it is to implement such ideas with present tools. In particular, Metasonic appreciated the construction of a model of their Pfaffenhofen office by QUT staff as an example of the capabilities of the technology. We view such a practical exemplar close to the experience of Metasonic as being a strong point of connection for their staff, helping overcome opposition to the new approaches presented. We recommend finding such touch points in research engagements, in order to ease any resistance to new ideas.

Acknowledgments The authors acknowledge the financial assistance of Metasonic GmbH in the development and evaluation of the virtual world tool in this project.

References

Barwise J, Perry J (1981) Situations and attitudes. J Philos 78:668–691

Bose R, Mans R, van der Aalst W (2013) Wanna improve process mining results? In: 2013 IEEE symposium on computational intelligence and data mining (CIDM), pp 127–134

Brown JS, Collins A, Duguid P (1989) Situated cognition and the culture of learning. Educ researcher 18(1):32–42

Brown R, Rinderle-Ma S, Kriglstein S, Kabicher-Fuchs S (2014) Augmenting and assisting model elicitation tasks with 3D virtual world context metadata. In: Meersman R, Panetto H, Dillon T, Missikoff M, Liu L, Pastor O, Cuzzocrea A, Sellis T (eds) On the move to meaningful internet systems: OTM 2014 conferences, vol 8841. Lecture notes in computer science. Springer, Berlin, pp 39–56

Burdea G, Coiffet P (2003) Virtual reality. Wiley, New York

Dunkl R (2013) Data improvement to enable process mining on integrated non-log data sources. In: Moreno-Daz R, Pichler F, Quesada-Arencibia A (eds) EUROCAST 2013, LNCS, vol 8111, Springer, Heidelberg, pp 491–498

Fleischmann A, Schmidt W, Stary C, Obermeier S, Boerger E (2012) Subject-oriented business process management. Springer Publishing Company, Heidelberg

Galitz WO (2007) The essential guide to user interface design: an introduction to GUI design principles and techniques. Wiley, New York

Glenberg AM (1997) What memory is for: creating meaning in the service of action. Behav Brain Sci 20(1):41–50

Grosskopf A, Edelman J, Weske M (2010) Tangible business process modeling methodology and experiment design. In: Rinderle-Ma S, Sadiq S, Leymann F (eds) Business process management workshops, vol 43. Lecture notes in business information processing. Springer, Berlin, pp 489–500

Guo H, Brown R, Rasmussen R (2013) A theoretical basis for using virtual worlds as a personalised process visualisation approach. In: Franch X, Soffer P (eds) CAiSE workshops 2013, LNBIP, vol 148. Springer, Heidelberg, pp 229–240

Herrgard T (2000) Difficulties in diffusion of tacit knowledge in organizations. J Intellect Capital 1(4):357–365

Hutchins EL, Hollan JD, Norman DA (1985) Direct manipulation interfaces. Hum-Comput Interact 1(4):311–338

Jestice R, Kahai S (2010) The effectiveness of virtual worlds for education: an empirical study. In: Proceedings of the sixteenth americas conference on information systems (AMCIS), association of information systems. http://aisel.aisnet.org/amcis2010/512

Kabicher S, Rinderle-Ma S (2011) Human-centered process engineering based on content analysis and process view aggregation. In: Mouratidis H, Rolland C (eds) Advanced information systems engineering, vol 6741. Lecture notes in computer science. Springer, Berlin, pp 467–481

Lave J (1990) The culture of acquisition and the practice of understanding. In: Stigler JW, Schweder RA, Herdt G (eds) Cultural psychology. Cambridge University Press, Cambridge, pp 309–327 (Cambridge Books Online)

Leidl M, Roessling G (2007) How will future learning work in the third dimension? In: Proceedings of the 12th annual SIGCSE conference on innovation and technology in computer science education. ACM, New York, ITiCSE'07, pp 329–329

Margaria T, Boßelmann S, Doedt M, Floyd B, Steffen B (2012) Customer-oriented business process management: vision and obstacles. In: Hinchey M, Coyle L (eds) Conquering complexity. Springer, London, pp 407–429

Miller GA, Gildea PM (1987) How children learn words. Sci Am 257:94–99

Nunberg G (1978) The pragmatics of reference. Indiana University Linguistics Club, Bloomington

Oppl S, Stary C (2011) Effects of a tabletop interface on the co-construction of concept maps. In: Campos P, Graham N, Jorge J, Nunes N, Palanque P, Winckler M (eds) Human-computer interaction INTERACT 2011, vol 6948. Lecture notes in computer science. Springer, Heidelberg, pp 443–460

Parsaye K, Chignell M (1988) Expert systems for experts. Wiley, New York

Polanyi M (1967) The tacit dimension. University of Chicago Press, Chicago

Rubin DC (2006) The basic-systems model of episodic memory. Perspect Psychol Sci 1(4):277–311

Shneiderman B, Plaisant C (1998) Designing the user interface: strategies for effective human-computer interaction, 4th edn. Addison-Wesley Longman, Boston

Stone D, Jarrett C, Woodroffe M, Minocha S (2005) User interface design and evaluation. Morgan Kaufmann, Los Altos

Vom Brocke J, Rosemann M (2010) Handbook on business process management. Springer, Heidelberg

Weller M (2007) Virtual learning environments: using, choosing and developing your VLE. Routledge, London

A Tangible Modeling Interface for Subject-Oriented Business Process Management

8

Christoph Fleischmann

Abstract

Processes are an important part of every organization's value creation and therefore have to be executed in the most effective and efficient way. Process Analyses are a first step of Business Process Management to identify weak spots and potential improvements within processes. Even a rough documentation of processes in a graphical way, a so-called process model, raises process awareness and transparency for all involved parties. However, it is not as common as one might think that an organization has all processes documented in a complete and up-to-date form or documented at all. In reality even existing process models might not properly reflect the executed processes because the involved process actors are not part of the process survey. And even if they are involved, the complexity of most modeling notations and their respective tools can have a deterrent and overwhelming effect on the user. For executing process surveys we offer a tangible modeling tool that provides a modeling framework and enables even modeling novices to directly model their own part of the process, the S-BPM Buildbook. The method and the notation are based on Subject-oriented Business Process Management and its low complexity of only five symbols. The modeling process itself is completely detached from any kind of software to further lower the complexity and instruction time and to increase intuitiveness. We are aware that for process management steps, like a detailed analysis, documentation or implementation, some kind of software support is required. For this a recognition algorithm was developed that converts the tangible process model into a digital form as a generic XML file. The XML file can then be imported into the software tool in use. Two case studies were

C. Fleischmann (✉)
Josefstraße 8/8, 3100 St. Pölten, Austria
e-mail: chris.fleischmann@gmx.net

© The Author(s) 2015
A. Fleischmann et al. (eds.), *S-BPM in the Wild*,
DOI 10.1007/978-3-319-17542-3_8

executed to examine the S-BPM Buildbook. The first case study evaluates the tool regarding its intuitiveness and usability to describe real-life processes. The second case study compares the time needed for instructions and the actual modeling process while using the S-BPM Buildbook, with a pen and paper approach.

8.1   Introduction

Today, processes are a very important, if not the most important part, of an organizations value creation. Every organization, be it charitable, commercial or otherwise, executes many different processes on a different bases. However, from our own experiences in the fields of industrial engineering and informatics, we have recognized that this does not necessarily mean that neither the processes are executed in an effective or efficient way, nor the process executors are aware of their involvement in a process. Independently from the actual field of application it is crucial to execute processes as effectively and efficiently as possible.

In general this task is accomplished through Business Process Management (BPM) activities, even though the term process is not restricted to specific fields or divisions and can represent, among others, a business process, a development process, a production process, or the process of process improvement itself (Fischermanns 2006). A first step for an ongoing process analysis is to survey and document the processes in a graphical way, the process model. Even a rough process model increases the level of transparency and helps all involved parties to better understand existing and future processes (Fischermanns 2006; Horváth and Partners 2005). However, business practice has revealed that process models are often outdated, incomplete or nonexistent. So for the necessary steps of process analyses it is important to keep process models up to date and ensure that the models include all relevant process information necessary to describe and execute the processes. But why is this often not the case? One reason for this is the fact that the actual "end users are typically not participating in the modeling process" (Mutschler and Reichert 2013). This means that the one element that actually executes the process, which is responsible for it and may provide the most experiences and knowledge regarding a process, is excluded from the process survey: the process actor.

By actively incorporating the process actors into the survey and modeling phase it is possible to directly document relevant process knowledge and experience, and validate the gathered knowledge (the process model) at the same time. However, the complexity of most modeling notations and their respective tools often has deterrent and overwhelming effect on the user (Horváth and Partners 2005). This includes novices and experts alike. For instance, the Business Process Model and Notation (BPMN) applies 40–170 symbols, depending on how one counts. Although everyone might learn the most complex modeling language and tool, a common process actor rarely is an expert in modeling, and neither has the time nor the desire to learn a complex modeling tool (Turetken and Demirors 2013). In addition, organizations often focus on the technical application of the tool instead of fulfilling the requirements for an efficient application of the modeling procedure and the resulting process models (Schmelzer and Sesselmann 2013).

These aspects has led us to develop a tool that provides a framework for process modeling and directly involves the process actor in the modeling process. The tool has to be intuitive to understand in a way that even process modeling novices are able to use it in an intuitive way. The modeling design and notation have to be as simple as possible but still convey all relevant process information. Furthermore, for simplicity reasons the modeling process itself should be as far as possible detached from any kind of software. By using the notation of the Subject-oriented Business Process Management method and its five symbols (Fleischmann et al. 2012) we developed a tangible modeling interface which we term the "S-BPM BuildBook" (Fleischmann 2013; Fleischmann and Bachinger 2014; Fig. 8.1).

On the following pages we will explain the development of the S-BPM Build-book in detail. We will describe the development of a prototype and the final version of the tool, present the notation for modeling, and provide some design rationale. Furthermore, we will present two case studies. The first case study evaluates the intuitiveness of the S-BPM Buildbook, involving a group of testers (Fleischmann 2013), and the second one compares the S-BPM Buildbook with a traditional pen and paper approach (Aumayr and Bloderer 2014). Hereby, the process management steps following the process survey cannot be neglected. Phases like documentation or implementation are often accomplished with the support of software-based tools. For this instance we have developed a recognition algorithm that allows us to convert the tangible process model into a generic XML file via camera or mobile phone.

Fig. 8.1 The S-BPM Buildbook

8.2   Defining a Framework for Modeling: Design and Notation

S-BPM allows us to decompose a process into subjects and to describe each subject behavior as its own part of the process (Fleischmann et al. 2012). In this way S-BPM enables each process actor to model his part of the process by himself/ herself. So why not just give the process actor a pen and some sheets of paper and say "Go for it!"? Everyone knows how to use a pen, no instructions required, and the modeling process is as intuitive as it can get. That is true, if we only regard the perspective of the process actor. But someone, namely the modeling expert, has to read and interpret all the different subject behaviors to bring them together and to create a whole process. Two experimental case studies executed by Recker et al. (2010) and Weitlaner et al. (2013) show that if there is no framework for the modeling process the same process will be modeled in many varying designs, ranging from "all text" to "all graphics" (Fig. 8.2).

These different designs make it particularly difficult for third parties to interpret and understand the process models and bring the various process parts together. Consequently, modeling without any restrictions might meet the requirement for intuitiveness, because no instructions are needed, but fail for structured working conditions for the modeling expert. At least some degree of framework is required to provide such conditions. According to these case studies, Flowchart Design (Recker et al. 2010) is considered the most intuitive and also the one leading to models with the best process quality. In this case quality refers to the relevant process information contained in the process model as well as the understandability of the process models for third parties.

A Flowchart Design mainly consists of abstract graphics (i.e., rectangles) and text to describe processes. It uses none or a negligible amount of concrete graphics. The latter supports the S-BPM notation through abstract symbols and by documenting concrete process information, like message or subject names, in textual form. The S-BPM notation uses five symbols which keep the complexity of the notation relatively low. Three symbols visualize the "function" state, the "send" state and the "receive" state, one symbol the subject, and one symbol (an arrow or

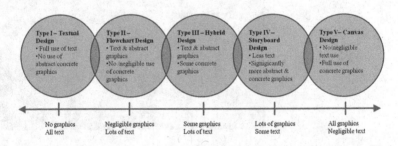

Fig. 8.2 Process design archetypes (Recker et al. 2010)

Table 8.1 S-BPM
Buildbook notation
(Fleischmann 2013)

S-BPM Buildbook notation	S-BPM notation
Green plug	Receive message state
Red plug	Send message state
Yellow plug	Function state
Grey plug	Message/transition
The letter case	The subject

comparable) state transitions and messages (Fleischmann et al. 2012). Based on the S-BPM notation and the Flowchart Design we have developed the S-BPM Build-book (Table 8.1).

8.3 Developing the S-BPM Buildbook

Existing tangible modeling tools like tabletop concept mapping (TCM) already apply S-BPM in conjunction with a tangible modeling interface to model processes by arranging blocks on a digitally augmented tabletop (Oppl and Stary 2009; Oppl 2011). So why should we develop another tangible tool? Well, the TCM tool still requires input via keyboard and mouse, in addition to the tangible blocks, to enter concrete subject names, message names or other process information. Hence, TCM does not allow a complete detachment from a software suite, and still requires at least one expert who can operate the software during the modeling process.

The goal of using a tangible interface without any kind of software resulted in the application of a letter case as basic structure. The process is modeled by arranging different colored plugs on the surface of the letter case. The application of the Flowchart Design and the S-BPM notation resulted in the following notation for the S-BPM Buildbook (Fleischmann 2013; Fleischmann and Bach-inger 2014).

The modeler can then write relevant process information, like names of the states or messages, on top of the plugs by using an overhead marker. For the basic structure when modeling the size of an average laptop was used for initial orientation.

8.3.1 The First Version

The first prototype had a size of $450 \times 250 \times 40$ mm (closed) and was made out of a material called "Corian" (Fig. 8.3; cf. Wikipedia 2014). The plugs are held in place on a predefined grid by magnets inside the plugs. This ensures that the plugs cannot move by accident and still enables the modeler to change the created model anytime.

Fig. 8.3 The first prototype
of the S-BPM Buildbook
(Fleischmann 2013)

However, with a weight of 6.5 kg the first prototype was too heavy, the transition plugs were too small to write on, and the measurements of the state plugs
were too space consuming given the limited space of the frame. These findings have
led to the development of the second version of the S-BPM Buildbook.

8.3.2 The Second Version

For the second version of the S-BPM Buildbook all plugs were changed, resulting
in a uniform size, achieved by smaller state plugs and bigger transition/message
plugs compared with the first version (Fig. 8.4). The overall height could be
reduced to 19 mm (from 40 mm) by using a construction of alternating layers
(corian-metal-corian) instead of steel balls. This also resulted in a weight reduction,
down to 3.6 kg.

The use of software tools for more advanced process management phases could
not be neglected. In order to support them we developed a "tangible to digital"
conversion interface allowing the user to import the tangible process model into a
software-based tool by making a picture of the S-BPM Buildbook. The step of
converting the tangible process model into a digital one is still completely detached
from the actual modeling process.

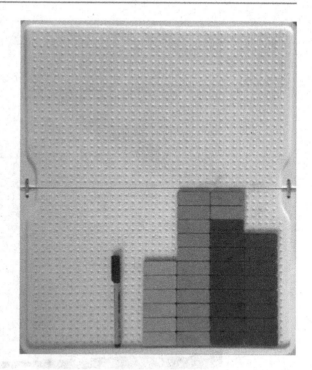

Fig. 8.4 The S-BPM Buildbook with the different colored plugs (Fleischmann 2013)

8.4   Tangible-to-Digital Process Model Conversion

Utilizing the concrete orientation of the plugs through the grid, the small number of symbols, and the clear differentiation of states by color, an image detection algorithm and an appropriate interface for a digital conversion was developed. By taking a picture via camera or mobile phone it is possible now to document and convert the process model from the S-BPM Buildbook into a generic XML file (Fleischmann 2013; Fleischmann and Bachinger 2014).

Figure 8.5 shows the subject behavior of a generic supplier. After receiving an order the supplier calculates the price and depending on the actions taken by the ordering actor either starts negotiations and prepares the delivery, or ends the process (Fig. 8.5).

In a second step the picture has to be loaded into the recognition software. The textual information on the plugs has to be entered manually on the right side of the user interface. This includes the information for each plug and the name of the state-transition plugs (Fig. 8.6).

After manually adding the textual information the XML file can be generated (Fig. 8.6, on the right). The plugs are identified via an ID and their state is defined by the color. Due to the generic XML format it is possible to import the file into practically any software suite—assuming that a proper interface exists.

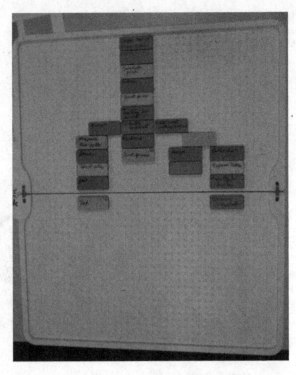

Fig. 8.5 Supplier process modeled with the S-BPM Buildbook

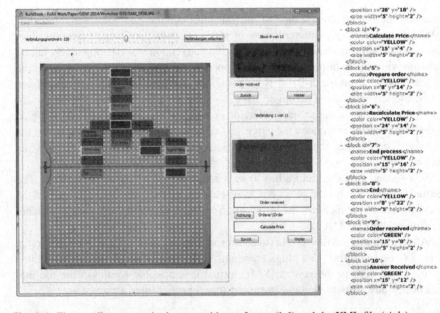

```
<position x="28" y="18" />
<size width="5" height="2" />
</block>
- <block id="4">
    <name>Calculate Price</name>
    <color color="YELLOW" />
    <position x="15" y="4" />
    <size width="5" height="2" />
  </block>
- <block id="5">
    <name>Prepare order</name>
    <color color="YELLOW" />
    <position x="8" y="14" />
    <size width="5" height="2" />
  </block>
- <block id="6">
    <name>Recalculate Price</name>
    <color color="YELLOW" />
    <position x="24" y="14" />
    <size width="5" height="2" />
  </block>
- <block id="7">
    <name>End process</name>
    <color color="YELLOW" />
    <position x="15" y="16" />
    <size width="5" height="2" />
  </block>
- <block id="8">
    <name>End</name>
    <color color="YELLOW" />
    <position x="8" y="22" />
    <size width="5" height="2" />
  </block>
- <block id="9">
    <name>Order received</name>
    <color color="GREEN" />
    <position x="15" y="0" />
    <size width="5" height="2" />
  </block>
- <block id="10">
    <name>Answer Received</name>
    <color color="GREEN" />
    <position x="15" y="12" />
    <size width="5" height="2" />
  </block>
```

Fig. 8.6 The supplier process in the recognition software (*left*) and the XML file (*right*)

A first version of such an interface was developed for the Metasonic Suite (Metasonic GmbH 2014), which is a software tool specifically developed for S-BPM. Figures 8.7, 8.8 and 8.9 show how the supplier process can be imported into the software suite with only a few mouse clicks.

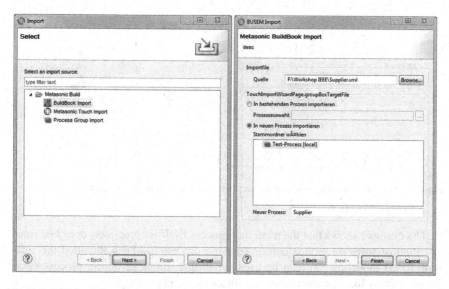

Fig. 8.7 Buildbook import into the Metasonic Suite

Fig. 8.8 The automatically generated subject interaction diagram in the Metasonic Suite

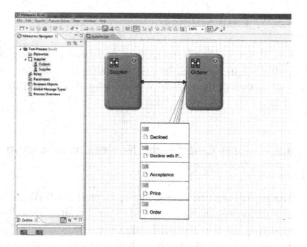

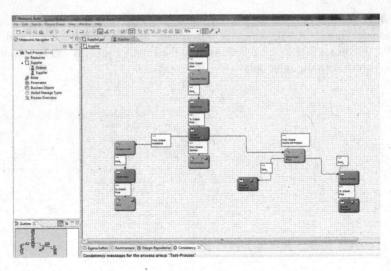

Fig. 8.9 The automatically generated subject behavior diagram of the Supplier

The example shows that the modeling process itself is completely detached from any kind of software requirements. After the process has been imported the software-based modeling tool can be used for further, more advanced, process management steps like documentation, optimization or even integration.

So much for the theory; but how does the S-BPM Buildbook work in an actual process survey? Two case studies are reported in the next sections.

8.5   Case Studies

Would the S-BPM Buildbook be as intuitive as intended? Two case studies were performed in the field, one in the course of a diploma thesis (Fleischmann 2013), and another in the course of a bachelor thesis, both intended to examine the intuitiveness of such a new tool.

8.5.1   First Case Study: Novices in Modeling and the S-BPM Buildbook

The goal of the first case study was to test the S-BPM Buildbook during a practical application regarding its usability and intuitiveness. The interviewed actors were modeling novices and had little or no knowledge regarding process management and process modeling. To evaluate the intuitiveness of the S-BPM Buildbook we created a questionnaire the respondents had to answer after performing the survey.

The case study was carried out at the "Center für industrielle Produktivität" (Center for Industrial Productivity, CiP) at the Technical University Darmstadt. The CiP is an initiative by the TU Darmstadt and McKinsey & Company with the goal to educate and research in the fields of real-life production processes. The surveyed process represents a production process for hydraulic cylinders, including the delivery of the raw material, the manufacturing of the single components, the internal logistics, and the final assembly of the cylinders. The production process, the various workstations (the subjects) and their interactions are clearly defined, although not documented in an explicit form.

The four participating actors received a 20-min introduction into the S-BPM method and the S-BPM Buildbook. Each of the participants is an actor in the production process and any actor is able to operate at any workstation. After the introduction each actor was assigned to one of the working stations (each representing a subject) and was given the task of modeling his respective subject behavior by using the S-BPM Buildbook.

After approximately two hours all actors had completed their respective process models.

Figure 8.10 shows two out of five subject behaviors modeled in the course of the field study. The subject behavior on the left side describes the production. The subject behavior on the right side captures the internal logistics.

The sample survey and the results from the questionnaires seem to confirm the S-BPM Buildbook's intuitiveness. The actors began to model their processes simultaneously and during the survey the actors autonomously began to mutually review each other's process models. Even if we consider the fact that each actor is able to execute any part of the process we may assume a level of intuitiveness of the design and notation in this behavior. Real life experience has shown that even modeling experts are not always able to understand a process model that was modeled by a different person, even if both know the process and the notation. The questionnaires show that the modelers rate the letter case as very intuitive and flexible to operate and easy to understand. They actually commented that the S-BPM Buildbook is fun to work with, in our opinion a claim not many modeling tools can make.

However, as promising as this evaluation might seem there are several factors that have to be considered. In order to collect sufficient data for a proper evaluation it is necessary to examine the S-BPM Buildbook in connection with different processes. There are many different process types (like management processes, production processes, etc.) with varying degrees of complexity. Production processes tend to be highly structured, which make them relatively simple to document. Surveys with more abstract processes, like management processes, have to be executed as well to elevate the S-BPM Buildbook's application with any kind of process survey.

In the performed survey all the process actors represented "working level" employees from the production line. This allows no conclusion on how employees from the higher management level would work with the Buildbook, or how a

Fig. 8.10 Two subject behaviors that were modeled during the first case study (Fleischmann 2013)

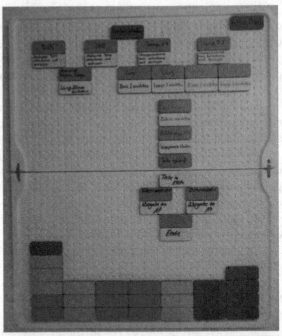

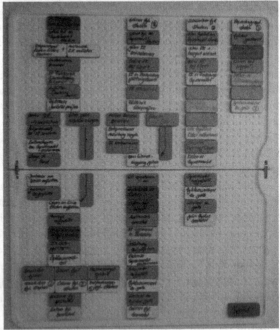

survey would work with a mixture of different employee levels. Finally, there were only four process actors involved, a number too small for any quantitative or qualitative evaluation.

8.5.2 Second Case Study: "Pen and Paper" Versus "the Buildbook"

In the second case study a process survey executed with the S-BPM Buildbook is compared to a survey done with pen and paper. To create an identical starting point the surveys were done in a company which consists of two independent business areas. Although they are in different business areas the executed processes are practically the same. The only differences were the actual employees, allowing us to compare the same process surveyed with different tools and different people.

All process participants modeled their respective part of the process either with pen and paper or with the S-BPM Buildbook. In a second step the process models were transferred in a process modeling software by modeling experts. The measuring points for the comparison were the time needed for instructions, the time needed for the process actors to finish their process models, and the time needed to transfer the process models into a software tool. This includes the time required for additional questions addressed to the process actors because of obscurities. Please note that at the time of this case study the tangible-to-digital interface for the S-BPM Buildbook was not completed. The process models were transferred to the software tool manually.

The surveyed process is a process used to create proposals. The involved subjects in this process are the secretary, the technician and the CEO.

In the beginning of the survey all participants got a brief introduction to business processes and process documentation. This general introduction took 30 min. The instruction for using the S-BPM Buildbook took 30 min while for the pen and paper method the instruction time was practically zero. Each process actor modeled his or her process isolated from the other participants. This measure was deemed necessary to prevent the process actors from communicating with, and so influencing, each other, although under normal circumstances it is recommended to allow and support communication between all process modelers. In the following the direct comparison is provided of the process models that were created with the respective tools, as well as a brief description of each part of the process (Aumayr and Bloderer 2014).

The process begins as soon as the secretary receives a customer request either by e-mail, mail, fax or phone. The secretary verifies the customer data for correctness and completeness. If the customer is not in the system a new entry is created for the customer and the request is forwarded to the technician. If the order is taken the secretary has to verify the technician's price calculation (Fig. 8.11).

After the technician receives the customer request he will communicate with the customer to specify the specific requirements. The technician then decides whether

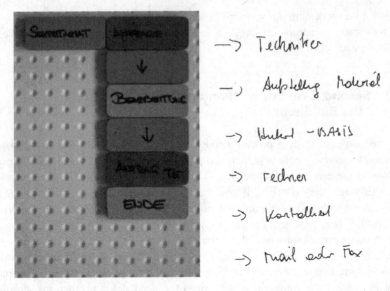

Fig. 8.11 Subject behavior of the secretary; S-BPM Buildbook (*left*) and pen and paper (*right*) (Aumyar and Bloderer 2014)

the order can be fulfilled according to the requested specifics. In case the order is taken and all details with the customer have been clarified the technician creates a first cost estimation which the CEO has to verify in case the order value is higher than 5000 €. If the technician receives a positive answer from the CEO he calculates the actual price and sends it to the secretary for confirmation. If the calculation is confirmed by the secretary the technician sends it to the customer (Fig. 8.12).

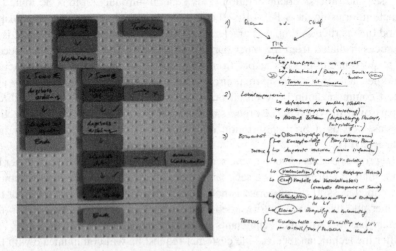

Fig. 8.12 Subject behavior of the technician; S-BPM Buildbook (*left*) and Pen and paper (*right*) (Aumayr and Bloderer 2014)

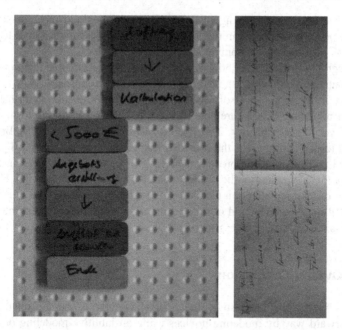

Fig. 8.13 Subject behavior of the CEO; S-BPM Buildbook (*left*) and Pen and paper (*right*) (Aumayr and Bloderer 2014)

If the estimated order value is higher than 5000 € the CEO has to verify the order for the technician (Fig. 8.13).

Table 8.2 shows the overall time needed for each step for both of the used modeling methods.

The pen and paper method did not require any instructions as everybody is familiar with the use of pen and paper. About 30 min were needed to explain the S-BPM Buildbook and how to use it. The overall time needed to model the processes required about 45 min with pen and paper and 40 min with the S-BPM Buildbook. The actual difference between the two methods was the overall time needed for the process conversion. To completely understand the various parts of the process modeled with pen and paper and transfer it to the software an overall time of 120 min was needed. This was due to the fact that the process actors had to

Table 8.2 Time comparison of both modeling methods

Modeling tool	Pen and paper	S-BPM Buildbook
Instruction time (min)	–	30
Overall modiling time (min)	45	40
Overall conversion time (min)	120	45
Total	165	115

Aumayr and Bloderer (2014)

be contacted and questioned again to clarify obscurities and misunderstandings. Using the processes modeled in the S-BPM Buildbook the time required to transfer the process information was only 45 min.

Although the S-BPM Buildbook requires more instruction time than a modeling method using pen and paper, the overall time required is still far less than the time needed for instructions for a software tool. In addition, the case study has shown again that modeling novices are able to use the S-BPM Buildbook to model processes of varying complexity. The biggest advantage of the S-BPM Buildbook compared to pen and paper is the provided framework which helps third parties to understand and interpret the process models. This can be clearly seen in the time needed for the conversion of the process models from tangible to digital. However, some kind of learning effect on the side of the modeling experts (the interviewers) could result in a shorter period of time required for understanding and interpreting the process.

8.6   Overall Conclusion

As shown in the first case study the S-BPM Buildbook can be operated in a straightforward way by modeling novices using an intuitive modeling design and notation. The predefined design and notation serve as guideline, to prevent inconsistencies between different users and ensure the highest possible quality of the resulting process models. The S-BPM Buildbook provides a framework to modelers to create non-redundant and syntactically correct process models while being detached from software-based input to model processes. The tool can be provided to several modelers simultaneously, thus supporting a subject-oriented approach for collective process surveys.

The first case study gives a first insight regarding the practical application of the S-BPM Buildbook. Although the participants were modeling novices, all process actors were students and the CiP represents a laboratory environment. Additionally, there was no possibility to evaluate whether the quality of the surveyed process models is sufficient for moving on in business process management.

The second case study also shows that it is possible for modeling novices to use the S-BPM Buildbook after giving only a brief introduction. Furthermore, the S-BPM Buildbook provides a proper framework for process modeling that supports third parties that are not involved in the actual process understanding and in interpreting the process. Further case studies have to be performed, especially to gain insight in how to model larger and more complex processes when using the S-BPM Buildbook.

References

Aumayr N, Bloderer K (2014) Computerunterstützte Prozessoptimierung in Klein- und Mittelunternehmen. Bachelor thesis ed. Linz, Austria (in German)

Fischermanns G (2006) Praxishandbuch Prozessmanagement, 6th edn. Verlag Dr. Götz Schmidt, Gießen (in German)

Fleischmann C (2013) Subject-oriented process survey—an approach and modeling tool for executing subject-oriented process surveys. Diploma thesis ed. Vienna, Austria

Fleischmann C, Bachinger A (2014) Subject-oriented process modeling interface: a tangible approach for subject process modeling. In: 2014 IEEE 16th conference on business informatics on business informatics (CBI), vol 2. IEEE, ed. Geneva, Switzerland, pp 108–112

Fleischmann A, Schmidt W, Stary C, Obermeier S, Börger E (2012) Subject-oriented business process management. Springer, Heidelberg

Horváth and Partners (2005) Prozessmanagement umsetzen – Durch nachhaltige Prozessperformance Umsatz steigern und Kosten senken. Schäffer-Poeschel Verlag, Stuttgart (in German)

Metasonic GmbH (2014) Metasonic Suite. [Online]. http://www.metasonic.de/metasonic-suite

Mutschler B, Reichert M (2013) Understanding the costs of business process management technology. In: Business process management. Springer, Berlin, pp 157–194

Oppl S (2011) Subject-oriented elicitation of distributed business process knowledge. In: S-BPM ONE-learning by doing—doing by learning. Third international conference, S-BPM ONE 2011. Springer, Ingolstadt, pp 16–33

Oppl S, Stary C (2009) Tabletop concept mapping. In: Proceedings of the 3rd international conference on tangible and embedded interaction (TEI'09), Cambridge, UK, pp 275–282

Recker J, Safrudin N, Rosemann M (2010) How novices model business processes. In: BPM 2010. LNCS, vol 6336. Springer, Heidelberg, pp 29–44

Schmelzer HJ, Sesselmann W (2013) Geschäftsprozessmanagement in der Praxis-Kunden zufriedenstellen, Produktivität steigern, Wert erhöhen, 8th edn. Carl Hanser Verlag, München (in German)

Turetken O, Demirors O (2013) Business process modeling pluralized. S-BPM ONE 2013-running processes, CCIS, vol 360, Springer, Berlin, pp 34–51

Weitlaner D, Guettinger A, Kohlbacher M (2013) Intuitive comprehensibility of process models. S-BPM ONE 2013—running processes, CCIS, vol 360, Springer, Berlin, pp 52–71

Wikipedia (2014) The free encyclopedia; Corian. [Online]. http://en.wikipedia.org/wiki/Corian

A Reference Model for Maintenance Processes

9

Christoph Piller

Abstract

Effective maintenance has become increasingly important the last few decades. Competition is increasing because of globalization. Therefore, production is confronted with increasing requirements. In particular, machinery and plants have to produce faster and in greater volume. Nowadays, the high availability of equipment is a prerequisite to compete. In recent decades, maintenance has become its own business area. The Lean Management method Total Productive Management (TPM) provides a guideline for effective maintenance. The maintenance process itself is not adequately described in the literature. However, it is an efficient means of addressing unplanned maintenance tasks. This is the reason for creating a reference model for the maintenance process that can be implemented in companies. The process model is described using the language of subject-oriented business process management (S-BPM). This process language meets the requirements of TPM and maintenance experts. S-BPM is a communication system which focuses on the individual actors. Furthermore, the message flow of the communication is displayed to provide a structured and clear understanding of messages required within the reference model. The reference model created was verified by maintenance and S-BPM experts and is seen as a positive and important development in the field of maintenance. It is also pointed out that this reference model needs to be customized for every customer. Then it facilitates responding to customer requirements.

C. Piller (✉)
UAS Technikum Wien, Ferdinand-Maria-Straße 17, 85095 Ingolstadt, Austria
e-mail: chpiller@gmx.net

© The Author(s) 2015
A. Fleischmann et al. (eds.), *S-BPM in the Wild*,
DOI 10.1007/978-3-319-17542-3_9

9.1   Importance of Maintenance Processes

The DIN EN 13306 standard defines maintenance as the combination of every technical and administrative measure, as well as management measures, implemented to maintain a perfect condition or recreate a perfect condition during the entire lifecycle of a unit with the aim that this unit can fulfill its function (Beutler 2008; Arnold et al. 2008). Effective maintenance has become increasingly important over the last few decades. Competition is increasing because of globalization. Therefore, production is confronted with increasing requirements. In particular, machinery and plants have to produce faster and in greater volume. Nowadays, the high availability of equipment is a prerequisite to compete. In recent decades, maintenance has become its own business area (Arnold et al. 2008; Ijioui et al. 2010).

Thus, "doing more with less, better and smarter" has become the new slogan for maintenance (Matyas 2013). In 2008, 250 billion euros were invested in maintenance by German companies. Approximately 45 billion euros could be saved. It was detected that 18 % of the maintenance tasks executed by companies are not required and ineffective. In addition, up to 30 % of breakdowns could be avoided if the maintenance process was executed in a more intelligent way. By increasing the effectiveness of maintenance, workforce could be reduced in the maintenance field by 30–70 % (Kuhn et al. 2008).

Nowadays, maintenance has become very important to organizations. Not only are the availability of maintenance objects and the costs of maintenance activities of considerable interest, but also considering effectiveness, product quality, the maintenance service and safety is important. This means that the availability of required resources must be ensured to guarantee the availability of the maintenance object. The main objective of maintenance is the preservation of the availability and functionality of a unit (Arnold et al. 2008; Matyas 2013).

The Lean Management method supports companies in fulfilling these new market requirements and improving the effectiveness of production. As the name of this method suggests, production and the company as a whole are made lean. This means that the stock of a company should be as small as possible and the lead time should be as short as possible. Theoretically, equipment availability needs to be 100 % because any failure of a maintenance object leads to an increase in lead time. Every increase in lead time increases the amount of stock; that is, the link between Lean Production and maintenance, i.e., providing an efficient maintenance process, overproduction, large amounts of stock, inefficient processes, etc. can be prevented (Matyas and Sihn 2011).

Total Productive Management TPM is a Lean Management tool developed especially for maintenance to ensure the availability of equipment (Matyas 2013). According to Matyas (2013 p. 191), TPM relates to productivity-orientated maintenance which allows the efficiency of plants and machinery to continuously improve with the help of all employees. Thus, the aim of TPM is to achieve perfect

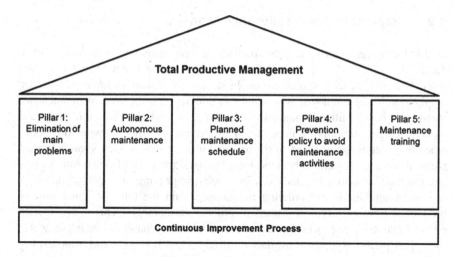

Fig. 9.1 Pillars of TPM [modified from Matyas (2013)]

equipment availability. The productivity orientation and the inclusion of all employees are two very important aspects not only for TPM but also for the entire set of Lean Management methods. The precise TPM process can be described in relation to five pillars. As can be seen in Fig. 9.1, the foundation of TPM is the Continuous Improvement Process (CIP) (Kamiske 2010).

The first pillar requires the elimination of the main problems that occur in production to reduce the difficulty of maintenance tasks and prevent breakdowns, unplanned down time, etc. The next step is autonomous maintenance, in which standard maintenance tasks (e.g., refilling engine oil, regular cleaning, etc. in the automotive industry) is carried out independently by the workers. This requires maintenance plans as illustrated by the third pillar. The fourth pillar goes further and relates to the creation of a prevention policy. This means that during the planning and construction phases, aspects of maintenance should be considered, e.g., the accessibility of parts. The fifth pillar recommends maintenance training for employees to prepare personnel. With the implementation of TPM, corrective maintenance activities can be minimized. Furthermore, the occurrence of unplanned repair activities can be avoided (Kamiske 2010).

Following Lean Production methods, especially TPM, a company is perfectly prepared for maintenance tasks, besides accidents, which lead to unplanned down time. Exact measures for handling such cases are difficult to define, because unplanned down time, by its nature, cannot be planned for and tends to be due to random accidents. Nonetheless, reducing and managing unplanned down time is addressed in the model proposed herein.

9.2   Importance of a Reference Model

In 2009, Moayed presented a comparison of lean-producing and non-lean-pro-
ducing companies. He recognized four main factors which have to be improved
when becoming a lean manufacturer. First, it is important to have well-trained
employees. Every employee who comes in contact with the area of maintenance
should be given additional maintenance training. Second, the amount of stock and
work in progress are highly important. Furthermore, the time between the occurrence of a failure and ordering of the required maintenance activity is an important
factor if companies want to become lean. Finally, "the ratio of down-time to production time" is also a key factor. In particular, improving two specific factors—
time between failure and ordering maintenance and the ratio of down time to
production time—are typical aspects of process management. This means that an
efficient maintenance process should be created in a way that it can be implemented
to support perfect equipment availability (Matyas 2013; Matyas and Sihn 2011).

There already exists a standard model for the maintenance process. This model
was created by Matyas (2013 p. 178ff) and is described using an event-driven
process chain (EPC). In this paper, it serves as a basic model for the creation of a
reference model. Matyas (2013 p. 178ff) defines eight main steps in maintenance:
Identify, Plan, Prepare, Execute, Restart, Check functionality, Approve and *Close*.
These eight sub processes were chosen based on the examination of maintenance
projects that were based primarily on them (Matyas and Sihn 2011). This overview
of the maintenance process is similar to the overview provided by Liebstückel
(2011), who defined five steps: notification, planning, control, implementation and
completion. These steps are a summary of the steps described by Matyas and
confirm the eight sub processes.

However, only the functions and activities of the maintenance process are shown
and described by Matyas (2013), as seen in Fig. 9.2. Little information is provided
about the messages which have to be sent or received to run the process, or about
the business objects which are necessary to complete the process in an effective
manner. Furthermore, there is little information concerning the process participants.
The lack of this information means that the maintenance process cannot be
implemented and used by a company. However, the description of the maintenance
process using an EPC can be used to present the concept of maintenance, giving the
responsible maintenance personnel a first impression of maintenance activities
(Weske 2007).

In summary, the standard model provided by Matyas represents the process
stages of maintenance and serves as a form of overview in case the maintenance
process is unknown. This description does not provide sufficient details to serve as a
reference process.

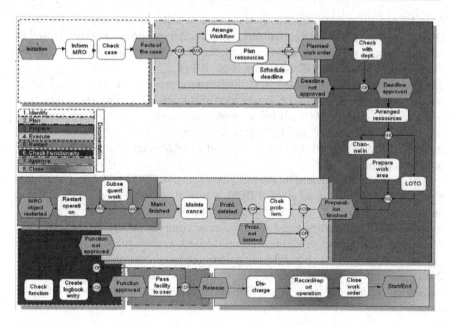

Fig. 9.2 Maintenance process according to Matyas and Sihn (2011)

9.3 Selecting S-BPM for Representation

For the creation of the reference model, S-BPM has been chosen. This process language meets both TPM requirements and reference model requirements as described now. The S-BPM notation consists of three core elements: subjects, predicates and objects (Fleischmann et al. 2011, 2013a, b). The EPC is a function-orientated process language and focuses on the functions and activities of a process. The participants and messages are less important and hardly considered. This means the EPC concentrates on the predicate of a sentence. In this approach, the process is built around the data structures which display the required operations (Fleischmann et al. 2011).

Subjects are the most important element in S-BPM. This means that each subject required for a process is defined and determined and each role must be defined before a process description can start (Fleischmann et al. 2013a, b). The central element of Lean Management methods is the active participation of employees (Kamiske 2010). The subject-orientated view of processes in S-BPM promotes this requirement. Accordingly, S-BPM seems to be suitable for implementing maintenance when viewed from the perspective of TPM. The second element of S-BPM is the predicate, which represents the subjects' behaviors. The behavior of each subject is described, which means that every subject knows exactly which activities and tasks are to be performed. Again, S-BPM supports the subject-based view of

Lean Management methods. The third element of S-BPM is the object. (Business) Objects are transferred between subjects. Objects can comprise messages as well as tangible goods, such as maintenance objects, etc. Objects are elements that are manipulated by subjects (Fleischmann et al. 2011).

One of the drawbacks of the EPC maintenance process was the lack of object representation. Less information is provided about objects if a process is described using an EPC (Weske 2007). If business objects and their flows are not created, a process cannot be created in S-BPM (Fleischmann et al. 2011). Unlike the standard model, S-BPM fulfills all the requirements of Lean Management methods and the maintenance process itself.

To transform the standard model described using an EPC by Matyas (2013) into a reference model described using S-BPM, a helpful case study was found in Cakar and Demirörs (2014). In this study, important transformation rules are given. Rules for basic structural elements and rules for more complex structures are listed. The creation of the reference model was initiated based on these rules. Furthermore, ten experts stemming from five different companies were interviewed (Aigner et al. 2014; Heimhilcher and Schwarz 2014; Matula and Markus 2014; Szalay 2014; Reinert 2014), in order to obtain qualitative verification of the constructed reference model.

9.4   The Maintenance Process Reference Model

In this section, the reference model is presented. First, the Subject Interaction Diagram (SID) created is shown. In Fig. 9.3, the SID of the reference model can be seen. For the maintenance process, five subjects have been defined: *Working System, Operations Manager, Maintenance Manager, Maintenance Workers* and *Warehouse/Procurement.*

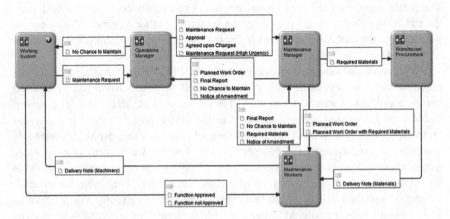

Fig. 9.3 SID of the maintenance process

The process starts with the subject *Working System*. The contact subject for the *Working System* is the *Operations Manager* who is responsible for a functioning operation. The Maintenance Manager is the responsible subject for maintenance activities. This subject creates maintenance plans, coordinates these plans and exchanges them with the *Operations Manager*, engages the *Maintenance Workers* to perform the maintenance activities, and orders the required materials from the *Warehouse/Procurement*. As can also be seen in Fig. 9.3, the *Maintenance Manager* is a central subject and therefore is important in this process. The *Warehouse/Procurement* is responsible for the correct delivery of the required materials. The *Maintenance Workers* are responsible for the maintenance activities. The contact subject for the *Maintenance Workers* is the *Maintenance Manager*.

We now turn to the behavior of each subject to explain the entire process and the messages required.

9.4.1 Subject Behavior Diagram (SBD) of the Working System

In Fig. 9.4, the behavior of the subject *Working System* can be seen. When a failure occurs or is detected, a report has to be filled out and appropriate activities must be set. The failure report consists of data such as details concerning the reference object available at the time, for example, data on the malfunction and details about the location and responsible persons. Appropriate activities are tasks which should be executed by the workers, and tasks which protect the machinery against additional damage.

When these initial tasks have been completed, a maintenance request is sent to the responsible *Operations Manager*. This is the first message sent by the *Working System* and can also be seen in the SID (see Fig. 9.3).

Then, the *Working System* receives either a note of the delivery of the machinery by the *Maintenance Workers* or the *Working System* receives the message that the machinery can no longer be maintained. If the *Working System* receives the latter message, the process ends at this point for this subject. Otherwise, if the *Working System* receives the machinery delivery message, the machinery has to be controlled (evaluated and monitored) in the next step.

If the functioning of the machinery is not approved by the *Working System*, a message is sent to the *Maintenance Workers*. In this message additional information, e.g., what exactly still does not work, is included. Then the *Working System* again waits for the completion of the maintenance. If the functioning of the machinery is approved by the Working System, confirmation is sent to the *Maintenance Workers* and the maintenance process ends at this point for the *Working System*.

As can be seen in the SID (Fig. 9.3) and in the subjects' behavior (Fig. 9.4), the following messages can be sent by the *Working System*: a maintenance request, an approval, and a non-approval message. The following messages can be received by the *Working System*: a no-chance-to-maintain message and a machinery delivery note.

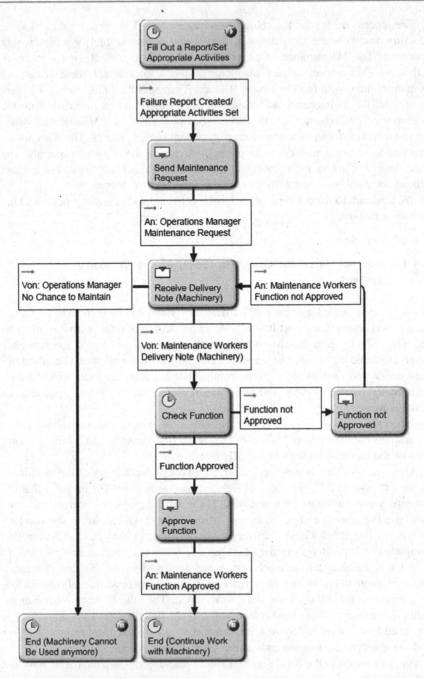

Fig. 9.4 SBD of the working system

9.4.2 SBD of the Operations Manager

As can be seen in Fig. 9.5, the process starts with the receipt of a maintenance request by the *Working System*. After receiving the message, the maintenance request has to be checked. If this request is not a high urgency request, all missing data is added, and the request is finally sent to the *Maintenance Manager*.

In the next step, the planned work order created by the *Maintenance Manager* is received. This work order consists of the time in which the maintenance is to be executed and the personnel and material are required. If any of these planned resources have to be changed by the *Operations Manager* because of other important tasks being accomplished by the responsible department, these changes are filed, and sent to the *Maintenance Manager*.

If the planned work order is checked and approved, an approval is sent to the *Maintenance Manager*, which can be seen as an order. This communication between the *Operations Manager* and the *Maintenance Manager* is the coordination of planned work orders. Then, the production plan is updated to change important scheduled tasks and shift resources in time. If the maintenance request by the *Working System* is a highly urgent request, an order is sent immediately to the *Maintenance Manager* and the production plan is then updated. When the production plan has been updated, the *Operations Manager* receives a response from the *Maintenance Manager*. There are three possible messages: a notice of amendment, a no-chance-to-maintain message, or a final report.

If a notice of amendment is received, the production plan has to be updated again. This notice of amendment can be a change of the completion date or a change in human and material resources required. If a no-chance-to-maintain message is received, the *Working System* has to be informed and the maintenance process ends. If a final report is received from the *Maintenance Manager*, the process is also complete.

The following messages can be sent by the *Operations Manager* (see Figs. 9.3 and 9.5): a maintenance request, a maintenance request of high urgency, an approval, an agreed-upon-changes message, or a no-chance-to-maintain message. The following messages can be received by the *Operations Manager* (see Figs. 9.3 and 9.5): a maintenance request, a planned work order, a notice of amendment, a no-chance-to-maintain message, or a final report.

9.4.3 SBD of the Maintenance Manager

As can be seen from Fig. 9.6, the process involving the Maintenance Manager starts with the receipt of a maintenance request from the *Operations Manager*. It is initially controlled (evaluated) whether it is a simple request or a highly urgent order. In case the message received is a simple maintenance request, the maintenance is scheduled. Human resources, necessary materials and a schedule have to be determined and summarized in a prospective work order. This work order is sent

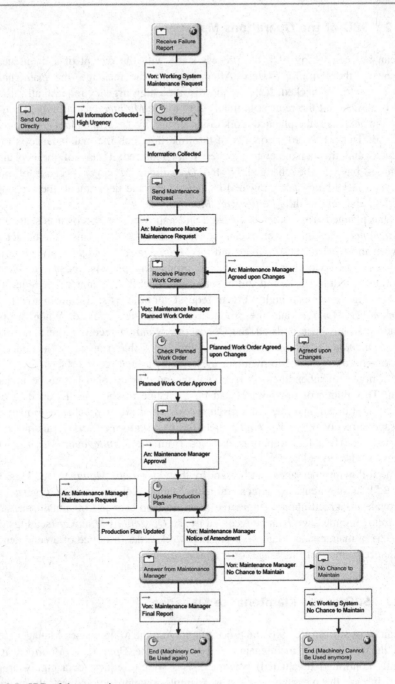

Fig. 9.5 SBD of the operations manager

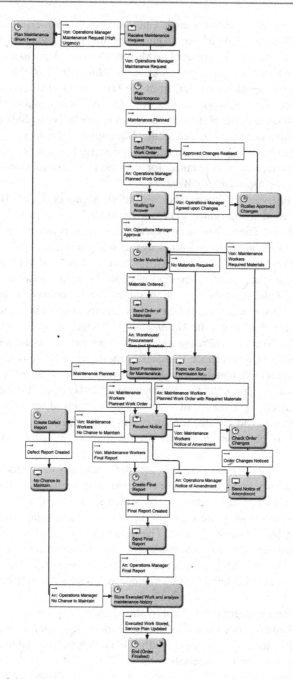

Fig. 9.6 SBD of the maintenance manager

to the *Operations Manager*, who sends either an agreed-upon-changes message or an approval. If some changes are required by the *Operations Manager*, these changes are realized and the updated work order is sent again to the *Operations Manager*. It also coordinates the *Operations Manager* and the *Maintenance Manager*. If an approval is received from the *Operations Manager*, the materials required are ordered. It is important that this order not only contains the necessary materials but also the place of delivery and responsible persons. Subsequently, the permission for maintenance is given to the *Maintenance Workers*.

If the *Operations Manager* has sent an order directly because of a high degree of urgency, the maintenance is planned for the short term and permission is sent immediately to the *Maintenance Workers*.

Four of the interviewed experts (see Appendix), Aigner et al. (2014), pointed out that, before a good maintenance plan can be made, an expert has to check the maintenance object. The maintenance expert, i.e., an expert in the machinery, is the only person with the appropriate knowledge to select relevant personnel, materials and time in the best way. Furthermore, two interviewed experts, Matula and Markus (2014), proposed that better differentiation could be made between maintenance orders. For example, different escalation stages can be defined in terms of how urgent a maintenance order is and how many experts are required, etc.

When permission is given, the *Maintenance Manager* waits for an answer from the Maintenance Workers. There are four possible answers: an order for materials, a notice of amendment, a no-chance-to-maintain message, or a final report. If an order for materials is received, materials are ordered from the *Warehouse/Procurement*. It is important that in this case the *Maintenance Workers* be informed when the material is ordered. If a notice of amendment is received, the necessary order changes are checked and the amendment is sent to the *Operations Manager*. These amendments can be either a change in the human resources required or a postponement.

If the *Maintenance Workers* confirm that the machinery cannot be repaired, the *Maintenance Manager* creates a defect report and sends the message to the *Operations Manager*. The executed work is then stored and the maintenance process ends. The process steps are similar if the Maintenance Manager receives a final report from the *Maintenance Workers*. The final report is completed and sent to the *Operations Manager*. The executed work is stored and the process ends. According to Matula and Markus (2014) and Heimhilcher and Schwarz (2014), it is important to analyze the work executed for every maintenance object to create perfectly tuned service plans.

The following messages can be sent by the *Maintenance Manager* (see Figs. 9.3 and 9.6): a planned work order (to the *Operations Manager* as well as to the *Maintenance Workers*), a notice of amendment, a no-chance-to-maintain message, a final report, or an order for materials.

The following messages can be received by the *Maintenance Manager* (see Figs. 9.3 and 9.6): a maintenance request, a maintenance request of high urgency, an approval, an agreed-upon-changes message, a no-chance-to-maintain message, a notice of amendment, an order for materials, or a final report.

9.4.4   SBD of the Maintenance Workers

The maintenance process for the Maintenance Workers starts with the receipt of a maintenance order by the *Maintenance Manager* (see Fig. 9.7). If extra material is required to handle this order, it is mentioned in the order and the material is received from the *Warehouse/Procurement*. In the next step, all the resources required have to be arranged. This includes not only material required but also the tools, as well as responsible persons and specialists. Then the maintenance work itself can be started. In this case a checklist can be created, which the *Maintenance Workers* can go through during the maintenance procedure. This checklist can consist of points such as correct channeling in, preparation of the work area, lockout–tagout (LOTO), etc.

During the maintenance process two possible issues can occur. First, additional or further material may be required. In this case an order is sent to the *Maintenance Manager* and the material is received from the *Warehouse/Procurement*. Second, a complete defect may be detected. In this case, a message is sent to the *Maintenance Manager*. The workplace is then discharged and cleaned up, and the maintenance process ends.

If the maintenance can be completed and the functioning of the machinery is checked by the *Maintenance Workers*, a delivery note is created for the Working System. After the machinery is transferred to the *Working System*, the workplace should be cleaned up completely and an answer from the Working System is awaited. If the Working System does not approve the functioning of the repaired machinery, maintenance work recommences. If the functioning of the machinery is approved, a final report has to be created, generating a timeout of 24 h. This means that no more than 24 h can pass before an answer is received from the Working System to ensure the process is completed as fast as possible. The final report is sent to the *Maintenance Manager* and the maintenance process ends here for the *Maintenance Workers*.

Four of the interviewed experts, Aigner et al. (2014), pointed out that the final inspection of a maintenance object is not done by the user alone, but together with the responsible maintenance worker. This should be marked in the process by companies in terms of how it is done, as Heimhilcher and Schwarz (2014) pointed out that the inspection of their products takes between one and two months. In this case, it is nearly impossible for the responsible maintenance workers to undertake this final trial together with the customer; furthermore, a timeout function seems to be unnecessary.

The following messages can be sent by the *Maintenance Workers* (see Figs. 9.3 and 9.7): a delivery note of the repaired machinery, a no-chance-to-maintain message, an order for materials, a notice of amendment, or a final report. The following messages can be received by the *Maintenance Workers* (see Figs. 9.3 and 9.7): a maintenance order, a delivery note of the materials, an approval, or a non-approval message.

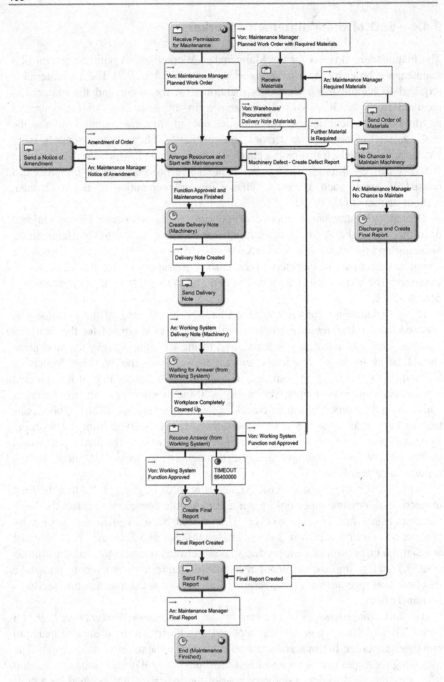

Fig. 9.7 SBD of the maintenance workers

9.4.5 SBD of the Warehouse/Procurement

As can be seen in Fig. 9.8, the process starts with the receipt of an order for materials from the *Maintenance Manager*. The materials required are sent to the *Maintenance Workers* and the process ends because the order is complete as far as the *Warehouse/Procurement* is concerned. There is one message, which can be sent by the *Warehouse/Procurement* "no delivery of materials" and one message which can be received by the *Warehouse/Procurement* "an order" for materials (see Figs. 9.3 and 9.8).

This SBD completes the reference model for the maintenance process. Each subject is solely responsible for its behavior. A technical verification was undertaken using the Metasonic Flow and the Metasonic Proof, both verification systems

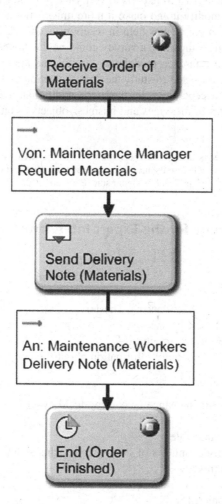

Fig. 9.8 SBD of the warehouse/procurement

included in the Metasonic Build. The process was implemented to detect logical errors. Furthermore, a qualitative verification was undertaken by interviewing maintenance and S-BPM experts.

9.5   Outlook

In this chapter a reference model has been introduced which can be implemented by companies in various sectors. The maintenance experts mainly appreciated this attempt and the model. They also mentioned that the reference model needs to be customized for each company when utilizing it. This indicates the next steps that need to be taken. There should be an intensive knowledge exchange between maintenance experts and S-BPM experts to verify the reference model in relation to different contexts, to modify it and make it more universally accepted. In addition, first implementations in companies help in receiving feedback on the model. With the consent of different companies, a survey could be developed to accompany the implementation of the reference model and examine its application. In this case, important data can be collected to study the "customization factor" of the reference model and its overall acceptability. Furthermore, additional investigation would be worthwhile in the areas of messages and business objects as only a short overview is given in this chapter.

Appendix: Guideline for the Expert Interviews

Interviewer: Date:
Experts: Company:

- Introduction (name, UAS, Master's Thesis)
- Objectives of the expert interviews
- Usage of this interview in the thesis
- No internally or confidentially information about the company necessary
- Agenda

1. Standard model of maintenance (according to Matyas)
   (a) Presentation
   (b) Process understandable
   (c) Advantages, disadvantages of implementing this standard model
2. Created reference model
   (a) Presentation
   (b) With "Metasonic Flow"

   (c) Gaps, complaints, suggestions for improvement
3. Messages within the reference model
   (a) Existing parameters sufficient?
   (b) Additional documents necessary?
4. Organisational embedding
   (a) Confrontation of internal and external processes (Service Level Agree-ments
   (b) Advantages, disadvantages of the implementation
   (c) Is an improvement of maintenance possible?

Date, Signature

References

Aigner G, Brandstätter K, Fleischmann C, Kloibhofer C (3 April 2014) Interviewees, Experteninterview-Referenzmodell für den Instandhaltungsprozess (Interview) (in German)

Arnold D et al (2008) Handbuch logistik. Springer, Berlin, pp 3–136, 534–547 (in German)

Beutler R (2008) IHRUS-Instandhaltung Rad und Schiene (Online). Available http://www.ihrus.ch/index_htm_files/100908%20IH-Begriffe.pdf (in German) (Zugriff am 14 03 2014)

Cakar B, Demirörs O (2014) Transformation from eEPC to S-BPM: a case study. In: LNBIP 170: S-BPM ONE scientific research. Springer, Eichstätt, pp 53–73 (in German)

Fleischmann A et al (2011) Subject-oriented business process management. Carl Hanser, Munich (in German)

Fleischmann A et al (2013a) S-BPM illustrated-an illustrated storybook about business processes. Institute of Innovative Process Management, Ingolstadt

Fleischmann A et al (2013b) Subject-oriented modeling and execution of multi-agent business processes In: 2013 IEEE/WIC/ACM international conferences on web intelligence (WI) and intelligent agent technology (IAT). Atlanta, pp 138–145

Heimhilcher E, Schwarz W (8 April 2014) Interviewees, Experteninterview-Referenzmodell für den Instandhaltungsprozess (Interview) (in German)

Ijioui R et al (2010) Globalization 2.0-a roadmap to the future from leading minds. Springer, Heidelberg, pp 1–20, 207–216

Kamiske GF (2010) Lean management. Carl Hanser, Munich (in German)

Kuhn A et al (2008) Gute Instandhaltung-Erfolgsfaktoren für die Produktion. In: Management circle Jahrestagung summit maintenance 2008. Munich, pp 3–8, 28 (in German)

Liebstückel K (2011) Plant maintenance with SAP. Galileo Press Inc., Boston (MA), pp 129–136

Matula C, Markus P (7 April 2014) Interviewees, Experteninterview-Referenzmodell für den Instandhaltungsprozess (Interview) (in German)

Matyas K, Sihn W (2011) Standardization and optimization of maintenance processes in lean manufacturing systems. In: Stuttgart: 21st international conference on production research

Matyas K (2013) Instandhaltungslogistik-Qualität und Produktivität steigern. Carl Hanser, Munich (in German)

Reinert M (9 April 2014) Interviewee, Experteninterview-Referenzmodell für den Instandhaltungsprozess (Interview) (in German)

Szalay NSB (24 February 2014) Interviewee, Experteninterview-Referenzmodell für den Instandhaltungsprozess (Interview) (in German)

Weske M (2007) Business process management concepts, languages, architectures. Springer, Berlin, pp 25–69, 125–226

Role and Rights Management

10

Alexander Lawall, Thomas Schaller and Dominik Reichelt

Abstract

Role and rights management of today's IT landscape is a challenging task that causes problems concerning the redundancy of organizational knowledge. This knowledge is the basis for specifying access rights and task assignment. As a consequence, the widespread technological methods are prone to inconsistencies on organizational changes, such as employees leaving, joining or moving within the organization. For this purpose, an approach is needed that offers both a comprehensive organizational meta-model and a declarative organization query language. The central meta-model helps to partially overcome the redundancy problem. In conjunction with the organization query language, the problems caused by redundancy is minimized. A query language expression describes formally characteristics of agents that are assigned to access rights, or tasks. Accordingly, this new approach uses a *descriptive* approach instead of *total enumeration* as required by other approaches. Thus, query expressions stay unmodified even if the organization changes.

A. Lawall (✉) · T. Schaller · D. Reichelt
Institut für Informationssysteme der Hochschule für Angewandte Wissenschaften Hof,
Alfons-Goppel-Platz 1, 95028 Hof, Germany
e-mail: alexander.lawall@hof-university.de

T. Schaller
e-mail: thomas.schaller@iisys.de

D. Reichelt
e-mail: dominik.reichelt@hof-university.de

© The Author(s) 2015
A. Fleischmann et al. (eds.), *S-BPM in the Wild*,
DOI 10.1007/978-3-319-17542-3_10

10.1   Role and Rights Management

This section describes what role and rights management in business process management is about and focuses on typical problems that companies have to face in this area. We will show the reasons for these problems and discuss solutions. At the end a novel, S-BPM-like organization server for role and rights management is presented.

10.2   Motivation

Looking at the various applications and systems needed for running a business, one thing becomes obvious: In almost every application, there is the need to maintain a model of the organizational structure including roles the agents. This model is required in order to define access rights or assign tasks to agents (in the case of a workflow management system). These redundancies lead to a great maintenance overhead that—even for small businesses—can grow to a great burden.

Another issue is that almost all applications try to model an organization as hierarchy or tree. But organization theory literature reveals that companies tend to be multidimensional graphs rather than just trees. In practice, this leads to a lot of workarounds within the used software components that are also not easy to maintain.

A general security problem is the result. Because of the complexity of the management task, nobody is able to guarantee that the agents only see the data that they are supposed to see. Often, the process of granting access to data items is well organized in companies. However, a proper process for revoking access rights in case an agent is transferred to a new position or is leaving the organization is missing.

10.3   What Role and Rights Management Does

Role and Rights Management is involved, within a business process, (1) when a subject has to be mapped to a concrete agent and (2) for determining access rights to data objects.

10.3.1 Business Processes

Figure 10.1 shows the typical process of a business trip approval. When it is filled out, the request has to be sent to the subject "supervisor". The role and rights management has to determine which agent can take over the task of the subject "supervisor". At first glance, this seems to be easy. In reality, however, it is often the case that the boss is not available and a deputy has to be determined.

Fig. 10.1 Approval of a
business trip (adapted from
Fleischmann et al. 2011),
subject behavior diagram.
© 2011 Hanser Munich,
reproduced with permission

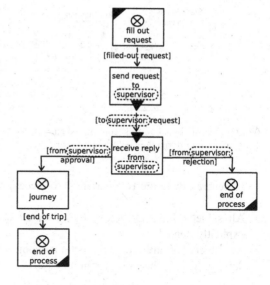

Which agent actually is the supervisor can also depend on the context a subject is acting in. If an employee is working within different projects at the same time, the request has to be approved by the leader of the project that defines the context for the business trip.

10.3.2 Data Access

There are different approaches for defining access rights. The most widespread are the access control matrix and the role-based access control (RBAC) model. The access control matrix simply describes which subjects have access rights to what data objects. Subjects can be agents like users, processes or even hardware components (e.g., a printer or a fax machine). Data objects can be files, tables, processes and so on (Fig. 10.2).

<table>
<tr><td rowspan="4"></td><td colspan="6" align="center">objects</td></tr>
<tr><td colspan="3" align="center">files</td><td colspan="3" align="center">processes</td></tr>
<tr><td>f1</td><td>f2</td><td>f3</td><td>p1</td><td>p2</td><td>p3</td></tr>
</table>

		f1	f2	f3	p1	p2	p3
subjects	u1	{write}	{write}			{execute}	
	u2		{read, write}		{execute}	{execute}	
	p1		{read}	{write}			{execute}

Fig. 10.2 Access control matrix (Seufert 2001). © 2002 Steffen Seufert

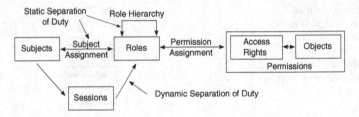

Fig. 10.3 Role-based access control (adapted from Ferraiolo et al. 2001). © 2001 ACM Transactions on Information and System Security

In general, there are two variations of access rights:

- All subjects have all access rights on all objects, except for rights that are explicitly denied.
- No subject has any access rights on any object until the access right is explicitly defined. This is the more common case.

In role-based access control (RBAC), permissions are not directly assigned to agents, but are instead accumulated in roles (Ferraiolo et al. 2001). Users are then assigned to these roles, thereby acquiring the roles permissions. A role typically contains all clearances needed in an organizational unit or for a specific job function. As the number of roles is usually assumed to be considerably lower than the number of agents, the number of administrative tasks required for maintaining the permissions can be reduced.

There are several extensions of the presented core RBAC. In Chen (2011) and Chen and Zhang (2011), the extensions of RBAC include role hierarchies, constraints and the combination of role hierarchies and constraints (cf. Fig. 10.3). Role hierarchies are used to inherit access rights. For example, a head of a department is superior to his clerk and has also access to all objects which the clerk is assigned to. With constraints, subject assignment and role relations can be restricted via the use of predicates.

10.4 Current Problems and Possible Solutions

10.4.1 Redundancy

Independently of the question of which access control mechanism to use, the problem remains that the role subject assignment has to be done in all application systems. This can grow to a great burden and is a source of security problems if not all policy definitions are kept up to date. We think that it is a good idea to think about an organization server that centralizes the task. This way, all organizational and policy definitions are defined and maintained in one location, reducing

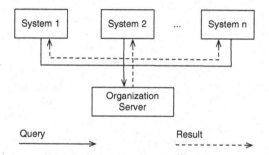

Fig. 10.4 Outside view of an organization server (Schaller 1998). © 1998 Thomas Schaller, reproduced with permission

Data Object	Read	Write
Daily Financial Report	Manager(*).(Now() - Manager.HiringYear) > 0,5 OR Manager(*).ReadFinancialReport==TRUE	Manager(Controlling) OR Clerk(Controlling).WriteFinancialReport==TRUE

Fig. 10.5 Access control matrix (Lawall et al. 2012). © 2012 Springer-Verlag Berlin Heidelberg, reprinted with permission

redundancy and enabling a higher level of security. Since the early 1990s, science has brought up different ideas of how to implement such a server.[1] It is funny, however, that this issue is not recognized in industry. Instead, the users are left alone with their maintenance problem.

Figure 10.4 shows the embedding of such a server. From an outside view, the server fulfills two tasks. First, it maintains the agents of the company, such as users, applications or systems. Secondly, it provides a language that makes it possible to "talk" with the server using an Organizational Query Language (OQL). As a simplified example, an expression in OQL could look like "clerk(claims department).(Now() − clerk.HiringYear) > 10". This means that we are looking for all clerks in the claims department of an insurance company that have been on the job for more than ten years. This language enables clients to specify access rights or task assignments according to the real-world needs. Let us first examine a simple policy definition scenario. In Fig. 10.5, OQL expressions are used for defining access permissions. Let us look at the read policy. The general rule is that all managers that have been with the company for more than half a year can read the daily financial report. The "OR" term of the expression defines an additional policy exception rule by referring to a specific "ReadFinancialReport" flag. At the moment a user would like to have access to the secured data object "daily financial report", the client application passes the OQL statement to the organization server. The server resolves the expression to a subset of matching agents, which is passed back to the calling application (client). The client will grant access if the agent is an element of the returned subset.

---

[1]For further reading please see Bussler (1997) or Schwab (1998).

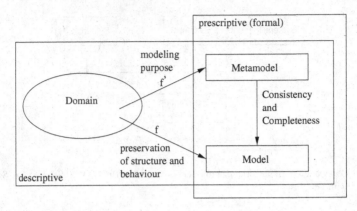

Fig. 10.6 Model and meta-model (Schaller 1998). © 1998 Thomas Schaller, reproduced with permission

The case of task assignment is very similar. In S-BPM, the subjects fulfilling a task are specified by an OQL expression.[2] This expression is passed to the organization server when the task has to be executed. The organization server returns a set of agents that satisfy the specification. Based on additional information, e.g., the employees current workload, the workflow management system decides which members of this set the task will be assigned to.

10.4.2 Wrong Models and Meta-Models

Previously, we argued that it is good to have **one logically central** organization server that is responsible for policy resolution and based on an organizational model. In order to work properly, this model has to be semantically and syntactically correct. Semantic correctness means that the structure and the behavior of the organization is represented correctly in the model, according to a defined modeling purpose. Syntactic correctness means that the model is set up consistently according to a given meta-model that defines how the building blocks of the model can be combined.

According to Fig. 10.6 there are two problem domains.

- Maintaining a wrong model (arc f).
  This situation often happens when the model is set up wrong initially or if the model is not kept up to date. Especially the second point is an issue for companies. As already described, they have to deal with multiple role and rights management systems and it is very hard to keep all of them up to date.

---

[2]In Fig. 10.1 the receiver of the send request task can easily be specified using the expression *supervisor (initiator)*.

- Choosing the wrong meta-model for the modeling task (arc f').

  The widespread stereotype for modeling organizations is the hierarchy (mathematically a tree).[3] This may come from the early days of computer science, when a lot of things were organized as trees, like the file systems of a computer. Another influence may be the fact that companies often represent their organizational structure as hierarchies. Consequently, it is not a big step to use these representations as a basis for the role and rights model. Organization theory reveals that companies are often not structured as hierarchies. This is because of things like projects, councils, divisions and so on. The elements of this so-called *shadow organization* lead to the fact that an employee can have multiple supervisors, depending on a given context. The result is not a tree but a general graph that is—due to different relationship types like deputyship, supervision and so on—multidimensional. Due to the wrong meta-model, the administrators have to build workarounds to map the organization to the tree structure. The result is an unsophisticated representation of the company that is a source of security issues and business process exceptions.

10.5   Requirements for an Organization Server—A Case Study

Let us have a look at a real-world scenario within an insurance company. According to the organization handbook, a claims department has a manager, a number of clerks and a lawyer. Generally the lawyer is the deputy of the department head, cf. Fig. 10.7.

We examined two concrete departments: One being responsible for "Car Damages", the other for "House Damages". Compared to the general structure and policies, we observed some differences (cf. Fig. 10.8). At "Car Damages", there was an additional secretary position. In the absence of the manager, organizational tasks were assigned to the secretary position. There was a change in the deputyship between the department head and the lawyer as well. Byron, the lawyer, had been working in the department for only three weeks and therefore was not very experienced. The clerk Winter had been working in the department for over ten years. Based on that constellation, the department head Smith decided that Winter should be his general deputy. Hinton was as well a deputy for Smith, but only depending on some constraint information, such as for instance the cash value of a claim (constrained deputy relation in Fig. 10.8).

Looking at these two departments, we also found an interesting mutual deputyship between the lawyers of the two departments (cf. Fig. 10.8). This observation becomes important when thinking about dividing the organization

---

[3]This can especially be found in RBAC-based approaches.

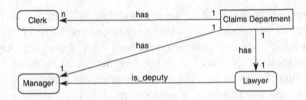

Fig. 10.7 Claims department in general. © 1998 Thomas Schaller, reproduced with permission

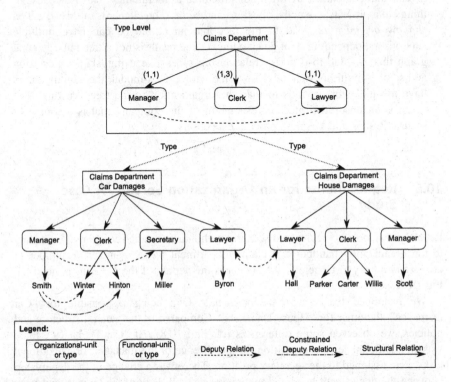

Fig. 10.8 Type and instance level of the example (adapted from Lawall et al. 2014a, Fig. 3). © 1998 Thomas Schaller, reproduced with permission

system into types or classes on the one hand and instances on the other. Please note that the relationships defined until now are specified on different levels of abstraction (roles and agents).

The observation made gives us some insights about the requirements an organization server and its meta-model has to meet.[4]

---

[4] A complete overview can be found in Schaller (1998).

10.5.1 Knowledge Hierarchy

As we have seen, there are different levels of organizational knowledge. On the top level, general structural assertions like "a department consists of one to three clerks" are dominant. We call this level the *type* or *template* level. Knowledge on this level is based on experience and is changed seldom as time goes by. Looking at real-world departments—we will call them *instances*—things become more concrete and specialized. There are concrete positions and relationships between them. Finally, agents are assigned to the concrete positions. The organizational structures on this level are changing more frequently according to the demands of the daily business.

10.5.2 Relationships

An organizational structure is formed by elements and relationships between them. It is important to realize the existence of several relationship types like "is_part_of", "is_deputy", "is_supervisor", "reports_to" and so on.

Positions[5] are abstractions of agents having a defined skill set fulfilling specific tasks. These abstractions help to define a more stable model of the organization that is independent of employee turnover. Relationships can be defined between abstract positions or on the concrete agent level.

Relationships are rarely of a general nature. As discussed in our example, relationships depend on specific constraint information like the cash value of a car claim. Even the "is_deputy"-relationship can depend on projects or products if you think in the terms of a matrix organization. They can also be valid only for a fixed time period.

10.5.3 Intelligent Subject Resolution

If a client system asks the organization server to resolve the OQL expression "Manager(Claims Department Car Damages)", an intelligent resolution algorithm has to be applied that uses the described knowledge hierarchy (Lawall et al. 2014a, b). By traversing the graph in Fig. 10.8, the algorithm moves to the department "Claims Department Car Damages", looking for a position "Manager". After that, the algorithm determines all the agents assigned to that position, finding manager Smith. If Smith is on the job, his identification is handed back to the client system and the search ends. In the case that Smith is not available (e.g., due to vacation or sickness), the algorithm searches for deputy relations between Smith and other agents. Obviously, there are two relations. Whether Winter and Hinton both appear in the search result depends on the constraint on the relation to Hinton and whether they are on the job. In the case of an empty set, the algorithm moves to the position "Manager",

---

[5]We make no difference between the term "role" and the term "position".

looking for a deputy relation and finds the position "Secretary" assigned to Miller. If Miller is on the job, her identification will be returned to the client system. If not, the algorithm has the alternative of determining a valid deputy on the type level. Let us assume that the department is linked to the department type as depicted in Fig. 10.8. Within this type, the algorithm finds the lawyer as a deputy. It moves back to the instance "Claims Department Car Damages", and checks if there is a position with this name and an agent assigned to that position who is available. If Byron is on the job, his identification is returned. Otherwise, the lawyer of the "Claims Department Car Damages" has a two-way deputy relation with the lawyer of the "Claims Department House Damages". If this position has an agent assigned to itself and the agent is available, the algorithm will hand back his identification (here Hall, the lawyer of the "Claims Department House Damages"). Otherwise the returned set is empty. In this case, the client has to postpone the execution of the task.

10.5.4 Multidimensional Organizations

Even in organizations that are structured hierarchically at first glance, there are structures belonging to the so-called secondary ("shadow") organization comprising committees, commissions, boards and so on. The positions and functions of the secondary organization are assigned to the employees. This leads to a multidimensional organization in every case.

10.6 The Organization Server C-Org

Within the S-BPM Research an Organization Server called C-Org was developed. It implements the requirements discussed in the foregoing section and offers central role and rights management to arbitrary clients (see Fig. 10.9). The system was developed at Hof University in Germany. Up to now, C-Org has been connected to several systems like

- Metasonic S-BPM Suite
- Microsoft's Active Directory
- Bonita Workflow
- Process Maker
- The telephone private branch exchange Asterisk
- Database management systems via an adapted JDBC driver (prototype stage)

Thanks to a small interface, the integration of C-Org into an existing IT environment is simple. Clients send OQL expressions to the server and receive the identities of agents that fulfill the expressions. The test drive has been used successfully to demonstrate how consistent role and rights management can look like in the future. If the organization changes, only the central model has to be altered and from that moment on all systems are up to date.

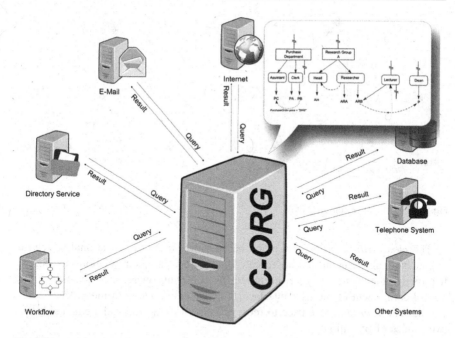

Fig. 10.9 C-ORG as central organization server

10.6.1 Implementation

Figure 10.10 shows the administrator user interface of C-Org (see also Lawall et al. 2014a). It contains a *model* editor, a *search* area, a *tree-navigation* as well as an *attribute pane* and a *relation list* for a selected organizational element.

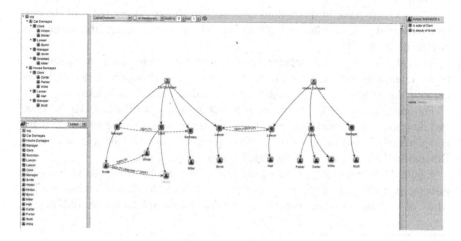

Fig. 10.10 Screenshot: administration view

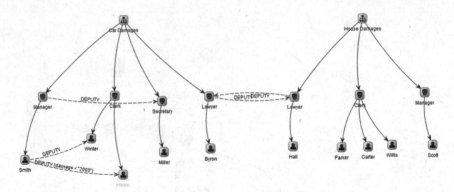

Fig. 10.11 Model region of C-Org

The *model editor* provides a graph-based view on the organizational structure. Organizational elements are represented as nodes and their relations as edges. It provides means to navigate the model by centering on selected nodes. As the central component of the user interface, it is discussed below in more detail.

The *search area* can be used to retrieve a list of organizational elements. It has two modes of operation:

1. It provides a simple text index search for attribute values, e.g., entering "Wi*" will yield Winter and Willis.
2. It can also be used to evaluate OQL expressions. An expression is entered and the result set for the current state of the organizational model is shown.

The *tree-navigation* maps the concrete organizational structure on a tree. Consequently, entities are duplicated in the projection if they can be reached on different paths.

The *attribute pane* in the bottom right section shows the attributes of the currently selected node or relation. It allows a quick modification, e.g., the assignment of a predicate to a relation.

The *relation list* lists all relations of the currently selected node, independently of the relation-types hidden in the model editor. This allows access to connected nodes and significantly reduces the time required to alter existing relations.

For quick access, elements can be dragged from any of the outer GUI sections and dropped into the model editor. If the elements have existing relations to the nodes already shown in the model editor, these relations will be shown as well. Otherwise, the elements are represented as unconnected nodes.

Figure 10.11 provides an enlarged view of the model editor. It contains the instance part of the example model of Fig. 10.8 with the desired[6] relations. The editor also shows concrete constraints (predicates) on relations, e.g., the deputy

---

[6]The relation types to be shown can be selected.

relation with *damage* < "2000" between *Smith* and *Hinton*. Users perform most modifications of the organizational model via this component. In addition to navigating the model, they can create, modify and delete organizational elements and their interconnections.

10.6.2 Usage of C-Org

From an architectural point of view C-Org can be used as a dedicated server within a company network. Another possibility is to use it as a cloud service within the IBM Bluemix environment.

10.6.3 C-Org from the Viewpoint of S-BPM

C-Org focuses on the subjects and their relationships rather than the organization's hierarchy. The end users are able to specify policies and roles according to their daily needs in a decentralized manner (if they are allowed to). In routine cases, like defining a deputy, a manager can react agilely without involvement of the central IT department. The specific resolution algorithm guarantees that if there is a specific policy on the instance level, it will be used (Lawall et al. 2012). Overall, the approach reduces the workload of the administrators and makes the life of the business people easier.

10.6.4 Additional Features

Despite the task of role and rights management C-Org offers some additional features.

- It can replace the classical mailing lists that have to be maintained by hand. Instead of returning identities, C-Org returns the mail addresses of the agents specified by an OQL expression. In place of enumerating the recipients, the client just describes which persons to write to. Because of the central organization database, the description is always up to date—which is not always true for hand-maintained mailing lists.
- Another nice function is the connection of a telephony server. For example, if a called agent is not available, his deputy can be called instead. This redirection can be fine-tuned by using context information added to the deputy relationship. Another idea is to implement a group call functionality, where all phones of the group members are called and the call will be routed to the first responding agent.

- Discussions with several banking companies revealed that C-Org is also very interesting for compliance management. Based on the central model, C-Org offers a new way for the management and documentation of policies.

10.7   Conclusion and Takeaway

This section is directed at IT architects, system administrators and CIOs who want to have a consistent way to reference organizational elements. This approach can be used to specify organization-wide access rights and policies with minimal maintenance effort. The reference, expressed by the organization query language, remains unchanged in the case of organizational changes. There is no need to alter existing role assignments.

It is also relevant for process owners and modelers who want to find a more descriptive way to define process stakeholders. This allows for a more flexible task assignment based on organizational relations. There is no need for technical workarounds to describe such relations, e.g., a table for supervisors, but the organization server can be asked for the specific case.

In addition to access rights and task assignment, the organization server can also be used for content generation (e.g., intra- and internet pages, customer relationship management systems, etc.). The contents can just be described using the organization query language and is resolved to the current values (e.g., team members, phone numbers, e-mail addresses, etc.).

Similarly to task assignments in processes, recipients of messages (e.g., e-mails) can be described using OQL. This can replace mailing lists and their maintenance. Not just functional e-mail addresses, like mailing lists, can profit from this, but also functional phone numbers.

In all of these application cases, the organizational information is current and does not have to be maintained manually in the individual systems.

References

Bussler C (1997) Organisationsverwaltung in Workflow-Management-Systemen. Ph.D. thesis, Universität Erlangen (in German)
Chen L (2011) Analyzing and developing role-based access control models. Ph.D. thesis, University of London
Chen L, Zhang Y (2011) Research on role-based dynamic access control. In Proceedings of the 2011 iConference. ACM, New York, USA, pp 657–660

Ferraiolo David F, Sandhu R, Gavrila S, Kuhn DR (2001) Chandramouli Ramaswamy: proposed nist standard for role-based access control. ACM Transactions on Information and System Security (TISSEC), pp 224–274

Fleischmann A, Schmidt W, Stary C, Obermeier S, Börger E (2011) Subjektorientiertes Prozessmanagement. Mitarbeiter einbinden, Motivation und Prozessakzeptanz steigern. Springer, Heidelberg (in German)

Lawall A, Schaller T, Reichelt D (2012) An approach towards subject-oriented access control. In: Stary C (ed) S-BPM one—scientific research. LNBIP, vol 104, Springer, Berlin, pp 33–43

Lawall A, Schaller T, Reichelt D (2014a) Enterprise architecture: a formalism for modeling organizational structures in information systems. In: Barjis J, Pergl R (eds) 10th International workshop, CAiSE 2014, LNBIP, vol 191, Thessaloniki

Lawall A, Schaller T, Reichelt D (2014b) Local-global agent failover based on organizational models. In: 2014 IEEE/WIC/ACM international joint conferences on web intelligence (WI), intelligent agent technologies (IAT), brain informatics and health (BIH) and Active media technology (AMT), pp 420–427

Schaller T (1998) Organisationsverwaltung in CSCW-Systemen. Ph.D. thesis, Universität Bamberg (in German)

Schwab K (1998) Konzeption und Implementierung von computergestützten Kooperationsmanagementsystemen. Habilitationsschrift, Universität Bamberg (in German)

Seufert S (2001) Die Zugriffskontrolle—Eine Bestandsaufnahme relevanter Ansätze und deren Weiterentwicklung zu einem Konzept für die Ableitung von Zugriffsrechten aus der betrieblichen Organisation. Ph.D. thesis, Universität Bamberg (in German)

Embodying Business Rules in S-BPM

11

Robert Singer and Stefan Raß

Abstract

The subject-oriented approach to model and execute business processes can be conceptually and easily combined with the business rules approach. Business rules are a mean to enhance the agility of workflows, as it should make the knowledge and decisions of an organization more explicit. As with the process model, ordinary users should be able to create, change and maintain the sets of rules in an idealized scenario. We demonstrate a real case for the beneficial use of business rules in the case of process automation and show a practical integration with an S-BPM reference implementation. Based on experiences in the field, we also point out that there is still serious lack of knowledge about actual trends and technologies in the context of the digital transformation of a business. The contribution is intended for practitioners with some interest in IT support for business process management.

11.1 A Business Rules Primer

Business rules and business processes are concepts which are closely connected. Nevertheless, we see the domain of business process management (BPM) as a general concept to manage a firm and business rules (BR) as a *refinement* to make BPM a more agile approach—especially in the case of the automation of (parts of)

R. Singer (✉)
FH-Joanneum—University of Applied Sciences, Alte Poststraße 147, 8020 Graz, Austria
e-mail: robert.singer@fh-joanneum.at

S. Raß
StrICT Solutions GmbH, Plüddemanngasse 39, 8010 Graz, Austria
e-mail: rass@strict-solutions.com

© The Author(s) 2015
A. Fleischmann et al. (eds.), *S-BPM in the Wild*,
DOI 10.1007/978-3-319-17542-3_11

processes. Business rules are—as will be discussed soon—a tool to give process participants more and easier control over their business processes. Business rules are also a means to collect and codify parts of the tangible knowledge of a firm or organization.

11.1.1 Introduction

All organizations operate in accordance with a set of underlying principles—that is what "organization" means. These principles define the "business logic" which controls the way the business conducts itself. Basically, a business rule (BR) is a compact statement about an aspect of a business and can be expressed in terms that can be directly related to the business. Business rules use simple and unambiguous language that's directly accessible to all interested parties in the organization.

Rules do not only articulate some constraints, but also provide a means of encapsulating knowledge about the business. Rules cannot stand in isolation but need to be rooted in a rich representation that captures the overall facets of a business. As rules are constraints, they define conditions that have to hold true in specified situations. Business rules and processes can be beneficially integrated for a more agile setting of models, defining how to conduct certain aspects of a business. In concrete, business rules can be integrated into a business process model in such a way that at a decision point in the model there is a reference to a concrete rule, the rule is evaluated and depending on the result (e.g., true or false) the process continues. For example, a rule could define the following logic: all purchasing orders exceeding a total amount of EUR 5.000 need to be confirmed by the department manager.

Business rules can be expressed using different levels (informal, formal) of expression as illustrated with the following examples:

```
The weight of a parcel has to be below or equal 32kg.
parcel.weight <= 32
```

One additional remark: it should be clear that such numbers (the 32 kg in the example above) should be handled as *business parameter* in the same way as rules; that means they are stored together with the rules and do not appear as *magic numbers* somewhere hard-coded in the source code. So, if the rule still applies, but the value changes, anybody can easily change the value, and from that moment on all business process instances with a reference to this rule will use it—voilà. No software developer is needed (as long as the front end to manage the rules follows common guidelines for usability).

11.1.2 Illustrative Example

Microsoft Outlook is a well-known desktop program to manage e-mail messages, appointments, contacts, and other facets of business life. The program integrates with other applications, such as *Microsoft Exchange*, to provide a range of facilities. Here—following the idea of Morgan (2002)—we are going to have a short look how *Outlook* uses rules to automate the handling of mail messages.

> Rules in Outlook are composed by using a "wizard" that provides an interactive dialogue from which you can define various parts of your rule. The interface design shows how a potentially complex and technical task can be made much easier for ordinary users ... (??)

Outlook is not a fully functional business rules system, but it demonstrates the core concepts and even is an example of compromises that may be found in your own applications.

Each rule statement is made up of a number of logically connected clauses. The first clause defines whether the rule applies to outgoing or incoming messages. There can be zero or more condition clauses which all together have to evaluate to true to activate the rule. At least one action clause has to be defined; additionally, zero or more exception clauses have to be false, or the rule will not be activated. A typical example for an *Outlook* rule might be

```
Apply this rule after the message arrives
where my name is in the To or Cc field
  and which has an attachment
move it to the folder attachments
  except if sent only to me
```

All possible conditions, exceptions, and actions are chosen from a predefined list. You can also use other mail clients to define your rules; rules can be client side (executed on your computer) or server side (executed on the mail server). It is clear that this way of defining rules needs to be implemented in the software application; there is code to execute the defined rules based on a predefined set of logical constructs.

11.1.3 Business Processes and Rules

Principally, integrating business rules with business processes is as illustrated in the *Outlook* case. What we need is a way for ordinary users to build rules based on predefined sets of clauses and parameters. The business rules concept should hide the implementation aspects from the users, giving them the possibility to define and change the behavior of a business process at defined decision points without coding. Nevertheless, the concept of business rules is a general purpose tool for software developers to generate more agile applications.

We demonstrate the concept with the help of a small process as depicted in Figs. 11.1 and 11.2. We intentionally use BPMN to emphasize that the integration of business rules and process is a general concept; in the next section we will discuss the integration using the S-BPM methodology as a foundation for *enforceable* business processes.

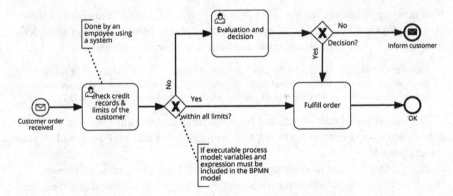

Fig. 11.1 Simple process model with a decision point. Technically, at the decision point the value of a variable is evaluated and depending on this value one of two alternative process paths is executed. The value is set in the preceding activity by a human agent

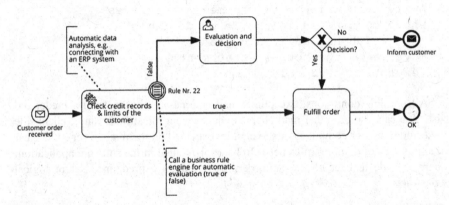

Fig. 11.2 The same process as in Fig. 11.1, but using a business rule for automation. After receiving a new order the data is analyzed and rule number 22 is called—using a business rules engine. The engine evaluates the rule and returns a value (true or false in this case) back to the instance of the process. Based on this result the process engine can decide which of the two alternative paths to choose. The rule itself is stored in a central repository and can be modified independently of the process model

There are several books about the topic available. The standard book and valuable first reader is *Principles of the Business Rules Approach* by Ronald (2003). The book *Agile Unternehmen durch Business Rules* by Schacher and Grassle (2006) gives a very good overview, but as the title shows, it is in German; the technical part is somewhat outdated.

11.2 S-BPM and Business Rules

11.2.1 Concept

How can we now integrate the business rules approach with the S-BPM methodology? Interestingly, there are two possibilities for how to integrate calls to a business rules engine:

As there are messages sent between subjects, we could define business rules to evaluate logical expressions based on business objects included in the messages. That means we could modify the message and or the content of a message (the business object) based on a set of rules; for example, we could *automatically* modify the receiving subject(s) depending on evaluations of the containing business object. So, if the business object holds information about a customer order we could change the *subject* depending on the amount of the order. Technically, there have to be some *locations* in the application from where we can call business rules (the business rules engine) (see Fig. 11.3 for illustration). A distributed environment can be established using, for example, web- or other service-oriented technologies. Depending on the process model we can think of local and global business rules. So we could define business rules valid for message exchange within an organization

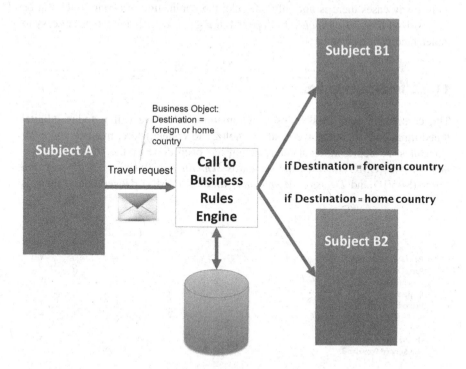

Fig. 11.3 If all messages would be routed over a central "rule box", depending on the message type and or business object or business object content one or more business rules could be applied

and with other organizations. This can be an interesting application for compliance or other topics.

Another possibility is to call business rules from function states defined in the internal behavior of a subject, i.e., using the concept of *refinements*, an integral part of the S-BPM methodology. In general, a *Refinement* is some extra code which can be invoked by a running instance. Depending on the result of the automatic evaluation of the rule, a decision can be made. One fact has not been mentioned yet: in many situations there is a decision tree built of more than one rule; this can be a chain of IF ... THEN ... ELSE ... clauses. The last ELSE could be used to initiate a human-based decision.

The elegance and flexibility of the S-BPM methodology can be seen once we recognize that an extra component is not needed to evaluate rules on the messages exchanged between subjects. So, we could define a subject *with the internal behavior of evaluating rules on incoming messages*. It is an integral part of the S-BPM methodology that a subject be a conceptualization of an agent—and an agent can be human, a physical machine (including an electronic interface for communication) or a software agent. Hence a software agent could be "intelligent", if we want to use a common term for agent systems. Hereby, we mean agents reacting on input of the environment and making autonomous decisions (but only based on internal behavior defined using an algorithm).

In many cases there is not only one rule; the application of certain rules can be summarized in *decision tables*, as depicted in Fig. 11.4. Decision tables are easy to understand (but can be large).

11.2.2 Implementation

The core idea of business rules is automation, or as we call it today "digital transformation"; therefore we need technology to collect, store, manage and evaluate rules. A step towards standardization has been done by the *Object Management Group* (OMG) defining the standards *Semantics of Business Vocabulary and Rules* (SBVR) and *Decision Model and Notation* (DMN). Nevertheless, there is

	Rules					
Conditions	1	2	3	4	5	6
C1. Parcel weight <WeightLimit	Y		Y	Y		Y
C2. Parcel size <SizeLimit		Y	Y		Y	Y
C3. Urgent Delivery			Y			Y
C4. Region 2	Y	Y	Y			
C5. Region 1				Y	Y	Y
Actions	1	2	3	4	5	6
A1. Use Service Provider 1	X	X				
A2. Use Service Provider 2			X			X
A3. Use Service Provider 3				X	X	

Fig. 11.4 A decision table is a matrix of rules and actions. For any possible combination of conditions, actions are defined

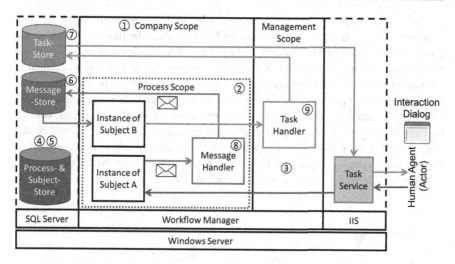

Fig. 11.5 StrICT architecture. The processes are executed server side and the workflows are coordinated through message exchange (*orange*). Task requests (*light green*) and task answers (*dark green*) are routed to a client via the task service

no one standard technology (implementation), but there are several—mainly commercial solutions—available.

We have integrated the business rules approach with the *StrICT*[1] S-BPM implementation (Singer et al. 2014; Singer and Raß 2015). The architecture is depicted in Fig. 11.5. Processes are hosted on an instance of the *Workflow Manager* (WFM), which is responsible for the hosting, administration and configuration of the subjects based on scopes, such as a *Company Scope* (1) for the processes of one organization, a *Process Scope* (2) for each process and a *Management Scope* (3). Each company has its own *Process Store* (4) and *Subject Store* (5); the same for *Message Store* (6) and *Task Store* (7). Each company has *Task Handler* (9) instances to generate new tasks and each process has *Message Handler* (8) instances to manage message exchange. *Task* and *Message Handler* are implemented as workflows. The mechanism of *Scopes* ensures full encapsulation of one company or organization by the other. Further, it allows permission management on a very fine granular basis for each activity; depending on the rights of a role, activities can be seen or not, executed or not.

The architecture of the StrICT Windows reference implementation is depicted in Fig. 11.5, as shortly discussed above. All messages of an agent are handled by a message handler (denoted by "8" in the figure). Within this handler we could implement a call to a business rules repository and an execution engine for evaluation. At this point the message itself and or the content, i.e., the business object, could be modified.

---

[1]StrICT = Structured Information and Communication Technology.

Such a mechanism would mean change to the architecture itself, so we decided in a first attempt to implement the use of business rules in function states of the internal behavior of subjects (see Fig. 11.6). This offers the flexibility—as discussed beforehand—to define so-called "intelligent" subjects. Subjects use rules defined in a business rules repository to *refine* their behavior, for example to make decisions based on rules or a set of rules. In this way we can define—as usually when using the S-BPM paradigm—human interaction processes or intelligent agents without human interaction. Technically, any subject is defined as a workflow, based on the *Microsoft Windows Workflow Technology* functionality which is implemented in the operating system routines (to be more exact: in the relevant .NET libraries) and the *Windows Workflow Manager* server component.

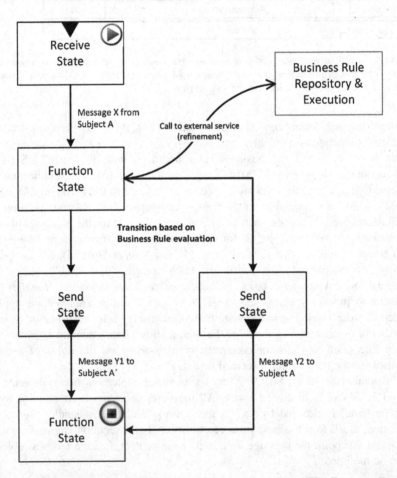

Fig. 11.6 A conceptual example of the internal behavior of a subject (SID). From any *Function State* we are enabled to make a call to a business rule system; depending on the result it is possible for us to make a decision

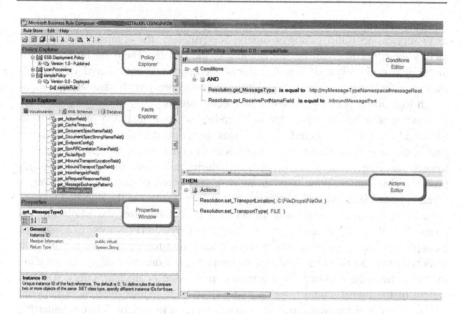

Fig. 11.7 The *BizTalk* business rule composer with sample example data for illustration purposes

Now, to enhance the actual architecture we can refer to the functionality of the *BizTalk* server component. This includes a business rules composer (see Fig. 11.7) to design rules, which are then stored in a database instance (SQL server instance). Rules can be evaluated, too. Additionally, the *BizTalk* server integrates with the *Microsoft Service Bus* component, an important aspect of the used reference implementation. An obvious disadvantage using the *BizTalk* composer is its poor usability; the composer needs a lot of technical skills and therefore we could not meet one requirement, namely the involvement of ordinary business users in designing rules. Nevertheless, that is one of the typical problems we experience in the field; not all problems can be solved immediately.

11.3 The Case of ABC Logistics

Now, let's look at a real-world project which addresses the discussed concepts. The project uses the discussed technology platform to execute S-BPM process models, including calls to a business rules execution engine (a technical prototype for further experiments):

The company *ABC Logistics*[2] offers the service of sending parcels all over the world. Towards customers they present themselves as a globally acting logistics provider collecting orders by web site (structured information) or e-mail

---

[2]The case is real, the company name has been anonymized.

(unstructured information). In reality the company is an intermediary using third party services to fulfill customer orders. Nevertheless, the company has its own facility for collecting, sorting and labeling of the parcels. There are no predefined limits in size or weight of a parcel; the core competence and offered value proposition (mainly towards business-to-business customers) is the knowledge about which logistics provider to choose in a specific setting.

Sending a pallet to Saudi Arabia? Sending a small and very urgent box to Shenzen? Sending a medium box with breakable content to Kenya? *ABC Logistics* knows the best (in a holistic view) provider to contract—invisible for their customers. Such decisions are done manually during all stages of the core business process. This can be done only in an error-prone and costly way. Moreover, a recently installed automated packaging line cannot be used in the intended way, as there is no coherent and persistent data model available over the whole process chain—so, all data has always to be interpreted by human actors. Consider for example the worst case: a customer sends information for a parcel via e-mail; then somebody has to extract manually all the needed data from the mail, check the data, maybe contact the customer if information is missing or unclear, check size and weight of the parcel, contact the customer in case of serious differences between customer and real measures, decide which contractor to use for delivery, enter the data into the system of the chosen contractor, print out any documents and labels, and label the parcel. Currently there is a pool of about 15 service providers, all using their own IT systems.

The main tasks for a digitized business process for *ABC Logistics* now are:

- a single coherent data model, i.e., business object for the whole process
- as much as possible automated decision making to determine the optimal (cost and quality) service provider
- fully electronic integration of the packing line or other physical devices with the digitized process
- integration with the company web site (order management and customer service)
- integration with an ERP system, including bookkeeping

What are the promises of a fully digitized business process for *ABC Logistics*?

- mostly automated decisions about which service provider to use in a concrete transaction based on codified rules; the core idea is that the rules are readable and changeable by ordinary process participants
- efficient use of the investment in the automated packaging line
- reduction of errors based on an integrated information model
- reduction of transaction costs
- gained efficiency enabling growth, i.e., an increase of rate of transactions based on a decrease of throughput time
- increase of efficiency and reduction of errors based on the integration with other systems

In the following section we will discuss the first steps and findings towards a solution for *ABC Logistics* based on S-BPM, which conveniently offers all needed capabilities to digitize ABC's business processes.

11.4 Results

11.4.1 Impact of Actions

Now, what is the focus of *ABC Logistics* in this case? Interestingly, it is the focus on automation of the data transfer (the interface) to their service suppliers. They do not realize that an automatic data transfer is useless without a digitized business process.

Consequently, the first step in the project in the field is to study (technically) how to automatically exchange data with the logistics partner. At the moment most of any interaction with partners is done manually via web sites; in the worst case a remote connection and data entry on the remote server needs to be established. This is rather inefficient, but accepted by *ABC Logistics*. For an ideal solution of a human interaction workflow, in this case with as much automated decision-making and data exchange as possible, it is clear that this is a necessary part of the solution.

But this focus does not consider the following topics:

- Data collection and consolidation still has to be done manually
- Data exchange with suppliers and customers still have to be done manually
- The packaging line is still not integrated in the process

The reason of this managerial priority setting is the fact *that a well-designed and semi-automated business process is not seen as an asset*, but more or less as *nice to have*. Some sophisticated data interface, i.e., information technology, is seen as the benefit. That is somewhat surprising when reading all the books, papers, reports and blogs about business process management—however, that is the reality in the field.

So again we have an IT project without clear requirements and unclear business processes, and we have the feeling that it is of no good. What can be the conclusion? It still seems that there is a lack of understanding of the topic of business process management in the field—especially in the case of an integrated view with technology. No operational business process nowadays can function efficiently without support of technology.

The concept of our proposed solution could be as depicted in Fig. 11.8. In the beginning there should be a focus on the core processes (as they are now) to understand the information flow. This includes the design of the required business object, which results in a coherent data model for the process. In the first shot there will be no integration of external systems. Concurrently, there can be a start to the development of intelligent agents (a service composition) to handle messages from

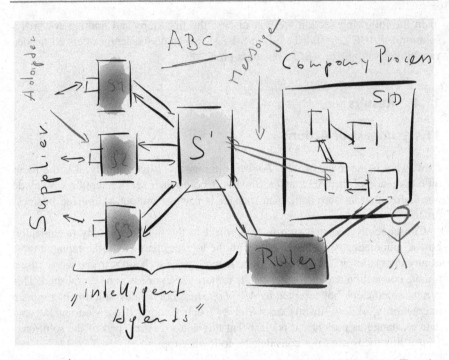

Fig. 11.8 A sketch on the napkin for a possible solution scenario for *ABC Logistics*. First, the end-to-end process of the company has to be modeled; afterwards or concurrently a set of business rules needs to be defined to model *decisions* in the business process. A technical challenge lies in the development of the *interfaces* toward the customer systems (*left* side boxes). The "*S*" denoted *box* represents an *intelligent* Agent (subject), the working horse for automated decisions based on the defined business rules set

other (human) agents to automatically transfer data from and to service suppliers. Later on, this network of agents can gradually increase its "intelligence" when more and more rules (knowledge) are incorporated in their internal behavior descriptions.

11.4.2 Open Issues

Nevertheless, to come back to the integration of business rules with subject-oriented business processes, it does not seem to be a great effort to integrate both concepts technically; however, there is still a lot to do to provide much software enabling ordinary process workers and responsible managers with convenient user interfaces. There also seems to be a real need in the field for a **better education of practitioners**, especially in small and medium enterprises (SME), as they usually do not have specialized staff for business process integration. It definitely is not sufficient for a CIO to be able to configure a mail or database server. All surveys of the last years stress the fact that IT departments also should focus on business and business process management—that includes deep knowledge and understanding of business process execution.

Now, some final technical remarks about business rules integration. Not considered yet in the reported case are topics, for example, such as *forward* and *backward chaining* of rules (Morgan 2002). There are also some more possibilities to collect and store business rules. Additionally, there are also several business rule execution engines available (open source and commercial ones). Another point not evaluated is performance; but we can expect a commercial product such as *BizTalk* server to be capable of evaluating a huge number of rules concurrently. These and other topics have to be evaluated in further projects.

11.4.3 Takeaway

Seen from a purely technical point of view the integration of business processes and business rules is ready for application. S-BPM is a perfect candidate for achieving that, as the concept of rule evaluation is inherently included in the concept of message exchange—a subject sends a rule (question) to a rule evaluation subject and receives the evaluated rule (answer = decision). This mechanism enhances the agility of business processes, as it should drastically reduce the effort to adapt process models. *Actors* should be given the tools to change process models more often without support of *Experts*. As demonstrated, there are many useful application scenarios in real-world business processes, especially also in the field of logistics and manufacturing—notably if we develop integration scenarios as discussed in the context of *cyber physical systems*.

References

Morgan T (2002) Business rules and information systems. Addison-Wesley, Boston
Ross Ronald G (2003) Principles of the business rule approach. Addison-Wesley, Boston
Schacher M, Grässle P (2006) Agile Unternehmen durch Business Rules: Der Business Rules Ansatz. Springer, Berlin (in German)
Singer R, Raß S (2015) Structured communication—approaching S-BPM with Microsoft technologies. In: Fleischmann A et al (eds) S-BPM in the wild. Springer, Berlin
Singer R, Kotremba J, Raß S (2014) Modeling and execution of multienterprise business processes. In: 16th IEEE conference on business informatics, workshop on cross-organizational and cross-company BPM (XOC-BPM). Genf, Switzerland, 14–17 July

Agents Implementing Subject Behaviour: A Manufacturing Scenario

12

Udo Kannengiesser

Abstract

This chapter presents a scenario for the use of agents in the implementation of subject-oriented process models. The scenario is set in a manufacturing company that has already used S-BPM in office-based business processes and now wants to apply this approach on the shop floor using agent technology. The chapter describes a project team meeting in which S-BPM specifications for a pressing process are developed and concepts for the agent-based implementation of that process are discussed. During the meeting, a number of issues are raised that are a consequence of using computational rather than human agents for implementing subject behaviour. The key issues include:

1. An open world of agents: Computational agents can be created on the fly, in various compositional structures and embodiments (virtual, physical, or both) that can change dynamically. As a result, mapping subjects to computational agents is typically more challenging than mapping subjects to human agents as human organisations are often assumed to pre-exist and remain relatively stable during process execution.
2. Access control mechanisms and cognitive capabilities: Explicit mechanisms for controlling which agent can execute a subject need to be engineered, taking into account process requirements, agent performance characteristics, and the current execution status. These mechanisms often require the implementation of some form of cognitive capabilities in the agents, including heuristic reasoning and planning—which are usually taken for granted in human-based processes.

U. Kannengiesser (✉)
Metasonic GmbH, Münchner Straße 29, 85276 Pfaffenhofen, Germany
e-mail: udo.kannengiesser@metasonic.de

© The Author(s) 2015
A. Fleischmann et al. (eds.), *S-BPM in the Wild*,
DOI 10.1007/978-3-319-17542-3_12

While these issues are discussed in a manufacturing scenario, they are generic in that they can be transferred to agent-based implementations in other process domains.

12.1 Introduction

It is 7:55 a.m. on a Monday morning. Peter Smith, 45, walks into his office, starts up his laptop and quickly grabs a cup of coffee from the kitchen next door. Peter is the CEO of a medium-sized manufacturing company producing parts for the automotive and aerospace industries. Today he is in an excellent mood, because a new project is about to commence that he recently proposed and he is very excited about: "Agent-based manufacturing processes" is the working title that Peter chose for his project. The kick-off meeting is in just a few minutes.

"Good morning," Peter says when entering the meeting room. The members of his project team are already sitting around the table: John, 53, production manager, Jerry, 34, automation engineer, and Diana, 41, head of purchasing. Peter sits down and says: "I already sent you an outline of the project, but let me recap what the project is about and why I chose you to be involved in it." "Yes, that would definitely be useful," John remarks, "as I haven't quite understood some of the things you mentioned in your email."

"I guess you mean the terms 'industry 4.0', 'cyber-physical systems' and 'agents'." Peter takes a sip from his coffee and then starts explaining, "OK, so let's start with giving you some background on these terms. Industry 4.0 is the name of what is often proclaimed as the next industrial revolution. I learned about it just a few weeks ago at a trade fair on production automation. Many of the speeches and even a whole section of the exhibition hall were devoted to that topic. It is essentially about enabling new models of production management by using embedded devices that monitor and control physical processes and communicate over wireless networks. These devices are called cyber-physical systems, because on the one hand they are physical objects, and on the other hand they have a representation in the virtual world—a second identity if you like. Almost any object you can find in a factory can be conceived of as a cyber-physical system: a sensor, an actuator, a conveyor belt, a product, a whole machine—."

"Uhm... hang on a second," John interrupts. "This sounds all great and futuristic, and I sort of heard about these things too. But what problem does it solve? What's the benefit of having all those cyber-physical systems everywhere?" "Well, I've been wondering about that too," says Peter. "At first glance, it seems to add a lot of complexity and communication overhead. On the other hand, cyber-physical systems allow you to decentralise your production planning and control, which gives you much more flexibility and agility. For example, these systems are able to sense unforeseen events such as new production requirements or breakdowns of individual resources, and then reconfigure the production process autonomously and in real time. Remember last month when we had to stop our whole production because of a defective sensor? We had to spend five hours searching for the problem and replanning the process. I believe this could have been handled much faster with the kind of self-organisation capabilities provided by cyber-physical systems." Peter pauses for a few breaths before continuing, "You could even endow cyber-physical systems with knowledge and goals—such as, 'I want to find the most energy-efficient path for the product through the production line'—so you could have some sort of intelligent behaviour. And this brings me to the concept of an agent. An agent is a piece of software that interacts with its environment in a goal-directed, autonomous way, often involving communication with other agents. It is often attributed to notions of human cognition and intelligent behaviour."

"Yes, agent-based systems have been around for quite a while," Jerry adds and adjusts his glasses, "I have already programmed such a system for my university thesis." "I know," Peter looks at him, "and that's why I involved you in this project. Your experience with agent technology will be extremely useful, because the goal of this project is to develop an agent-based cyber-physical production system and trial it on the shop floor." Peter turns back towards John and says "Don't worry, John, this will only be a pilot implementation involving a very small, isolated part of our production system. There won't be any risk of interrupting our core operations if things go wrong with our prototype. Only after extensive testing will we think about rolling it out on other parts of the shop floor."

Diana, who so far has only been listening, now joins the conversation. "Sorry, Peter, what I still don't understand is what my role is in all this. I have no experience whatsoever in agents or production engineering!" Peter looks at Diana and his eyes seem to twinkle. "But Diana... you are the most important person here! You will guide us in the development of a process architecture for our agent-based production system. This architecture is necessary to capture the bigger picture and specify how the system should work in terms of functionalities—and help us understand the impact of any system changes that may be required after implementation. We will use S-BPM for specifying the process architecture. This is because S-BPM has well-defined execution semantics yet can be easily used by domain experts without IT background. So people like John and myself can have a say in the system design, because we can understand and directly change the process model if we see a need for that."

As Diana still does not look convinced, Peter adds, "You will be the perfect facilitator for developing an S-BPM process model. Haven't you been in exactly that role in your department for many years now?" Diana thinks for a few moments. "Yes sure, I've been in this role, but the processes we are dealing with in the purchasing department are completely different from the ones in production. And our processes are all executed by humans, not machines or agents." Jerry quickly jumps into the conversation. "Well, on a conceptual level humans can be viewed as agents too. Agents can be any autonomous entity—human or computational. And in fact, most models and architectures of computational agents are inspired by psychological and social accounts of human agents."

"That's right." Peter looks at each team member to make sure he has their full attention before continuing, "What we want to achieve in this project is an agent-based system whose design and execution is driven by S-BPM models. Why S-BPM? Firstly, it puts a process layer on top of the specific technologies used, such as production technology and agent technology. This additional layer ensures everyone can easily understand the overall process and improve it when necessary. There's a close connection between S-BPM and multi-agent systems, as they share many fundamental ideas: decentralised control, autonomy, concurrent behaviour, and communication. And secondly, S-BPM models are unambiguous and directly executable; so the executed process is not just some IT guy's interpretation of a flow chart, but the result of an automatic, model-driven transformation. The constructs of the S-BPM notation are very generic and can be applied to any kind of process, no matter if it's a business process or a production process. We had excellent results introducing S-BPM in our purchasing department a few years ago—let's try and reap similar benefits with S-BPM in our production department!"

12.2   Specifying a Production Process in S-BPM

Peter takes a whiteboard marker and a set of blue magnetic cards in his hand. "So I thought of using parts of our pressing department as a test bed for an agent-based production system. What would an S-BPM model of the pressing process look like? What are the subjects?" John frowns and asks, "Sorry, can you remind me what subjects are?" Diana quickly replies, "Subjects are the active entities, or actors, in a process. But by subjects we don't mean any specific actor—we rather mean the abstract functionalities required in a process. So at the level of subjects, we don't really care about which actor or agent will implement and execute the functionalities. To give you an example, in a purchasing process we usually have a subject or functionality called 'Purchaser' and one called 'Approver'."

The frown on John's face slowly disappears. "OK, so in our pressing process, one obvious subject would be, I suppose, 'Pressing'." Peter writes the word "Pressing" on a blue magnetic card and sticks it on the whiteboard. "Well, and there are plenty of others," John continues to come up with possible subjects in the pressing process, now with increasing motivation as he begins to understand the notion of a subject. "Before we can use the press, we need to cut blank plates from a coil. These plates are then transported and placed into the press. The pressed part is transported to quality testing and then stored in a warehouse. So the subjects would be 'Blanking', 'Transportation', 'Quality Testing' and 'Storage', I reckon."

After writing these subject names on separate cards and adding them to the whiteboard, Peter says, "OK, so all these are subjects that provide services related to transforming physical materials. Do we need any subjects for providing information, like telling the other subjects when or how to provide these services?" John thinks for a while and then replies, "Well, we need functionality for scheduling the production, and perhaps one responsible for launching the individual production services." Peter writes "Production Scheduler" and "Production Service Launcher" on two magnetic cards and adds them to the whiteboard.

Peter and his team now go on and think about the messages to be exchanged between the subjects. After some discussion, they agree on a set of messages that Peter represents by drawing arrows that connect the different subjects on the whiteboard. The final subject interaction diagram is shown in Fig. 12.1.

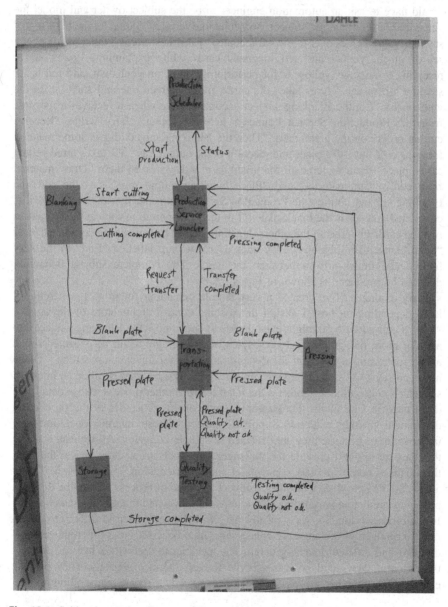

Fig. 12.1 Subject interaction diagram of the pressing process

Peter looks at Diana and asks, "What would you suggest as a next step after agreeing on the subjects and their interactions?" "Well, in our department we would now assign a subject owner to every subject and let them model their internal behaviour. So, uhm…" Diana stops talking and looks slightly confused by the whiteboard. "The problem here is that some of the subjects are machines, or software agents that control a machine, and we can't really ask, say, the blanking machine to model its own behaviour." "That's right," Peter nods, "in this case we would have to ask an automation engineer to be the subject owner and model the behaviour of the Blanking subject. Someone like Jerry…" "Sure, let me have a go," says Jerry and comes over to the whiteboard. "Take these cards," Peter hands over a set of green, yellow and red magnetic cards while explaining, "green is for receiving a message, yellow is for performing a task on your own, and red is for sending a message." Jerry takes the cards, picks a green one and sticks it on the whiteboard. "So, the Blanking subject becomes active when it receives a message from the Production Service Launcher to start cutting." Jerry writes "Receive cutting order" on the green card. "Then the Blanking subject draws some material from the coil, cuts off a piece and places it in the output tray." He takes three yellow cards, places them underneath the green card and writes on them "Draw material from coil", "Cut material" and "Place blank in output tray". "At the end, the Blanking subject notifies the Production Service Launcher that the cutting task is completed and sends the blank plate off to the Transportation subject." Jerry places two red cards underneath the others, labelling them "Notify cutting completed" and "Send blank plate". Finally, Jerry adds a yellow card labelled "End" to the very bottom and draws arrows between the cards. The complete subject behaviour diagram he produced is shown in Fig. 12.2.

Jerry explains, "I've created a very simple behaviour for now. I will refine it later, depending on how I design the specific control architecture of the agent." "Yes," Peter adds, "you might even decide to decompose the Blanking subject into a set of more fine-grained subjects. Each of them might again be executed by an agent, for example, an agent for the coil, an agent for the saw, and so on." Diana nods and says, "Yes, the Blanking subject would then be what is called an interface subject: A subject that establishes the interface to another process whose details we don't need to care about. For example, some of our processes in the purchasing department include external 'Supplier' subjects whose internal operations are unknown to us because they are executed in another company. All we care about is that they accept and provide the messages we expect from them and at the right time. This is one of the key concepts of subject-orientation." "That's right," Peter adds, "S-BPM provides a means to connect any kind of process, where the different processes are defined according to the different views and interests of stakeholders. In the business domain, we typically deal with processes across different companies. In production, we are more concerned with processes across different technical domains and different levels of detail. The mechanism with which we can connect the different views and processes is the use of interface subjects. They provide exactly what the other process needs to get or needs to know, and nothing more."

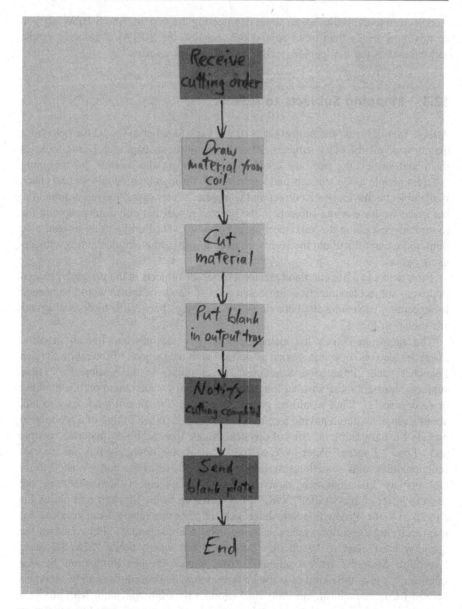

Fig. 12.2 Subject behaviour diagram of the blanking subject

"OK, but back to the question about how to specify the behaviour of a subject when it's not humans but agents who implement that subject," Diana says with a contemplative look, "We can't really decide on the final specification of behaviour before we know which agents will execute it." "Yes," Peter agrees, "behaviour models need to evolve as we go about engineering the system. And S-BPM lets you do this more easily than other approaches, because the S-BPM notation is simple and tailored to the first-person perspective of subject owners."

12.3   Mapping Subjects to Agents

After a 15 min break, the project team comes back together to model the behaviour diagrams of all the other subjects. After finishing these diagrams, Diana looks at them and says "OK, now we could already validate the models, by assigning different people to the subjects and let them play through their behaviour and check if all subject behaviours are correct and complete." Peter says, "I agree in principle, but given we have seven subjects in the process model but only four people in the room I suggest doing the validation later. For now, what I'd like to do instead is to think more carefully about the issues we need to solve when implementing subjects using agents."

Peter walks to a flip chart and creates a list of all subjects in the pressing process. For every subject he quickly writes down a set of agents he thinks would be needed for executing each subject's behaviour. His mappings between subjects and agents are shown in Fig. 12.3.

The agents in Peter's list include production machines and human workers. There are also two question marks, associated with the subjects "Production Service Launcher" and "Production Scheduler". Peter points to these subjects. "These subjects represent quite abstract functionalities—can we map them onto something more concrete?" "That would be good," says John, "because it's not easy to talk about a subject without having a concrete picture of it. When I think of a production process I usually think in terms of physical things, like machines, materials, people and so on." "I agree," Peter looks at John, "we should definitely link the abstract functionalities with something more tangible—because in the end we need to do that anyway. Functions need concrete actors that implement them, otherwise the process never comes to life." "OK," John walks up to the flipchart and places his hand next to the 'Production Scheduler' subject. "For this subject I can visualise our manufacturing execution system as being able to implement it." Peter crosses the question mark next to Production Scheduler and writes down "Manufacturing Execution System". Jerry continues, "And I reckon, the 'Production Service Launcher' is just some kind of software programme that coordinates all the services needed for manufacturing an individual product by communicating with all other subjects, including those that are implemented as physical resources like machines. But it would be nice to also have a physical identity or embodiment for this software programme—a physical object that is in contact with all other physical resources…" "Maybe it's the product being manufactured?!" John interrupts Jerry. Everyone looks astonished. After a short moment of silence Peter says, "Yes, the product being worked on could be the agent implementing the Production Service Launcher. Interesting idea, John! This fits nicely with a popular vision for future

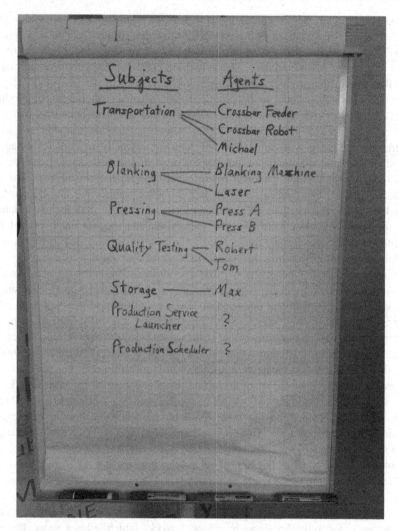

Fig. 12.3 Associating subjects with specific agents

manufacturing systems that I often heard in industry 4.0 talks: intelligent products determining their own path through the factory. By knowing their individual history, their current status and their target state, these products can dynamically react to changes or breakdowns by selecting alternative production paths."

Peter, John and Jerry look enthusiastic. Only Diana is still not convinced. "But the product doesn't really exist before executing the process. At the beginning, there is just this coil. Only when a piece of it is cut off could I imagine it to be a product-to-be." Jerry replies "Yes, the physical embodiment of the agent takes shape only during the process. But the agent can be instantiated in the virtual environment already before cutting the coil. It's like a ghost that is invisible at first but then slowly materialises as the production process unfolds." "You're a spook, Jerry!" Diana laughs, "But OK, I do think the whole process model now becomes much more tangible and intuitive. The only thing I still don't get my head around is how this ghost, this product agent, comes into existence in the first place. If you have hundreds of products to be produced, you also need hundreds of product agents. Who programs all these agents? And who can tell in advance how many of them will be needed?" Jerry points to the subject interaction diagram and says "Well, product agents wouldn't be pre-programmed manually on stock; every agent would be spawned when the production of a new product instance is launched by the Production Scheduler. This can be done automatically, as all instances of the product agent are identical in terms of their software architecture and their initial knowledge. We just need to define a template that is then used for instantiating product agents by some kind of agent factory. So the internal behaviour of the Production Scheduler subject might need to include an activity that creates a new product agent before sending the "start" message to that agent."

Diana scratches her head. "Wow, that's so different from the processes we're dealing with in the purchasing department, where all agents are human and cannot be just "spawned" or cloned on demand. We can only hire new people and then train them, and this often takes a very long time. We basically need to map our processes to an existing organisational structure that doesn't change much over the years. When you have software agents instead of people, the possibilities are almost unlimited—you can just create new agents in next to no time!"

Peter is impressed by the many ideas and insights generated by his team. "I like how we manage to bring the two worlds of subject- and agent-orientation together. I think we're onto something big here. I still have a question though. For implementing the 'Transportation' subject, we have three agents: A crossbar feeder, a crossbar robot, and Michael. But both the crossbar feeder and the crossbar robot can execute only some parts of the subject behaviour: transporting the blank plate from the blanking machine to the press, and transporting the pressed plate from the press to the quality testing station. This is because there are clear physical constraints that allow only certain movements on the shop floor. Moving the pressed plate to the storage area can only be done by manual work, which allows more flexible movements than crossbar feeders or robots. Of course it's not completely manual— when Michael moves the plates around, he uses a trolley for smaller plates and a forklift for larger ones. Now the question is, do we need some form of substitution mechanism to enable agents' replacing each other at execution time?"

Jerry thinks about this for a while and replies, "I think a much easier way is to create a new 'transportation' agent that is composed of three other agents—the feeder, the robot, and Michael. So this would be some sort of 'super-agent', a central control structure for a set of other agents or components specialised for different tasks. It's a bit like Michael who uses different tools for moving the pressed plates." Diana adds, "It's actually very similar to integrating S-BPM models in an IT environment where you also have many different IT tools for executing the same process. Many of our business processes, such as applying for vacation, need to be integrated with various email and calendar programmes, the time recording system and sometimes the project management system. No single IT system can support all tasks—they are all needed together for executing the complete subject behaviour. Our IT guys perform the IT integration by programming refinements for specific states in the behaviour specification." Jerry says, "You could either do that, or give the agent direct control over how it integrates the execution in its components. So rather than executing pre-programmed refinements, the agent could flexibly decide which component is best suited for the situation at hand. This would be useful when the agent needs to consider different alternatives for executing the same task, such as using either the feeder or the robot for transporting a blank plate to the press."

Peter summarises, "So, once again, we can see there's a great deal of design freedom in conceptualising and implementing agents for executing subject-oriented process models. We can view every single machine or person as an agent, or we can aggregate some of them to form a composite agent that has centralised control over its individual components. We can hard-code the physical or IT integration of an agent's behaviour at design time, or we can allow the agent to reason about and modify this integration at runtime."

12.4 Developing Control Mechanisms for Subject Execution

After another short break, it is John who resumes the conversation. "OK, so what exactly does the interplay between all these agents look like? Who exactly talks to whom? How can I ensure that I want to use Press A and not Press B for a particular product?" Diana answers, "In S-BPM when you send a message, you have the choice of who to send it to. You can either leave the recipient unspecified—in this case any agent associated with the receiving subject can choose to accept the message and thus commit to executing the subject—or you can send it to a specific agent or group of agents associated with the receiving subject." "Well, then again, what happens if you no longer have people but software agents to take this decision?" Jerry argues, "In the absence of human intelligence you need a well-defined mechanism for this kind of decision making."

Peter walks to the whiteboard and writes "Mechanisms" on top. "What kinds of control mechanisms for the runtime selection of agents can we think of?" Jerry quickly comes up with a few ideas. "So, in principle we could have a first-come-first-serve mechanism, just as it is now in Diana's department: When a message is sent to a subject, any agent associated to that subject can receive the message, and the first agent to take the message will be the agent executing the subject's behaviour. Of course, we might also think about randomising the message allocation, to prevent messages from being routed to agents simply on the basis of their different reaction times. Peter writes "1st-come-1st-serve" on the whiteboard, and then "Random" underneath. Jerry continues, "We may also think about introducing a system where agents can bid for receiving particular messages, using credits they earned by having done a good job in the past. The agent with the highest bid gets the new job—that means the incoming message in our case. Bidding mechanisms have already been applied for allocating manufacturing tasks among agents in the automotive industry." Peter writes down "Bidding" on the whiteboard. Diana asks, "Could we also have a mechanism similar to human decision making? One where different alternatives are compared and evaluated against some form of criteria?" "Well, I'm not sure if human cognition really works that way," Jerry adjusts his glasses, "there's actually strong evidence that suggests that humans typically use simple heuristics instead of complex analyses. But I do agree that some form of rational, analytical decision making would be useful for our system." Peter writes down "Heuristics" and says, "Let me call both just 'heuristics', without caring about whether they're simple or complex."

"By the way, 'first-come-first-serve' can also be seen as a heuristic," Jerry adds, "namely when the sender applies this mechanism to its memory of possible recipients. So the sender would choose the first agent that comes to its mind, perhaps based on some key feature that was used for cueing its memory. For example, when I'm asked to think about a city in Europe, the first cities popping up in my head would probably be Paris, Berlin or London, because they are among the biggest or the most popular ones."

Peter steps back from the whiteboard and looks at it from a little distance. "So, there's definitely some overlap between the mechanisms, but that's OK. Maybe they can also be combined. We can decide that later. But what I'm thinking now is that we might include a second dimension that is about where the execution of these mechanisms may be located: on the side of the sender or the receiver of a message." He writes "Sender" and "Receiver" in two new columns on the top of the whiteboard. Jerry adds, "And there might also be a third party, something like a facilitator, who can execute the mechanisms." Peter writes "Facilitator" in a new column, resulting in the table shown in Fig. 12.4.

"There may also be combinations within this dimension, where the sender and the receiver, and perhaps also a facilitator, cooperate on executing a mechanism," says Jerry. "A well-known example in agent-based systems is the 'Director Facilitator' approach. The facilitator can be thought of as the 'yellow pages' of the agent system. All agents must register their services with the Directory Facilitator. When you need a specific service, you can just ask that facilitator to give you a list of agents that provide that service, and you can then choose a specific agent or perhaps let the facilitator choose for you."

Peter is content with the table the team just produced. "We can use this table as a basis for developing control mechanisms for every message exchange defined in the subject interaction diagram. John, which of these mechanisms would be suitable for your problem of selecting the right press to send your blank plate to?" John thinks for a while and says, "I reckon it should be the heuristic approach, because there's a great deal of specific knowledge involved in selecting the press. On the one side we have product specifications and production requirements that need to be satisfied, and on the other side we have production services with their specific capabilities

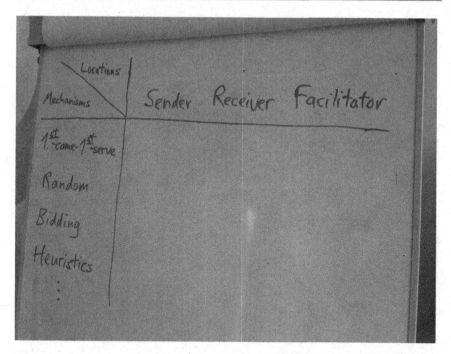

Fig. 12.4 A few possible mechanisms for selecting agents to receive messages, and possible locations of these mechanisms in the sender, the receiver, or a facilitator

and performance values. Both sides need to be matched. For example, if I need a specific product to be produced within a certain timeframe or satisfying certain quality constraints, some of the services might not fulfil these requirements." "Yes," Jerry remarks, "and the Directory Facilitator approach I was just talking about seems to be appropriate here, because the basic capabilities and many performance values of the production resources do not change over time, so they can be stored in a central directory."

Peter hands the whiteboard marker over to Jerry. "Could you try to model the process of querying and selecting a service via a facilitator—that is, selecting the agent providing that service? This would help us understand the selection process—besides making it ready for execution." "Sure," Jerry walks to the whiteboard and places three magnetic cards onto it. While writing on them he explains, "We need three subjects: a 'Service Requestor', a 'Directory Facilitator' and a 'Service Provider'." He quickly adds a few message arrows to produce a subject interaction diagram as shown in Fig. 12.5.

"The diagram is pretty self-explanatory," Jerry says. "The Directory Facilitator identifies the agents that can provide a specific service, and the Service Requestor selects from among these agents based on some criteria or priorities and finally asks for a commitment from the Service Provider to deliver the service." John remarks, "Well, the most frequently used criterion for deciding on a production service

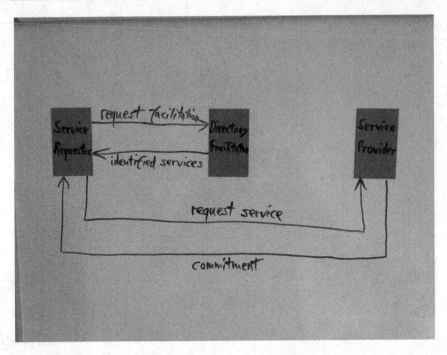

Fig. 12.5 Subject interaction diagram of an agent (service) selection process

would probably be the current availability of the service. If a press is busy with another production job, I usually need to select a different press—preferably one that's idle. Would the Directory Facilitator know about this status information?" After thinking for a short while, Jerry answers, "If the Service Requestor is executed by the same agent that also executes the Production Service Launcher in our main process—that is, the pressing process—then the agent can infer the current status of a machine from the status of the process instance." Jerry points to the subject interaction diagram shown in Fig. 12.1. "So, for example, if the Production Service Launcher was just told by the Transportation subject that the blank plate has been delivered to the press—using the message 'Transfer completed'—but is still waiting for the notification message 'Pressing completed' from the Pressing subject, then the Production Service Launcher can infer that the press is still busy."

Peter summarises, "So the logical connection between these two processes is established in the knowledge of the agents involved in them. The agent executing the Production Service Launcher would also need to execute the Service Requestor, because it knows that the results of the agent selection process are needed to perform its tasks within the pressing process." "Yes," Diana adds, "when people execute processes in our department, they also have a range of processes they can select. For example, before booking a business trip they might realise that they are running low on business cards, so they would run the 'ordering business cards' process before running the 'business travel booking' process, to make sure they get the new business cards before travelling. Of course, we might think of connecting the two processes on the modelling level, if there is a close connection between the two. Although in this example, I would say that these processes are quite independent of each other. So we wouldn't need to include a task in someone's travel booking behaviour to check if sufficient business cards are available and if not then to launch the card ordering process. We trust that our staff can organise themselves enough to make the connection between the processes in their minds and choose the right processes to be executed at the right time."

"Good observation," Peter compliments Diana. "So for our two separate models, we would need to implement some form of common sense reasoning in the agent to decide which process to execute at what point in time. Jerry, what are your thoughts on this?" Jerry answers, "That's certainly possible. Many agent architectures incorporate cognitive notions such as goals, beliefs and plans. We could use these architectures to represent the goals associated with different processes. Our two processes would then be connected with each other because the goal of one process is to support the other process."

Peter asks Jerry, "What other issues do we need to consider for implementing the agents and the control mechanisms we just discussed?" "Well, there are always a number of points to be thought about when implementing agent systems. For example, what specific decision-making mechanisms and learning capabilities should we implement? What are the real-time requirements? Do we want a closed system that has always the same set of agents, or an open system where new agents may come in dynamically? What are then the implications for interoperability; what types of knowledge can be predefined among the agents and what types of knowledge are unknown prior to running the process?" Diana agrees, "This is also important for defining data objects—or business objects, as we call them—that we need to add to the messages and behaviours in the S-BPM models."

Peter looks at his watch. "Well, it's almost lunch time, so let's wrap up our meeting. Today we outlined the major challenges to be addressed when designing and executing our agent-based production system based on the S-BPM approach. I think we are now in a position where we are able to define concrete work packages and schedule our tasks. But we will do this in our next meeting. For now, let me just summarise the main issues and what we learned from this morning's discussions."

12.5 Conclusion

Peter glances over the notes he took during the meeting. "There are quite a few interesting ideas that came out of our discussion. What I found most valuable are the issues arising from applying the S-BPM approach to a new domain, one in which processes are executed by computational agents rather than people."

Peter looks at Diana. "From the point of view of an S-BPM practitioner, what is probably most intriguing about agents is the almost unrestricted design freedom in mapping subjects to agents, because agents can be specified in so many ways.

In traditional S-BPM applications all you have is a set of people, grouped together in hierarchies, networks or geographies. So the organisational units and structures here are relatively fixed. Now what happens when we have agents instead of people? We can create our agent world in almost any way we can think of. Some agents can be embodied in the physical environment, while others have only a virtual existence. The embodiment of agents can even change during the execution of a process, for example, from being completely virtual to becoming both virtual and physical—cyber-physical—as we've seen in the case of our product agent. Multiple agents may be combined to form a composite agent, so that the individual agents are just like the tools of a Swiss army knife used by that agent. And one agent may even spawn other agents as needed during the process. All this is not possible in human organisations—or at least it requires a level of abstraction that is usually not needed in traditional business applications of S-BPM. So with such an unlimited set of possibilities in conceptualising agents, establishing mappings between subjects and agents may be difficult, especially if you haven't worked with agent-based applications before."

Peter pauses for a while, then continues, "The other thing that struck me is that many things we take for granted in people-based process execution need to be carefully engineered in agent-based applications. This includes devising mechanisms for controlling which agents are to be allowed to execute a subject's behaviour. The mechanisms vary based on the specific requirements associated with different parts of the process. For many agent-based applications, a simple first-come-first-serve mechanism is not suited as there is typically the need for more constrained access control based on specific performance characteristics and the current state of the production process. This often requires endowing agents with heuristic knowledge and decision-making capacities, and the ability to reason about the goals of different processes and how they relate to one another."

"I really want to thank you, Peter, for initiating this interesting project and inviting me to be part of it," Diana says. "I learned a lot today, because our discussions about agent implementations made me think about S-BPM in a more general way. I believe that some of the concepts we developed, such as the control mechanisms for subject execution, may even be useful for some of the business process applications in my department."

"Great," Peter smiles, "I'm looking forward to working with all of you to make this project succeed. I think the S-BPM approach helps us develop our agent-based prototype fairly quickly. But now let's have a well-deserved lunch!"

Acknowledgments The research leading to these results has received funding from the European Union Seventh Framework Programme FP7-2013-NMP-ICT-FOF(RTD) under grant agreement no. 609190.

Part III
Technical Execution Support

An Abstract State Machine Interpreter for S-BPM

13

Harald Lerchner

Abstract

Each business process management (BPM) approach requires a precise semantic specification scheme. Semantically, ambiguities can cause a lot of problems during the lifespan of a business process. As Abstract State Machines (ASMs) are grounded to subject orientation, we have explored their capabilities with respect to representing and executing Subject-oriented BPM (S-BPM) models. Based on the ASM method we implemented an interpreter which allows not only the proof of the S-BPM concept in terms of semantical preciseness, but also the automated execution of S-BPM models in terms of a workflow engine. This workflow engine serves as a baseline and reference implementation for further language and processing developments, such as simulation tools, as it has been developed within the Open-S-BPM initiative. This contribution focuses more on the use of the technique than on formal definitions.

13.1 Setting the Stage

Industry 4.0 is currently one of the most widely used keywords in industry. There are many events and conferences regarding this topic. Alessandro frequently attends such conferences. He is responsible as head of production in a typical SME company in the automotive industry. Concerning new ideas he is open-minded and always searching for new technologies and approaches to improve processes in the company. At one particular conference, Alessandro attended a presentation about

H. Lerchner (✉)
Department of Business Information Systems—Communications Engineering,
Johannes Kepler University of Linz, Altenberger Straße 69, 4040 Linz, Austria
e-mail: harald.lerchner@jku.at

communication-based business process management (BPM). This concept differed from the classical approaches with which he had been familiar. His staff has to communicate a lot with other departments. They are well equipped with IT-Systems, but he is aware of the many difficulties concerning the communication between the involved employees. He is enthusiastic about the idea of modeling business processes from a stakeholder's perspective.

After the presentation, Alessandro gets to know Bernardo. Bernardo is a scientist and is doing work in the field of S-BPM. After some general small talk they engage in an intense discussion. The following contains some parts of this conversation between Alessandro and Bernardo.

13.2   Conversation

Alessandro: I understood the general approach to S-BPM in the presentation, but I can't imagine how this could be useful, particularly with the behavior diagram of the subjects.

Bernardo: In order to accomplish a business goal a subject has to perform a set of interrelated activities in a certain sequence. A subject can be a human or a system. Each subject has an internal behavior and communicates with other subjects. The latter requires the exchange of messages between subjects. With these messages, the subjects synchronize their work. Modeling a process means that you have to be aware of your activities and the necessary communication between the involved subjects. This is a kind of reflection and is the first step in discovering new potential for improvements and optimizations. Such a model can be used for the purpose of documentation (e.g., as requirement of ISO certification), for process improvement discussion, or for the introduction of new employees.

A model is a representation of what is currently happening or what is intended to happen. But an S-BPM model is executable (Fleischmann 2012). Execution denotes the interpretation of the model by a workflow engine. At runtime it generates an instance of the process model, allowing for real-time access in order to control, monitor and manage the progress of each subject to execute. The information collected from one process instance or a set of processes can be analyzed according to both quantitative and qualitative aspects.

Alessandro: Quite understandable, but how could we use this for our production?

Bernardo: I mentioned already that a subject can be a human or a system. Regarding your production environment, a system could be a computer system like an enterprise resource planning software (ERP) or a milling center, or even a sensor. The product itself could also be seen as a subject.

Alessandro: I see. I find this perspective quite enlightening. You told me that you are working with a special state machine. How is this relevant to S-BPM?

Bernardo: That's a good question. For both modeling and execution you need a language. There are many such languages. Not all of these languages are applicable for both modeling *and* execution. The notation of the respective modeling approach has to be specified precisely, in order to enable proper usage, including communicating and sharing models. The lack of semantic precision entails the risk of misinterpretations in each phase of the lifecycle of the business process. For example, difficulties may arise in learning how to use a notation in the event that the notation itself is unclear. Different people could interpret the same model differently. At runtime several instances of the same business process could lead to inconsistent and unpredictable results. Finally, exchanging business models between different workflow engines could be hindered or could lead to unpredictable results. These are just a few examples of why precise semantics is necessary. S-BPM has been introduced to avoid the misinterpretations such as these in the various phases of the lifecycle of a process.

By means of validation, a process model is checked for whether it represents the intended process behavior. S-BPM validation can be supported by a tool featuring the direct execution of the model. I implemented such a tool. It is an interpreter which allows not only the proof of the S-BPM concept, but also the automated execution of S-BPM models in terms of a workflow engine. And this is where Abstract State Machines come into play.

Alessandro: Very informative! However, I am a little bit confused about the relationship between ASM and S-BPM.
Bernardo: OK, I will draw a sketch (Fig. 13.1) (Lerchner and Stary 2014) to show the components and their relations.

On the one hand, a business process model based on the S-BPM approach can be processed automatically, as it covers a complete control flow specification for execution. This is the existing S-BPM part. On the other hand we have the existing ASM components. In the middle there is an existing Abstract Interpreter for S-BPM (Fleischmann 2012). In this case, "Abstract" has the meaning that the interpreter is on a high level and contains no detailed information for an actual implementation. Since this Abstract Interpreter is based on the S-BPM approach, it enables validation of an S-BPM model. The interpreter itself is based on the ASM method which offers a mathematical framework. This method has been developed for system engineering of complex, discrete, and dynamic systems like business process management systems. I will explain the basics of the theory behind ASM afterward. For now I will give you just an overview. The developments of the ASM method in the resent years have led to tools that allow for execution of ASM specifications. For several reasons I have chosen CoreASM as such a tool. I have used this tool to transfer the theoretical approach of the Abstract Interpreter in order to develop an executable interpreter. This interpreter allows not only the proof of

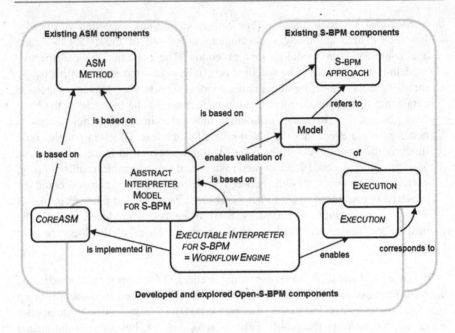

Fig. 13.1 S-BPM and ASM components and their relations

the S-BPM concept, but also the automated execution of S-BPM models in terms of a workflow engine.

The concept of the Abstract State Machine was developed by Yuri Gurevich 30 years ago (Gurevich 1985). The Abstract State Machine is a scientifically well-founded system engineering method. It allows developing formal descriptions of algorithms, thus reducing unintended or erroneous system behavior. ASM is also a universal mathematical framework for semantic modeling of discrete dynamic systems. ASMs are based on mathematic algebras which consist of a nonempty set with a collection of operations defined over this set. Sets and relations are supported and therewith complex data structures like graphs can be built. Due to enhancements in the resent years, the ASM method has matured to an engineering method which can be utilized for the development of software and embedded hard-software systems (Börger and Stärk 2003). On the one hand, it is used for formal specification and on the other hand for analysis (verification and validation). With the semantically well-founded form of pseudo-code, system engineers are able to transform descriptions expressed in application domain terms into precise abstract definitions.

An ASM consists of a set of states and transition rules. Contrary to Finite State Machines (FSMs), a state is a structure in the sense of mathematical logics. Only one state is valid at a particular time. Starting from a defined initial state, a transition to a subsequent state occurs only under a certain condition. A transition from one state to a subsequent one is driven by transition rules.

Basic ASMs consist of a set of such transition rules of the following format (Börger and Stärk 2003):

If *Condition* then *Updates*

A condition (also called a guard) is a Boolean expression. Updates refer to a finite set of assignments which are performed in parallel in the course of the transition. An ASM computation step in a given state results in executing simultaneously all updates of all transition rules whose guard is true in the state if these updates are consistent, in which case the result of their execution yields the next state (Börger and Stärk 2003).

In addition to basic ASMs, which are executed as "single agent ASMs", there exist enhancements to synchrony and asynchrony as well as "multi agent ASMs". These enhancements include also additional transition rules which define the syntax of ASM programs. The "LET" rule is exemplarily for those powerful rules.

LET rule: let x = t in P

This rule allows for the assignment of the value t to x, followed by the execution of P. Variable x is a logical variable and cannot be updated by a transition rule. The scope of x is P. P is a transition rule and t may be a value or the result of a function.

Using ASMs, algorithms can be specified on the level of abstraction, as determined by the application domain. Hierarchical system design is supported by two concepts, namely ground model and refinement. Due to the abstraction and formalization with ASM, an efficient tool for requirements elicitation and precise modeling is available. Due to its versatility ASMs are used for analysis, design, and verification of complex, distributed, and discrete systems.

ASM as a method for software design and analysis has three constituents. Besides the concept of an abstract state machine, the ASM method has the two concepts ground model method, for capturing requirements, and the refinement method, for detailing ground models stepwise toward implementation (Börger and Stärk 2003).

A transformation of natural language into a formal precise description occurs in the course of requirements elicitation. Such a description as the result of the elicitation process is termed ground model (Börger and Stärk 2003). It serves the purpose of bringing the domain expert and system designer to a common understanding. The model can be verified and validated at the level of abstraction determined by the application domain (Börger 1999). "Ground models come with a sufficiently precise yet abstract and unambiguous meaning to carry out an implementation-independent, application-oriented requirements analysis (i.e., both verification and validation) prior to coding" (Börger and Stärk 2003).

The stepwise refining of higher abstraction ASMs leads to a lower abstraction level or even to executable code. This approach is well documented and can be readily inspected by mathematical means.

The "freedom of abstraction" (Börger 2003, p. 244) enables the designer to determine the vertical and horizontal refinement steps, in order to synchronize the different abstraction levels starting with customer expectations and ranging to final code. You are able to produce a high-level description of a system at a much earlier point in the design process, before all of the details have been decided.

The possibility of validating and verifying systems with ASM specifications has led to the development of ASM languages, enabling the execution of such specifications. In order to keep our implementation of the executable interpreter as close as possible to the abstract interpreter model for S-BPM, the instruction set of a corresponding tool needs to follow the mathematical definition of pure ASMs. In addition, as open source it facilitates exploration, adaptation, and enrichment. Finally, individual adaption of such a tool should be enabled, either to support users with a distinct user interface, or to integrate it with an existing framework.

Since CoreASM is an extensible ASM execution engine (Farahbod et al. 2007), it is utilized as a tool for the implementation of the executable interpreter. It is itself an interpreter.

Alessandro: I understood that S-BPM is an approach for BPM, and that ASM is a system engineering method, which sounds very theoretical. How can I imagine the relation to an S-BPM model.

Bernardo: Each BPM language has certain rules which describe the function of the specific language constructs and how to proceed with the modeled single process steps. Those rules are implemented in the Interpreter.

S-BPM is an approach for modeling business processes from a stakeholder's perspective. It explicitly distinguishes between one's individual work and the communication among the involved parties that is required to successfully accomplish a business goal.

Subject-oriented business process management (S-BPM) has been triggered by natural language constructs, namely standard sentences. They consist of subject, predicate and object (Fleischmann 2010). In the notation of S-BPM, subjects represent the active part of the process and can be a human or a system. Each subject has an internal behavior and communicates with other subjects. The latter requires the exchange of messages between subjects.

In order to accomplish a business goal a subject has to perform a set of inter-related activities in a certain sequence. S-BPM distinguishes between three fundamental types of activities for modeling the internal behavior. These types are sending messages to other subjects, receiving messages from other subjects, and executing internal actions like a program script if the subject is a system, or a manual task if the subject represents a person. Activities are denoted by predicates, and an object is the target of an activity. As in a natural language with subject-predicate-object (Fleischmann and Stary 2012), the object is the target of an activity and is not mandatory. Objects denoted as business objects can be manipulated in the course of the internal action or can be sent from one subject to another subject. But for further explanation I will focus only on subject and predicate.

Alessandro: I have a current situation from our assembly line in mind. For my understanding it would be very helpful to use an example with which I am familiar. I will give you a brief explanation of our production process. Please try to envision a product which is processed in sequence by several machine tools during a production process. The product communicates with a measurement machine and the transport system. First the product requests measurement. The measurement machine takes the product from the transport system and conducts the measurement. When the measurement machine has finished, it puts the product back on the transport system and sends a report with the result of the measurement to the product. The product knows about the tolerance range and compares this with the received report. In cases where the actual measurement is within the tolerance, the product informs the transport system to move forward to the next production step. Otherwise, the transport system receives a command to drop the product from the production sequence.

Bernardo: This is a good example which we can use for further explanations. For reasons of simplicity I suggest that we neglect other subjects like ERP systems or quality management systems.

Alessandro and Bernardo develop the interaction diagram and the behavior diagrams together. The following diagrams show the result (Figs. 13.2, 13.3, and 13.4).

The behavior diagram of the subject Transport System is not depicted because it has no added value for further explanation.

Bernardo proceeds: For further explanation, I will focus on the behavior of the subject "Product," which is detailed in the Subject Behavior Diagram we have modelled (Fig. 13.4). Such a diagram can be interpreted as directed graph. A graph consists of nodes connected by edges. A node has at least one ingoing and one outgoing edge. The basic structure of a node is depicted in Fig. 13.5.

This concept must be extended (Fig. 13.6) because the behavior of a subject can be described using the three fundamental types of activities: send, receive, and action. Each node represents a state in terms of ASM. At each state the underlying subject performance of one of the three activities is assigned to the state. Only after you have finished an activity a subsequent activity can be started. One can understand an edge as a transition from one state to the next. A transition can only occur once the activity

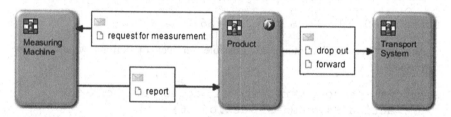

Fig. 13.2 Subject interaction diagram

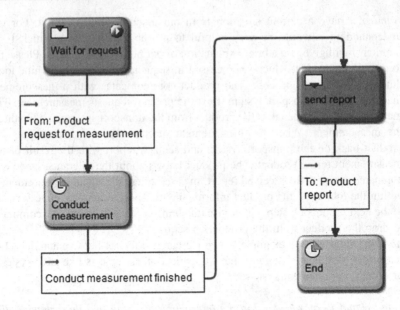

Fig. 13.3 Subject behavior diagram from subject measuring machine

assigned to a node has been completed. In order to manage alternative transitions, each edge corresponds to an exit condition of the executed activity.

Alessandro: With this information you are able to transfer the behavior diagram of a subject into a form which the interpreter can work with. Is that right?
Bernardo: That's absolutely right. Let me draw the transformation for the subject "Product" (Fig. 13.7).

Mathematically speaking, a Subject Behavior Diagram (SBD) is a directed graph. Each SBD is assumed to be finite and to have one initial state and at least one end state. More than one end state is acceptable. Each path leads to at least one end state. At a definite time a subject can have only one single valid state. Unfortunately the ASM cannot interpret this figure of the graph so we have to use a proper notation. Therefore I will explain it for node "S2," the most complex node in this example.

At first, we have to define general sets, which are a collection of possible values. The set "State" contains all nodes of the SBD of the subject "Product."

```
State = {S0, S1, S2, S3, S4, S5, S6}
```

The set "Services" contains all possible services or actions which can be performed.

```
Services = {send-S0, receive-S1, action-S2, send-S3,
       action-S4, send-S5, action-S6}
```

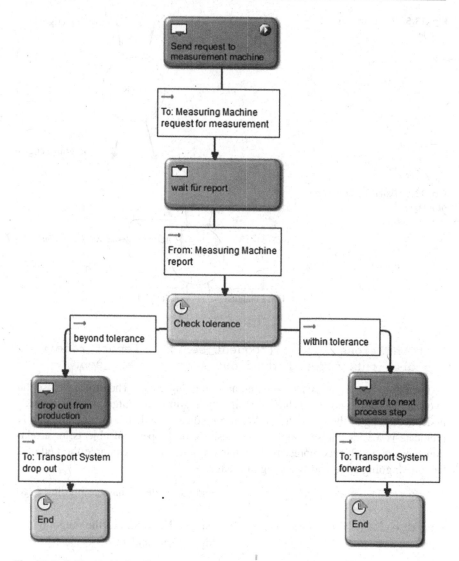

Fig. 13.4 Subject behavior diagram of the subject product

The set "Edges" contains all of the edges necessary for connecting the existing nodes in the given graph. An edge is denoted by the form *fromNode_toNode*. This means that the edge s0_s1 connects node S0 with node S1.

```
Edge = {s0_s1, s1_s2, s2_s3, s2_s5, s3_s4, s5_s6}
```

The possible exit conditions are enumerated in the set *ExitCondition*.

Fig. 13.5 Basic structure of
a node

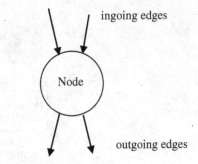

ingoing edges

outgoing edges

Fig. 13.6 Extended structure
of a node

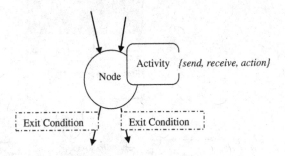

```
ExitConditions   =   {request_sent,   report_received,
     drop_out, forward, drop_out_sent, forward_sent}
```

Each node has to know its incoming and outgoing edges. Therefore, we use the two sets "InEdge" and "OutEdge" to assign the ingoing and outgoing edges to each node, according to the given graph. We use predicates to depict this assignment. A predicate is a verb phrase template that describes a property of objects, or a relationship among objects represented by the variables. In our example the node S2 has one ingoing edge and two outgoing edges.

```
InEdge(S2) := {s1_s2}
```
read as: Node S2 has the ingoing edge s1_s2

```
OutEdge(S2) := {s2_s3, s2_s5}
```
read as: Node S2 has the outgoing edges s2_s3 and s2_s5

A service or activity is assigned to a node. A service can be one of the three fundamental types of activity (send, receive and action). 'Service' is not further specified for the function activity. In a function state, the assigned service could perform several tasks. For instance, a user interface (UI) or an external program could be invoked, or made to wait until a specific period of time has elapsed (like ripening in process industry). 'Service' needs to be specified with further refinements. For our purpose we have to define a predicate for the assignment of a service to a node. It works in the same way as for *InEdge* or *OutEdge*.

```
Service(S2) := {action-S2}
```
read as: action_s2 is the assigned service to node S2

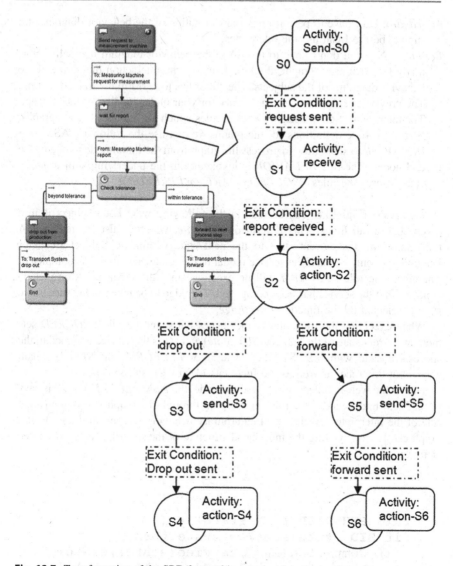

Fig. 13.7 Transformation of the SBD from subject product into the graph structure

Each edge needs to know its target node. Therefore, we use the predicate "target."

target(s2_s3) := {S3}   read as: the target node from edge s2_s3 is node
                            S3

It works the same way for all other nodes and edges.

Alessandro: Do I have to perform this transformation of the behavior diagram of a subject before I can use the interpreter?

Bernardo: No, you don't have to transform the behavior diagram manually. Normally you will use a graphical editor to model the interaction diagram and the behavior diagrams of the subjects. The editor has to perform the transformation. The previous explanation was necessary for your understanding of the concept. The interpreter itself consists of a set of rules which are applied on such graphs. Based on these definitions for the graph, we can use the following ASM rule *BEHAVIOR* to show how to process the graph from the initial node to one of the end nodes. The rule *BEHAVIOR* is invoked with the underlying subject and a state. It uses the rules *PROCEED, START, and PERFORM*.

This ASM (Fig. 13.8) can be read in the following way: Each subject is in a given state at all times. This is termed *SID_State*, which is also a predicate. A transition from the current state to the next state within the Subject Behavior Diagram can only occur if the service (equal to the assigned activity) is completed. Therefore, the rule *PERFORM* will be executed until the predicate "Completed" confirms that the service has been completed. The edge to be taken to the successive state is selected by the function *selectEdge*.

When executing the transition to the successive state, the rule *PROCEED* sets the new current state of the subject (*SID_State*) and starts the service assigned to the successive state with the "START." The rules *PERFORM* and *START* remain abstract at this time, as well as the functions *Completed* and *selectEdge*.

Due to the well-founded form of pseudo-code, the ASM rule *BEHAVIOR* is easy to read and understand. This rule for stepping through the graph is a fundamental rule of the interpreter. At this level an arbitrary behavior diagram in the form of a graph can be set up using the introduced structure of the nodes. This ASM can be stepwise refined.

```
rule BEHAVIOR(subj,state) = {
  if SID_State(subj) = state then
    if Completed(subj,service(state),state)
      then lete = selectEdge(subj,state) in
      PROCEED(subj,service(target(e)),
              target(e))
    else  PERFORM(subj,service(state),state)
  endif   }

rule PROCEED(subj, X, state) = {
     SID_State(subj):= state
     START(subj, X, state)   }
```

Fig. 13.8 ASM rule BEHAVIOR

Regarding our production example, the interpreter works as a workflow engine. Since there is no human involved the process runs automatically. If a human such as a quality employee would be involved in this process, the process would also run automatically. However, for activities which need human input the corresponding Subject Behavior Diagram awaits the input.

Alessandro: It is really manageable to follow the explanation on such an abstract level with the pseudo-code. How can I or others benefit from your work?

Bernardo: The result of this work will be accessible within the Open-S-BPM community. The Open-S-BPM project has been initiated to foster the spreading of the S-BPM concept and approach on a common theoretical and practical basis. It aims to establish a research platform for S-BPM developments. Within the S-BPM community, there are some projects focusing on the different activities of the S-BPM lifecycle (Fleischmann 2012). The development of the workflow engine is intertwined with some of these projects. The architecture is depicted in Fig. 13.9 (Schmidt and Fleischmann 2012).

In BPM business processes pass several phases of deployment, ranging from analysis to design, modeling, validation, execution, monitoring, and optimization. This concept is commonly known as the BPM lifecycle. In Fig. 13.9 several components are depicted which are necessary to support such a lifecycle. Some of the components are implemented by current projects. The workflow engine is the main component which is necessary for execution. The *Model Data* is the basic input for the workflow engine. It contains the S-BPM process model which includes the interaction diagram and the behavior diagram of each subject. The storage format corresponds to the directed graph, which has been explained already in

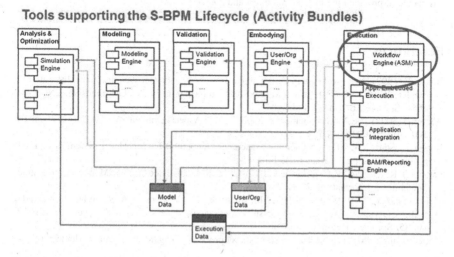

Fig. 13.9 Architecture in Open-S-BPM

detail. The organizational structure of an organization is also relevant for execution. It is necessary to assign users to the subjects of the processes. Therefore, *User/Org Data* contains the required data. Those data are provided from an organization engine. When the workflow engine executes a process, many status data can be collected and held in a database. Those data can be used for monitoring or for the calculating of key performance indicators (KPI). All the information can be used to simulate changes in your processes. This mechanism allows you to evaluate the effects of the changes before you deploy the process.

The workflow engine serves as a baseline and as a reference implementation, ensuring semantic soundness for further language and processing developments of S-BPM. Here the strength and advantages of the ASM method can be utilized.

S-BPM and ASM are completely different methods from different fields. But, they have some similarities which make them worth dealing with.

You, Alessandro, can benefit from future developments in all of the areas of the S-BPM lifecycle. And you can contribute to these developments through active participation within the S-BPM community. Particularly, practitioners are welcome to bring their perspective.

13.3 Closing

In the meanwhile, the last presentation of the day on this conference has finished, and the participants are on their way to a common evening event. Alessandro and Bernardo join the other participants and are going to have some other fruitful and interesting discussions.

References

Börger E (1999) High level system design and analysis using abstract state machines. In: Hutter D, Stephan W, Traverso P, Ullmann M (eds) Applied formal methods—FM-trends 98, LNCS, vol 1641. Springer, Berlin, pp 1–43

Börger E (2003) The ASM refinement method. Formal Aspects Comput 15(2–3):237–257. doi:10.1007/s00165-003-0012-7

Börger E, Stärk R (2003) Abstract state machines. A method for high-level system design and analysis (19 tables). Springer, Berlin

Farahbod R, Gervasi V, Glässer U (2007) CoreASM: an extensible ASM execution engine. Fundamenta Informaticae 77(1):71–103

Fleischmann A (2010) What is S-BPM? In: Buchwald H, Fleischmann A, Seese D, Stary C (eds) S-BPM ONE—setting the stage for subject-oriented business process management, LNBIP, vol 85. Springer, Berlin, pp 85–106

Fleischmann A (2012) Subject-oriented business process management. Springer, Heidelberg

Fleischmann A, Stary C (2012) Whom to talk to? A stakeholder perspective on business process development. Univ Access Inf Soc 11(2):125–150. doi:10.1007/s10209-011-0236-x

Gurevich Y (1985) A new thesis. In: Abstracts, American Mathematical Society, vol 6, p 317

Lerchner H, Stary C (2014) An open S-BPM runtime environment based on abstract state machines. In: IEEE 16th conference on business informatics (CBI), pp 54–61

Schmidt W, Fleischmann A (2012) Open-S-BPM white paper. Goals and Architecture. http://www.i2pm.net/open-s-bpm

Structured Communication— Approaching S-BPM with Microsoft Technologies

14

Robert Singer and Stefan Raß

Abstract

Many enacted business processes in the field use (more or less intense) communication to forward work to the next participant in an activity chain. Communication can be oral (personal, phone) or technically supported (e-mail, phone). It can be unstructured using natural language—typically text or spoken word—or structured using formal language (business objects) typically stored in systems. Based on decades of research in the domain of the social sciences, we know that an understanding of how organizations work are based on communication and language. Therefore any technology to support the execution of business processes should support communication between process participants. This is the concept of S-BPM. Here, we present the results of work in the field to develop a platform to model and execute business processes as interaction between actors. As process models predefine work we call this way of interaction *structured communication* (using standard e-mail exchange). To enable also cross-company communication (process orchestrations) we technically implemented the platform as a so-called *multi-enterprise business process platform* (ME-BPP) using cloud technology. The contribution uses a real-world case to demonstrate the need for a communication-based view on business processes. The case reflects the situation typically for large-scale international companies with world-wide activities and with focus on processes related to order fulfillment, including manufacturing. Further on, an IT architecture to support the enactment

R. Singer (✉)
FH-Joanneum—University of Applied Sciences, Alte Poststraße 147, 8020 Graz, Austria
e-mail: robert.singer@fh-joanneum.at

S. Raß
StrICT Solutions GmbH, Plüddemanngasse 39, 8010 Graz, Austria
e-mail: rass@strict-solutions.com

of such *distributed* processes is discussed. The contribution is intended for practitioners with some IT background and/or interests.

14.1   Introduction and Motivation

In this section we will report and discuss typical situations in the field—related to business process management in general and the execution of business processes in particular. These situations will provide the context and the motivational background for the analysis: the use of S-BPM as business process modeling and execution paradigm.

For example, let's think about a typical work situation in a manufacturing company.

When the phone rings it is always something urgent, but Bob, the planning manager of the company, has no choice and picks up the phone. The friendly voice of Pieter wishes him a good morning, but the strange feeling in his stomach remains. Pieter is responsible for consolidating orders from several industrial customers; this includes orders from the own sales organization (brand) and from OEM[1] customers. Pieter is located in another European country. In principle, he could simply enter all requests (new or changed sales orders) into the company's order system, according to some simple business rules, and the factory, represented by Bob, has to answer via the system (accept or reject). Several key performance indicators are automatically recorded via the system, measuring the flexibility and reliability of the manufacturing site. But because of a trusted relationship, Pieter typically informs the factory in advance and asks for feasible solutions: can you do more of this product in week 24? Can we change some quantities from type A to B in this month?

On this day he asks to start two weeks earlier with the production of a new product for a very important customer and he needs an answer within two hours. That needs a lot of hectic personal communication and commitment from engineering, production, purchasing and logistics. Will the manufacturing equipment be ready (e.g., moulds), can we conduct a trial run in advance (including losing capacity because of a lost shift), can we bring in the needed material in time, etc. And, if we cannot handle this situation, are there additional options like moving orders between European and Chinese locations? The one and only tool to solve such riddles is communication. Some of the communication threads are serial (first check this, then that), some are parallel (each department checks). Additionally, the communication thread spreads over many people for the issue to be discussed personally, by e-mail, or by phone; they use, send and receive data using simple office documents and or systems; and it involves people from outside the organization as well, e.g., suppliers, engineering colleagues or the logistics department in the business unit headquarters in Taiwan.

---

[1]Original Equipment Manufacturer.

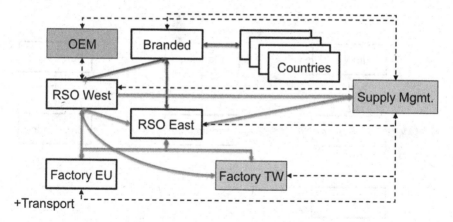

Fig. 14.1 Communication connections (relations) between the involved parties in the text case (business unit view). Each *box* represents a particular organizational unit, as described in the text. Abbreviations: *RSO* Regional Sales Office, *TW* Taiwan, *Countries* legal units in each European country. *Dashed lines* visualize further communication and line of command relations not explicitly discussed in the case

Bob will come up (as always) with an answer in time; after that, Pieter will discuss the committed proposal with the customer and, if they commit too, he will enter the agreed sales order (new or changed) into the system. Bob then will accept the changes in the system. To make it more complicated, the solution has to be communicated to and or committed with the business unit supply manager (Amy) located in Taiwan (possibly delayed because of time difference). Obviously, there are some interesting issues. An infamous point is that nobody knows what happens afterwards. There are private conversations and phone communications, notes on napkins and some or several e-mails all over the world. Maybe there will be trouble two months later with this order and the customer has to be informed that the order has to be postponed by two weeks. How to analyze what happened and why? The only visible fact is the acceptance of the new or changed order contradicting documented or undocumented policies or business rules. And—how to interpret the measured KPIs? If we try to visualize the "relations" and information flow between all involved **actors** of the *Order Fulfillment* process (on business unit level) we come up with Figs. 14.1 and 14.2.

Practice shows that such processes are the norm and can neither be modeled in full with "standard" modeling notations (such as *Business Process Model and Notation* (BPMN) or *Event-driven Process Chain* (EPC), for example) nor automatically executed based on these business process models—in this case, the organization has some documented business process description in RACI[2] form. As can easily be seen, we are confronted with a typical knowledge-intensive process; the main ingredient is **knowledge**, the output is a decision. But of course there is an

---

[2]Responsibility Assignment Matrix.

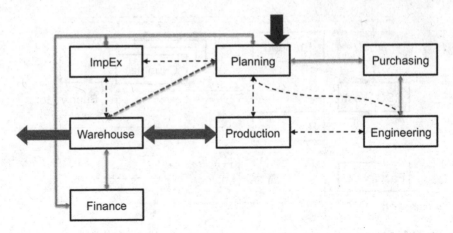

Fig. 14.2 Connections between the parties in the case (site view). Each *box* represents a particular department, as described in the text. Abbreviations: *ImpEx* Import and Export. *Dashed lines* visualize further communication relations not explicitly discussed in the case

inherent structure in such a change **case** and it should be noted that such change requests typically violate "standard" business rules and policies (fixed sales orders over a period of three months, for example). Any change therefore has to be evaluated on its own.

The question now is: Can we bring more structure into the work flow? Or, shouldn't we simply stick to a system, such as an *Enterprise Resource Planning* (ERP) system? The first question we will answer with "yes"—as we will discuss soon the second one with "no". The above case uses information and enters information into an ERP system, but that has no relation to any predefined work flow (but it is linked with the organizational structure and roles).

But there is actual IT support which works very well: E-mails! All involved parties (lets call them actors) can send any other actor a message. We can even cross organizational borders—and world-wide. It is also possible to send messages to people we do not even know, as long as somebody else knows them—so we can get answers to our questions from people we didn't know beforehand (we call this mobile messages). Additionally, we can send data together with our messages; any actor in the communication path can store or (depending on the data format) modify the data, which often are office documents: an actor, for example, can add a column in an *MS Excel* file and forward it to another actor. We can see from this that e-mail communication is a way for flexible—but unstructured—enactment of business processes. It can even be used to execute business processes we never thought about —it can *bootstrap* a process. Nevertheless, neither the communication thread nor the data is centrally stored—there is no central repository. It is therefore difficult to investigate what happened in the past; more or less forensic work—not so good if we are interested in compliance and process improvement.

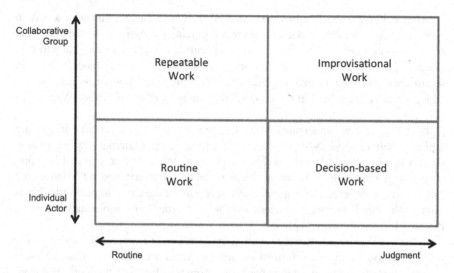

Fig. 14.3 A proposal of Davenport (2010) to categorize knowledge-based business processes

The predominant benefit of e-mail as business process execution tool is its flexibility and ease of use (a really flat learning curve); the disadvantage is that it is not efficient in cases when it is possible and wise to define a work flow (or parts of work flows) in advance. Not all business processes are purely ad hoc. These types of processes are typically expensive, as we need experienced and educated knowledge workers to evaluate the situation, develop a solution and make decisions—this can only be done by well-educated and empowered employees, who are typically also well paid. It is also difficult to agree on service levels for such processes.

We can see in Fig. 14.3 that business processes can be categorized (gradually) in two dimensions representing level of interdependence (number of actors) and complexity of work. Depending on the value of each dimension, a business process will have a more or less predefined structure.

14.2 Structured Communication

The question now is, how to create a system for structured communication? As methodology, *Subject-oriented Business Process Management* (S-BPM) seems to be the perfect foundation for such an approach—simply because it is structured communication: we have a network of actors (subjects are conceptualizations of actors), who are synchronizing their work through the exchange of messages. In the following paragraphs we will identify some (somewhat technical) requirements we have to consider for an implementation; and we want to create an IT platform for the execution of S-BPM models based as closely as possible on natural communication behaviors, and using as many already existing software platforms and applications as possible.

After collecting the requirements we will then be able to argue why a certain architecture is a feasible and useful approach to realize a solution for the execution of business processes. A business process execution system is an integral part of a business process management system and bridges the gap between models stored in repositories and their IT-enabled execution. It brings the information and knowledge, which is embedded in the model—the blueprint of the business process—to life.

In this context we understand a business process model as an entity for defining a plan to deliver services (or products) to customers, i.e., defining what we plan to do and in which logical order. If this sounds easy, let me assure you that it is not. Business processes are a means to manage service delivery, and as broad as the range of possible services is, the semantic spectrum of the term "logical order" is as broad. We therefore have to understand "logical order" in a more fuzzy way, as discussed in the previous section.

Therefore, business process execution systems need to support flexibility in the order of activities to be performed or needed. What we mean is, if we define a business process model, we define the future, how we plan to do the work. But from practical applications we know that we cannot plan all possible future situations. Depending on the type of service, organizational culture, or industry—the corresponding business process will create situations where we will not be able to stick to the predefined business process logic, simply because the concrete situation has not been considered appropriately. That means any business process execution system needs to facilitate this fact in some way. The typical case presented in the previous section is the context for the definition of the requirements of a fully featured business process execution system.

- Business process execution systems need to support **concurrency**. That means activities (or, synonymously, tasks) are executed simultaneously and potentially interact with each other; the simplest interaction would be synchronization after each concurrent activity has finished. In modeling notations this typically is reflected using symbols for AND-splits and -joins.
- Business process execution systems need to support **distributed** execution. Business processes cannot be seen as isolated workflows for administrative purposes only, but as a means to coordinate a value system with supply chain partners. That means actors in a business process are geographically distributed and not necessarily members of the same enterprise (e.g., manufacturer and supplier).
- Business process execution systems need to support **mobility**. This is a consequence of how we work today, but also leads to technical requirements for an implementation of a business process execution system.
- Business process executions systems need to support **flexibility**, i.e., the possibility of human process participants deviating from the predefined process path in case of an unexpected (and therefore not modeled) situation or exception—we need the capability to deviate from the path initiating so-called ad hoc activities while running a concrete instance of a process.

From these requirements we can conclude that BPMS based on any technology which executes business processes under the central control of some software (the process engine) cannot fulfill the criteria discussed above in its full consequence; this is especially true for the requirements *concurrency* and *distributed*, which lead to technical questions (Butcher 2014), which cannot be discussed here. Today such systems mainly focus on BPMN as modeling notation and more or less proprietary solutions to execute the models. Such "classical" workflow systems typically support office processes very well (for example the famous "application for leave" process) within one organization, but have serious difficulties executing real-world processes crossing organizational boundaries; additionally, from a socio-technical view on systems, we can also conclude that communication plays a central role in social interaction and therefore it is a natural way to think about the coordination of work.

Another issue we have to consider is the handling of data or **business objects**. Here we have the same issues as above: who stores the data and where? If we think of a process execution system as an ERP system it is clear that all data is centrally stored in exactly one database. This database is "owned" by one organization (even if it is located somewhere else) and the organization has full control over content and states of the datasets. But how do we handle the data we send to other process participants?

This demand is now reflected in new developments in the domain of BPM, such as *BPM Platform as a Service* (bpmPaaS), *Multi-Enterprise Business Process Platform* (ME-BPP), *Cloud BPM*, and *Social BPM*. The term bpmPaaS can be defined (Dixon 2012) as *"the delivery of BPM platform capabilities as a cloud service by a service provider"*. An ME-BPP is defined Dixon (2012) as a *"high-level conceptual model of a multistakeholder environment, where multi-enterprise applications are operated. Multi-enterprise applications are those purposely built to support the unique requirements for business processes that span across more than one business entity or organization. They replace multiple business applications integrated in serial fashion"*. Now, that is exactly what we are looking for: an ME-BPP. The next sections will discuss what we found on our *excavation* in the field.

14.3 How to Execute S-BPM Models

In this section we will sketch our journey towards a *Multi-Enterprise Business Process Platform* based on S-BPM (Singer et al. 2014), i.e., a so-called agent based approach. As already mentioned, one very important intention was to use as many available tools as possible in the field. Although this section contains some technical stuff, we do not have the intention to discuss things like code snippets in detail, but to give some deeper insight what is needed behind the scenes to **execute distributed and concurrent business processes**.

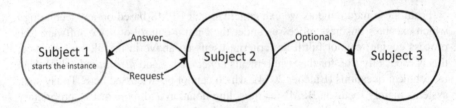

Fig. 14.4 An example of a *Subject Interaction Diagram*: it contains three subjects and all exchange messages. Subject 1 starts the process by sending a request to Subject 2; Subject 2 makes a decision, sends an answer back to Subject 1 and, in case of a positive answer, informs Subject 3 about the decision

An S-BPM process is defined via the communication exchange channels between subjects (agents are instantiated subjects in this context, or the other way round—subjects are generalizations of agents) (see Fig. 14.4). Additionally, each subject has a defined (but invisible to the outside world) internal behavior, which is determined as a process flow using states for receiving or sending a message (to another subject), and states in which the subject is doing some work (see Fig. 14.5). States can be flagged as starting or ending states and are connected using directed arcs.

A platform for enterprise use cannot be built from scratch, but has to be integrated with an available IT infrastructure (e.g., server platforms). Additionally, we need some business process execution technology we can use as a starting point; one prerequisite is that it must be usable in a software development platform (we need to write software using some functionality offered by others) and be able to run in a cloud environment (we will explain this later). Besides other points, and because there is already a platform available which is based on *Java* (but limited to running on *MS Windows*), we decided to start investigating other available technologies based on the *MS Windows* technology stack. Especially, the *Workflow Foundation* (a .NET programming framework) offers a promising starting point, as will be explained now. Principally any other workflow engine can be used, as long as it integrates with the used server platforms and offers similar functionality.

14.3.1 Workflow Technology

The *Workflow Foundation* (WF) workflow provides functionality to maintain state, get input from and send output to the outside world, provides control flow and executes code—this is done by so-called *Activities*. An *Activity* can be modified in any thinkable way and WF workflows can be graphically constructed within the development platform (*Microsoft Visual Studio* in our case). An example of a WF workflow is depicted in Fig. 14.6. The execution is done by the workflow engine, which is part of the operating system (the .NET environment).

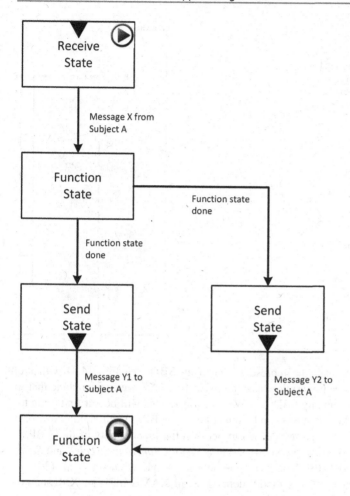

Fig. 14.5 An example of a *Subject Behavior Diagram*: *triangles* at the *top* symbolize *Sending*, *triangles* at the *bottom Receiving States*; other states are *Function States* and states in general are marked as starting or ending state (by *play* and *stop* icon). State transitions are modeled as directed arcs

If a process instance is not needed for the moment—e.g., because of waiting for a message from another process participant—the state of a workflow can be **persisted** (into a persistence store) and stored safely until the continuation condition (e.g., an arriving message) is met—an important functionality for **long-running processes**. Based on the requirements discussed above, a workflow might run on different threads in different processes and on different machines during its lifetime. Any application built on WF technology is therefore **scalable**, since it is not confined to a single process on a single machine. Furthermore, activities can be executed **concurrently**. The chosen *WF workflow* technology supports these requirements.

Fig. 14.6 The structure of a
WF workflow; all work is
done by activities. The
Flowchart Activity is enacted
by the WF runtime engine and
process flow can be routed
back to previous *Activities*

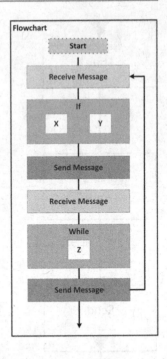

If we simply compare the representation of an SBD (see Fig. 14.4) with the
representation of the WF workflow as depicted in Fig. 14.6, we can conclude that it
may be possible to map any SBD to a WF workflow. This will be our first topic to
study and we will show that this can be done. For the S-BPM methodology to work
with WF, custom activities[3] are needed to perform the functionality of the S-BPM
states: so we need to write some code to get a custom *Function*, *Receive* and *Send*
Activity for standard S-BPM behavior, as defined by Fleischmann et al. (2012).
Technically, we get a process model defined as an XAML file[4] (an XML-based
language).

14.3.2 S-BPM as Windows Workflow Model

The mapping of an SBD onto a WF workflow can be done in the following way: there
are four elements in S-BPM which need equivalents in WF workflows: subjects,
states (send, receive, function), transitions and parameters (local, global). The WF
equivalent for a subject in general is a WF *Flowchart Activity*. Each S-BPM state and
its following transitions are a custom WF *Activity*. Parameters in S-BPM are

---

[3]From a programming point of view this means that we have to develop our own S-BPM classes
using the WF Activity classes as base classes.
[4]The *Extensible Markup Language* (XAML) is a *Microsoft* format to store executable program
code.

converted to variables in WF, which provide the same functionality. S-BPM parameters assigned to S-BPM states become WF variables assigned to WF activities.

As we need WF *Activities* with specific behavior, we need to "enhance" the standard *Activity* class (we use C#) with additional functionality. Not to forget, any *Function State* can include so called *Refinements*, that is, any additional functionality, for example, interacting with other applications or hardware.

All information about processes and their execution has to be stored in a proper way. Therefore, all defined processes as well as their running instances are stored within a central process repository on the server side. Additionally, we have to consider a mapping between organizational roles and subjects, i.e., a specific role is mapped onto a specific instance of a subject (an agent); roles are typically defined in the active directory structure of the IT infrastructure. Normally, a single user can be assigned to several subjects and a subject can be assigned to several users.

As we can see, it is rather straightforward to map an S-BPM model and it goes off without a hitch. It is therefore also possible to automatically transform S-BPM models from other platforms.[5] That means we have a general technology which is able to represent and enact *one* subject, i.e., we can map the internal behavior of a subject onto a Microsoft .NET workflow. The next step now is to find out how several subjects can interact with each other, or in other words, how we can map an entire business process onto WF workflows. As a reminder, any agent or actor in the case at the beginning represents a subject. It is important to understand, that the communicating subjects are *distributed*, that means we do not have a central control over them; each of them acts *independently* and *concurrently*.

14.3.3 The First Prototype (PROMI)

The basic component of our first architecture model is an application titled **Scheduler**, as it is responsible for scheduling all messages between the interacting subjects. The *Scheduler* represents the server-side execution environment for processes, while all necessary interactions with users are performed on the client side. The basic concept of this server component is depicted in Fig. 14.7. First of all, the *Scheduler* is acting as a host environment for all WF workflows. Each instance of an S-BPM process consists of several communicating subject instances (agents). The *Scheduler* manages loading, instantiating, termination, unloading, and the storing of workflows, including the synchronous or asynchronous execution of workflows. Furthermore, the *Scheduler* manages the message exchange between the subject instances (agents). Messages can be exchanged by the use of specifically designed activities from within the WF workflows. The *Scheduler* takes care that messages are delivered to the dedicated recipients.

The **message pool** concept is a central mechanism of S-BPM; in S-BPM all subjects have their own input message pool,[6] and message exchange between

---

[5]As proof of concept we imported a process designed in the Metasonic Suite (www.metasonic.de).

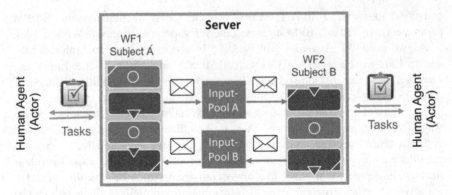

Fig. 14.7 The figure shows the execution of a process with two subject instances, i.e., agents (*Subject A* and *Subject B*). The behavior of each subject is defined by a sequence of custom activities defined by a WF workflow (*WF1* and *WF2*). The workflow activities can basically perform three different actions: send a message, do something and receive a message. Each subject has its own message pool. A workflow communicates with clients in the form of *Tasks*

subjects can be synchronous or asynchronous. We need both types, as subjects are instantiated as agents and an agent can be a human or a machine, or a service. Further, a subject has full access to all messages in its input pool and it can remove any of these messages for processing. This is a fundamental functionality for real-world business processes, reflecting the fact that a process participant (actor) decides which process to continue next (in general it allows setting of priorities).

Consequently, any agent can send messages to the message pool of another agent and take out messages from its own message pool. Workflow activities may require user interaction. In our implementation concept the user interaction is performed client-side. Therefore, the *Scheduler* generates a so-called *Task* for the responsible agent and also includes corresponding data fields (read and or write); in case of a human agent (user-task) this will typically lead to a form to be completed and returned to the *Scheduler*. The information flow between the components of the architecture is depicted in Figs. 14.8 and 14.9.

Based on these concepts we have built a platform to execute S-BPM process models. As *structured communication* is our motto, we use an enterprise e-mail infrastructure to start the processes and to answer the tasks. Following this approach there is no need to learn a new application and we can use the benefits of e-mail as a tool to execute processes, but in a (more) structured way. And, we have the possibility at any time to send an "unstructured" e-mail to anybody inside or outside the defined business process. This implements, in a very uncomplicated way, the S-BPM modeling approach "modeling by restriction" (Fleischmann et al. 2012): we gradually move from unstructured to structured communication.

---

[6]Since any technical implementation has limited resources, input pools are limited in their size. If a pool is full, no further message can be received and the situation has to be handled by the software. In worst case we have a deadlock situation: waiting for a message which never can be received.

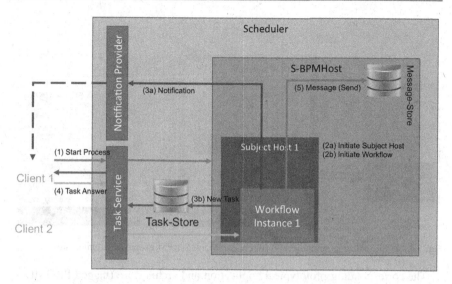

Fig. 14.8 Part 1: (*1*) a process is started by a user on a client. The system then (*2a*) instantiates the environment and (*2b*) the workflow, (*3a, b*) creates a *Task* for interaction with the user, (*4*) handles the answer and (*5*) generates a *Message* to be forwarded to the next *Subject* in the process

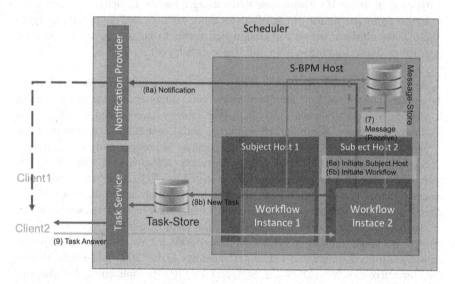

Fig. 14.9 Part 2: now, (*7*) the *Message* is forwarded to the next *Subject*, which means that it has to be instantiated first (*6a, b*), if needed. Then (*8a, b*) a *Task* is generated for interaction with an user via a client application (*9*). And so on

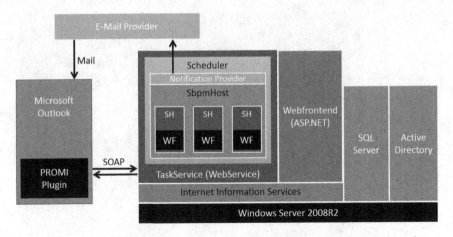

Fig. 14.10 Structured communication: overview of the S-BPM execution architecture

The corresponding prototypical application and architecture (named PROMI) is depicted in Fig. 14.10. Some components were not mentioned yet:

- A web-frontend can be used to answer *Tasks* via any web browser, if preferred (instead of using *MS Outlook*, or when using a mobile device).
- In this prototype we use *MS InfoPath* for more sophisticated data exchange types (business objects); so we can design rich forms to be sent to communication partners (basic forms can hold only basic data types).

As we have learned, *InfoPath* is not a very practical candidate as foundation for the exchange of forms; there are many restrictions (safety or documentation issues). It principally works, but we think that other solutions are needed to achieve the required ease of use, flexibility, performance and a cost-efficient implementation. *MS Outlook* is also not an easy candidate, because of programming restrictions.

S-BPM processes can be uploaded for execution (JPP or XAML format), all data (persisted instances, process models, etc.) is stored in a SQL database, a web server instance works as application host, role models from an active directory can be directly used to model the organization, and a mail server instance is used to handle message exchange between the subjects in the form of e-mails. The architecture resides on a server running *MS Windows Server 2008 R2 Datacenter* with *Hyper-V*; on this platform there are two virtual *MS Windows Server 2008 R2* servers running (one for active directory, DNS, IIS, SQL and the PROMI application, the other one hosting the *MS Windows Exchange* server). On clients we need *MS Outlook*, which uses a plugin to start S-BPM models (appears as a separate menu entry).

One very important aspect of using such a setting should not be neglected: integration of other software or hardware components; for example, we used *MS Dynamics NAV 2009* to demonstrate the integration of customer data via web service calls. Any software built on the *Microsoft* technology stack can be integrated without big hassle, as long as the interface is documented.

14.3.4 Moving into the Cloud

The PROMI architecture has some substantial limitations, thus we have to rethink some assumptions. Nevertheless, the core idea—to translate S-BPM models into WF workflows and use this as a foundation for an enterprise application to execute business processes—remains.

What do we need? To recap, we need an infrastructure which can be used by more than one company to define and execute integrated business processes crossing organizational boundaries. That means we have to create an architecture which does not run on only one company's server; from a technical point of view this means that processes running on the infrastructure of one company need to interact with processes running on the infrastructure of another company. Other requirements yet not or not fully considered:

- The platform needs to be **scalable**; that means it must be capable of handling processes with a small and a large number of instances and transactions per time frame.
- There must be a **security** concept which allows fine granular steering of user rights and visibility of business process models or instances, and access to data (business objects).

We believe that the only way to implement a *Multi-Enterprise Business Process Platform* is the use of an agent-based approach (in our case the S-BPM methodology) built on proper infrastructure. This can be for example a **public** or **private** cloud; the installation, running and managing of a cloud infrastructure as discussed in the following needs serious capabilities of an organization (money and people). We think that a public cloud has some beneficial features related to cost and as a foundation for new services and business models. We especially think, that a public cloud could have some advantages for SMEs. But there are also some drawbacks of a public cloud, as it needs additional efforts to integrate locally hosted applications with S-BPM processes hosted. If deep integration with other applications is needed, a local installation is preferred.

The whole new architecture is depicted in Fig. 14.12. Processes are hosted on an instance of the *Workflow Manager* (WFM), which is responsible for the hosting, administration and configuration of the subjects based on scopes (see Fig. 14.11), such as a *Company Scope* (1) for the processes of one organization, a *Process Scope* (2) for each process and a *Management Scope* (3). Each company has its own *Process Store* (4) and *Subject Store* (5); the same for *Message Store* (6) and *Task Store* (7). Each company has *Task Handler* (9) instances to generate new tasks and each process has *Message Handler* (8) instances to manage message exchange. *Task* and *Message Handler* are implemented as workflows itself. The mechanism of *Scopes* ensures full encapsulation of one company or organization by the other. Further, it allows rights management on a very fine granular basis for each activity; depending on the rights of a role, activities can be visible or not, and activities can be executed or not.

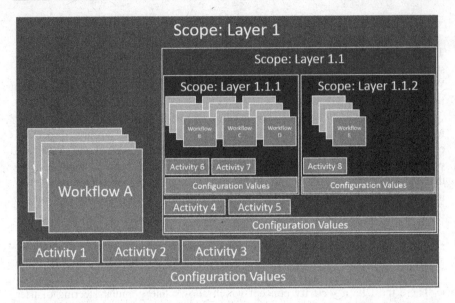

Fig. 14.11 Scopes are containers that may contain *Scopes*, *Activities*, workflow definitions, workflow instances and configuration settings

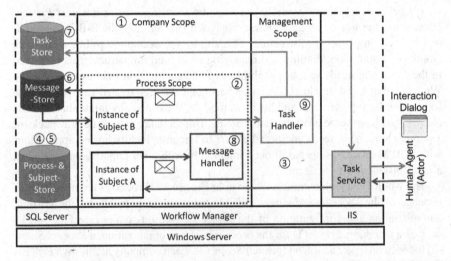

Fig. 14.12 StrICT architecture. The processes are executed server side and the workflows are coordinated through message exchange (*orange*). Task requests (*light green*) and task answers (*dark green*) are routed to a client via the task service

The new S-BPM architecture heavily uses fundamental functionality of the *MS Workflow Manager* (hosting of workflows) and the *MS Service Bus* (exchange of messages). The service bus provides relay and broker messaging functionalities that enable the exchange of messages between different services (see Fig. 14.13). It is

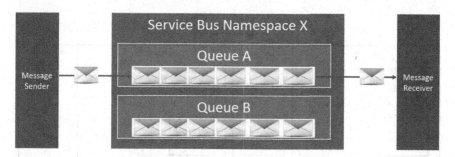

Fig. 14.13 Service bus namespace with service bus queues. Send messages to a transmitter queue, from which they are taken in the order received by the recipient

important to understand that the S-BPM architecture can be hosted on a server or a server farm (if scalability is needed) under the control of a company's IT department, or it can be hosted on a public cloud infrastructure provider such as *Microsoft Azure*. Any needed service (exchange, etc.) is available as a service in the *Azure Cloud*. A public cloud offers some additional possibilities for inter-company process execution, as will be explained later.

Communication between subjects—Messages to other subjects are routed via the internal *Service Bus* (part of *Workflow Manager*). The *Message Handler* is instantiated after receiving a message and forwards it to the correct input pool (*Message Store*) of the receiving subject instance; afterwards the instance is canceled. Subject instances have access to their own message pool and can choose any available message. Now, there is no central scheduler component any more; any subject conceptualizes an independent agent. This realizes an environment for distributed execution of concurrent business process tasks, which are synchronized via the exchange of messages. Messages are containers for data models, which means process actors exchange relevant business data (e.g., customer order, production order, invoice, ...) via message exchange.

User interaction—Interaction with process participants is done via the *Task Service*. A *Task* is a request to be processed by a user, typically to fill in some data into a form (or anything else). A user has full access to its list of tasks. Tasks can be routed as regular e-mails to a user according to the role in an S-BPM process. A task can then be answered again using a standard e-mail protocol.

Figure 14.14 depicts the routing of messages via an external service bus. In this way messages can be routed from the IT infrastructure of one company to another one. This realizes an execution scenario of cross-company business processes. Of course, the processes need to have an agreed common name (technically we also have to send a Globally Unique Identifier (GUID) to identify the instance, so we know for which running instance the answer is) and a compatible and agreed interface.

The modeling of process collaborations can be a difficult task, as it is not an easy task to check whether a model can be executed without dead- or life-lock (because of the distributed and concurrent nature we have no execution path under central control). Principally, there are methods to accomplish that in an automatic or semi-

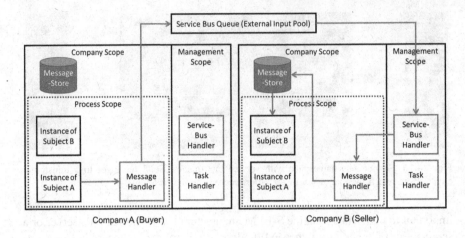

Fig. 14.14 Messages for external entities are passed to the input of the external subject

automatic way. As the processes are executable, they can be validated via simple execution (but, depending on the complexity eventually, not in a systematic way).

14.4 Results

14.4.1 Impact of Actions

Using the S-BPM methodology and the developed process execution platform it is an easy task to develop an enterprise application based on business process models. Now, we get an executable business process without coding; nevertheless, promising any complexity without coding is not credible. Especially if we need communication with other applications we will need to develop interfaces, or, if there are standard interfaces, we may need some coding to pack the data accordingly and make the correct calls writing some lines of code. Data, or business objects in general, typically call for technical skills for the design of the data models. Even if there is a tool to design nice forms for user interaction (generated by the *Task* service) knowledge about different data types is needed.

In the case of our example, in the beginning no highly sophisticated data model or extra lines of code are needed to demonstrate the functionality of the discussed and developed application. Nevertheless, a fully functional implementation of business processes needs interfaces to existing applications, such as an ERP or sales systems where customer data, purchase or manufacturing orders and other data is stored (depending on the needs of each collaboration participant). To design and discuss the process in collaboration between the interacting *Subjects*, simple data types can be used. If the process participants—we mean the people doing the process—have developed a common understanding over the supply chain, IT can support the business process by connecting process activities with other systems; but only if needed.

Now, back to the introductory case. There are several involved subjects which coordinate work through the exchange of messages. For clarity we focus on the exchange of messages only and do not discuss the internal behavior of all subjects as it does not add any additional experiences. Following the modeling guidelines discussed by Fleischmann et al. (2012) we focus on the interface behavior, i.e., message exchange. If one is interested in similar scenarios as discussed here, we suggest also having a look at the book *S-BPM Illustrated* from Fleischmann et al. (2013).

For a compact visualization[7] of the process participants (*Subjects*) we use a BPMN conversation diagram as depicted in Fig. 14.15. This visualizes the case in a similar way as a *Subject Interaction Diagram* but without a detailed view of all *Messages*. It is interesting to see that the S-BPM concept to define business processes corresponds with a very similar representation defined in the BPMN standard; we see that the S-BPM concept is not something esoteric, but contrary to BPMN conversation diagrams S-BPM allows for a direct enactment of the modeled business processes.

The presented cloud implementation as discussed in the previous sections is capable of fully realizing an IT-based implementation of the case process. In Fig. 14.15 the subjects *Customer*, *Regional Logistics*, *BU Logistics* and *Factory Planning* represent cross-company process partners. Each of them has its own *Scope* in the cloud architecture, which represents its very own area to model and execute processes; no data can be interchanged between different scopes. It is also possible that any involved organization hosts its own copy of the architecture on separate hardware. Each organization models only its own processes and defines its communication partners as interface subjects.[8] Messages during execution are routed to the correct process partner (subject) as elaborated in Sect. 14.3.4 and depicted in Fig. 14.14. Further, the process execution is done via e-mail exchange (the client side). That means starting a process, interacting with tasks via forms and message exchange are done via e-mail (we developed a Microsoft Outlook plugin for this, as discussed in Sect. 14.3.3).

14.4.2 Open Issues

At the end of this practical case, some words about open technical issues.

Performance: we did not execute any performance tests, specifically performance depending on the number of running instances in total and of a process model. Even the architecture *should* be scalable, this has to be confirmed based on scientific and technical best-practice principles.

---

[7]The case discusses a so-called *Process Network* as described in Chap. 5 in Fleischmann et al. (2012).

[8]*Interface Subjects* regulate cooperation and facilitate the synchronization of process network partners (Fleischmann et al. 2012).

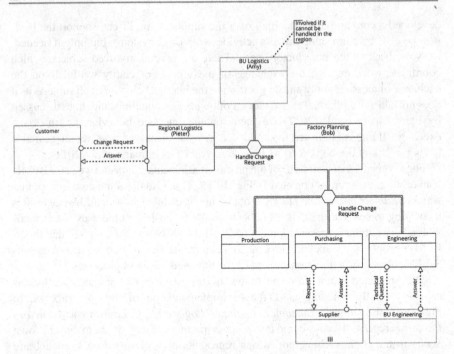

Fig. 14.15 The case visualized as BPMN conversation diagram. This representation cannot be directly converted into an S-BPM process representation and is therefore not directly executable

Modeling: at the time of writing, the modeling tools are not in a mature state; the development of models is done in a browser window based on *jsPlumb*[9]; the models are stored in the cloud infrastructure and can be uploaded for execution.

Business objects: there are two ways to work with data; messages can hold simple data types (numbers, text) or complex data types based on *JavaScript Object Notation* (JSON) data structures, a readable and compact data format designed for the exchange between applications. In this context there are some open technical questions to be solved.

Usability: as the application is intended to be used by *non-technical* people, heavy research towards usability has to be done. This includes questions about *semantic transparency* of the modeling language as discussed by Singer (2014), the design of data models and forms for user interaction.

---

[9]http://jsplumbtoolkit.com.

14.4.3 Takeaway

Practical work based on real-world problem settings has shown that all tools (applications) to build a multi-enterprise business process platform are available. In our case we have demonstrated that using the available server and programming tools from *Microsoft* it is possible without large effort to build an S-BPM platform based on cloud technology. The benefit and intention of choosing these platform products was to get an architecture for any size of business, even the largest. All used server applications are available as services on the *Microsoft Azure Cloud* and are therefore highly scaleable. The drawback of the presented approach is that it may be a too "fat" (i.e., not lean) solution for small and medium enterprises. Especially, if there are only simple processes based on some few subjects, the platform could be too expensive based on cost per transaction.

But we also have learned that execution is not everything—there is also a great need for modeling tools, not only for process models, but also to design data structures and forms. The execution platform is not visible to any stakeholder, but only to IT staff. Nevertheless, for daily and practical use also well-designed interfaces for using a business process system are needed with plenty of functionality; for example, users want and need to *search* for transactions (instances) and the related data. A very good approach is the idea of exchanging messages via e-mails. This leads to a mix of structured (the processes) and unstructured communication with high acceptance by the involved users.

References

Butcher P (2014) Seven concurrency models in seven weeks. The Pragmatic Programmers. LCC, www.pragprog.com

Davenport TH (2010) Process management for knowledge work. In: vom Brocke J, Rosemann M (eds) Handbook on business process management, vol 1. Springer, Berlin

Dixon J (2012) Hype cycle for business process management. Gartner, Stamford

Fleischmann A, Schmidt W, Stary Ch, Obermeier S, Börger E (2012) Subject-oriented business process management. Springer, Berlin

Fleischmann A, Raß S, Singer R (2013) S-BPM illustrated. Springer, Berlin

Singer R (2014) User centered development of agent-based business process models and notations. arXiv:1404.2737

Singer R, Kotremba J, Raß S (2014) Modeling and execution of multi-enterprise business processes. In: 16th IEEE conference on business informatics, workshop on cross-organizational and cross-company BPM (XOC-BPM), Genf, Switzerland, July 14–17

ERP Integration in S-BPM Processes

15

Max Dirndorfer

Abstract

Introducing a standard ERP system gives best-practice processes to companies; but what if a company has developed a better practice and wants to implement it? ERP projects are often very time and resource consuming. One alternative opportunity is the use of S-BPM together with ERP systems. In this article, several ways are shown how this interaction can be realized. Practical examples are presented based on SAP ERP. The intention is to empower readers to apply the shown concepts to their projects.

15.1 Introduction

Over the last decades companies have invested large amounts of money in their ERP (Enterprise Resource Planning) systems (Monk and Wagner 2013). Along with the license fees for the systems, the money was mainly spent either to adapt the ERP systems to the companies, needs or to adjust the companies to fit the ERP systems processes. Often a mixture of both can be found. Even though ERP systems are established in many companies now, this does not mean the story ends here (Leon 2014).

There are still several reasons why processes within ERP systems have to be re-vised or updated, e.g., to keep up with the market and future requirements. Furthermore there are often processes or process parts that are not supported by the ERP system itself. These are often performed within further systems, which can

M. Dirndorfer (✉)
Technische Hochschule Deggendorf, Edlmairstraße 6 und 8, 94469 Deggendorf, Germany
e-mail: max.dirndorfer@th-deg.de

lead to isolated data islands (Müller and Loeblich 2013). This contradicts the paradigm of central data storage as it is proposed by ERP systems.

These are some reasons showing that there is still much space for ERP projects. In praxis, traditionally ERP projects are realized in one of the following two ways:

1. The ERP is complemented with the needed functionality. In SAP ERP environments this means individual ABAP program code. The strategy can lead to several disadvantages like the risk of making the system incompatible with vendor updates.
2. Additional systems for particular tasks with interfaces to the ERP system are introduced (e.g., special CRM systems). Possible disadvantages of this solution can be that those additional systems also may not fully support the requirements, which leads to similar problems as those with the actual ERP system.

Due to the disadvantages of these two methods the idea came up to use the features of S-BPM and the Metasonic Suite to describe and run additional functions extending the ERP systems standards while being able to use the agile and holistic features of S-BPM (Fleischmann et al. 2013; Obermeier et al. 2014).

15.2 Project SUGGEST

To accomplish the idea of using S-BPM along with ERP systems, Project SUGGEST[1] was initiated. It was a research project located at TH Deggendorf conducted in cooperation with Metasonic AG with a term of about one year starting in March 2013. The project was under the scientific direction of Prof. Dr. Herbert Fischer on the university's side and Nils Meyer (CTO) on the side of Metasonic. The purpose of project SUGGESTS was to elicit the interaction between S-BPM and ERP systems, especially SAP ERP. With the goal of implementing real working examples a team of one scientific associate as well as two student apprentices were settled at TH Deggendorf. The team worked closely together with the software engineers and consultants of Metasonic. At every stage of the project the expertise of various experts was involved, including experts from consulting as well as IT and process staff from corporate users.

The first investigations were aimed to find out which basic kinds of interaction between S-BPM and ERP systems can be useful. In small workshops with ERP and S-BPM experts it was discussed what forms of interaction can add a reasonable value for practice. Initially, five relevant categories were identified; see Fig. 15.1. Those simply describe how the S-BPM processes and the ERP systems are related:

1. *Upstream processes*, meaning an overall process starts outside of the ERP system in an S-BPM process and at a certain point the process execution and the

---

[1]SUGGEST is a German abbreviation. In English it means something like subject-oriented design of ERP systems.

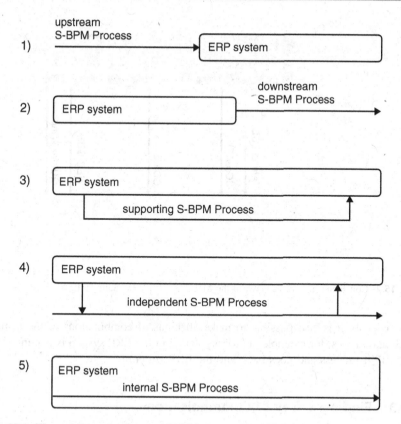

Fig. 15.1 Ways of interaction between S-BPM processes and ERP systems

collected data are passed to the ERP system. These can be preparing processes, e.g., to collect data outside of the ERP system by users with no ERP access.

2. *Downstream processes* are started within the ERP system. In the next step an S-BPM process is triggered and relevant data is passed over. The area of application is similar to the upstream processes, except that they are for follow-up tasks.

3. *Supporting processes* are processes running basically in the ERP system. At predetermined points S-BPM processes are started to support the main process.

4. *Independent processes* run from start to end outside of the ERP system but data is read from or written to the ERP. For example, this can be a process that replaces a standard ERP process without compromising the integrity of the data of the ERP system.

5. *Internal processes* stand for the use of S-BPM to describe and run processes inside the ERP system. This requires a strong interweaving between the ERP system and S-BPM.

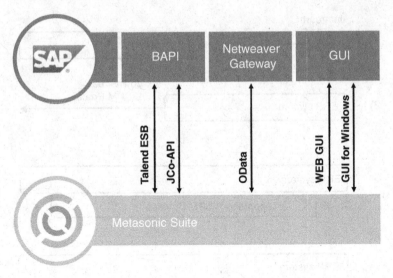

Fig. 15.2 Considered interfaces between the Metasonic's S-BPM Suite and SAP ERP

Obviously it is also possible to make all kinds of combinations of the named integration types; for example, a process started in the ERP system is continued in an S-BPM process and goes back into the ERP system.

15.3 Finding a Way of Communication

After knowing in what ways the integration between S-BPM processes and ERP systems can be useful in praxis the next step was to find out how the communication between the different systems can be realized. To keep the project manageable the context was reduced from ERP systems in general to SAP ERP, but always by cross-checking with other solutions so as not to lose the overall picture.

Relevant interfaces were identified by obtaining expert knowledge and literature reviews. Interfaces on both sides, the SAP system and the Metasonic Suite, were identified. Figure 15.2 gives an overview of the finally considered interfaces. The interfaces (displayed as black arrows in Fig. 15.2) are described as follows from left to right.

15.3.1 Talend ESB

Talend ESB[2] is an Enterprise Service Bus which is available in different versions. Some are under open source license and for some a subscription is needed (those

---

[2]http://www.talend.com/products/esb.

include extra features). The ESB uses a graphical mapping to design and configure services for the interaction between different systems. Talend ESB offers Connectors to address SAP systems. Via graphical connectors the data from SAP BAPIs (Business Application Programming Interfaces) can be mapped to S-BPM business objects and vice versa. The advantage of communicating with BAPIs is that the integration takes place on business level (inherent part: e.g., data checks and transactional access) and BAPIs are very well documented.

The Metasonic Suite offers the option to directly integrate talend ESB services. Without any line of code it is possible to call talend services. Therefore an interface description is required in the talend ESB which can be generated automatically while defining an S-BPM process with the Metasonic Suite. The generation is done based on the description of business objects that are defined in the respective S-BPM process.

15.3.2 JCo-API

The second method considered is the use of the API (Application Programming Interface) JCo (Java Connector). It is a Java library offered by SAP to its customers with appropriate licenses. It allows any Java program to access SAP BA-PIs and other remote enabled SAP function modules. Talend ESB described in Sect. 15.3.1 also uses JCo, but abstracts the Java programming part.

With the Metasonic Suite every state in the internal behavior of a subject can call a refinement. A refinement is custom Java code that is executed when the state is entered during the execution of an S-BPM process. To realize the communication between SAP and the Metasonic Suite, again the data objects are mapped to the interfaces of SAP BAPIs. This is realized within the Java code by the use of the library. With this method data can be exchanged between SAP and S-BPM processes not noticed by the user.

15.3.3 OData

The third way of integration is via the OData web service protocol. OData services for accessing data from SAP systems can be generated with SAP NetWeaver Gateway. OData services can be integrated in S-BPM processes via refinements by the use of OData4j (Java library). OData is XML-based and uses the REST (Representational State Transfer) concept.

15.3.4 Web GUI

The next way considered is the use of the SAP Web GUI. SAP offers a browser-based user interface. It is a one-to-one implementation of the GUI for Windows. This user interface can be directly embedded as an external application via its URL in a state in an S-BPM process. This can be used for processes running mostly outside of SAP. In a particular process step an SAP transaction can be called directly and viewed by the user within the Metasonic GUI. It is also possible to pre-allocate fields in the SAP GUI with data collected in the S-BPM process.

15.3.5 GUI for Windows

Similarly to the Web GUI integration, it is also possible to open the SAP GUI for Windows from an S-BPM process. This is realized by the generation of an SAP shortcut which is generated and opened in a process step. Again, SAP transactions can be accessed directly and fields can be pre-allocated.

15.4 Practical Application

For each of the integration options described in Sect. 15.3, a prototype implementation was created based on a practical use case. The results were shown to corporate users. Thereby important clues could be identified about which integration forms are particularly suited for what purpose and what further forms of integration are required. Some improvements have been transferred directly back into the prototypes.

All prototypes are based on the same use case. An employee can make a purchase requisition (BANF). For this purpose he or she must specify the relevant data such as material number, quantity, or delivery date. After that the requisition has to be released by his line manager if it is higher than a certain amount (e.g., 500 EUR); otherwise it is released automatically. All necessary information has to be stored in the SAP system.

15.4.1 Prototype Talend ESB

In this prototype the talend ESB has to technically interact with two systems, the SAP ERP and the Metasonic Suite. The talend ESB has the main advantage that there is no need to write program code.

First of all an S-BPM process model was designed; see Fig. 15.3. It uses three subjects, two for human participants, "Purchaser" and "Approver", and one fully automated for the SAP system. The SAP system does not necessarily have to be a separate subject, but the communication with the SAP system could also be handled via the internal behavior of the human subjects. By using a separate subject all technical data exchange with the SAP system is encapsulated.

The second step is to establish the connection between the S-BPM process and the ESB; see Fig. 15.4. This is handled via the internal behavior of the SAP subject. In the state calling an ESB service, a business object has to be chosen as the source, for the service input data, and one as the target of the service output data. The necessary schema for talend can be generated and imported in talend ESB.

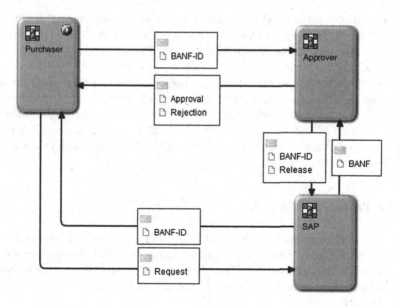

Fig. 15.3 S-BPM subject interaction diagram for Talend Prototype

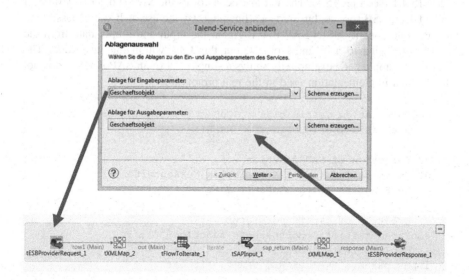

Fig. 15.4 Talend ESB service calling an SAP BAPI mapped to a business object from an S-BPM process

The third step is the realization of the communication between talend ESB and SAP ERP. The lower part of Fig. 15.4 shows the model of the talend ESB service. The service gets the data from a business object of the S-BPM process. This data is mapped and sent via a "tSAPInput" connector to an appropriate SAP BAPI. The answer of the BAPI is mapped back to a business object of the S-BPM process and the data can be used in the next S-BPM process. The users of this prototype only use the GUI of the Metasonic Suite with no need to open the SAP GUI.

This approach has one big advantage: The graphical mapping needs no programming skills to integrate S-BPM with SAP ERP. However it must not be assumed that it can be realized by any employee of any department. At least some affinity towards IT and familiarization with the talend ESB is required. Thus the integration is realized on the BAPI layer of SAP ERP; this approach makes use of their inherent business logic and control mechanisms.

15.4.2 Prototype JCo-API

The second prototype uses the JCo-API. This means some source code has to be written. The Metasonic Suite allows running custom Java code as refinements from any state of an internal behavior. The advantage is that there is no need for third-party software. The communication is realized directly between the Metasonic Suite and SAP ERP.

The basis for this prototype is the same S-BPM model as that used in Sect. 15.4.1 (see Fig. 15.3). The internal behavior of the SAP subject now doesn't call a talend ESB service, but starts a refinement. By the use of JCo it is possible to use the functionality of an SAP BAPI. Again the input and output data from the BAPI is mapped to a business object, but this time within the Java code. The following sample code exemplarily shows a simple call of an SAP BAPI and is not the detailed implementation used in the real prototype.

```
...
JCoDestination destination = JCoDestinationManager
  .getDestination(DESTINATION_NAME);

// selection of SAP function
JCoFunction function = destination.getRepository()
  .getFunction("STFC_CONNECTION");

// creation of import parameters
JCoParameterList importparam = function
  .getImportParameterList();
importparam.setValue("REQUTEXT", "foobar");

// function call
function.execute(destination);

// reading export parameter (response)
JCoParameterList exportparam = function
  .getExportParameterList();
String resptext = (String) exportparam.getValue("RESPTEXT");
String echotext = (String) exportparam.getValue("ECHOTEXT");
...
```

In the example above a very simple BAPI "STFC_CONNECTION" is called. The BAPI has one plain import parameter, REQUTEXT, and two plain export parameters, ECHOTEXT and RESPTEXT.

From within the refinement, access to business objects is granted via the Metasonic Suite APIs. So the mapping from import and export parameters can be handled. For the user the process runs exactly the same way as the one using the talend ESB. The users only see the GUI of Metasonic process runtime.

As with the integration via talend ESB, JCo also uses the BAPI layer; this means things like data checks and transactional access are supported. The advantages of this approach are that there is no need for additional software products and existing Java knowhow can be used directly.

15.4.3 Prototype OData

The third prototype is realized with the OData protocol. SAP NetWeaver Gateway enables SAP ERP to use OData. The internal SAP processes need not be known. The integration is done via a web service. The web services can be generated from BAPIs or can be programmed based on ABAP Objects.

Again the same process model is used (see Fig. 15.3), but the internal behavior of the SAP subject is adjusted. Once more a refinement is coded. The information objects from the SAP system have to be mapped to the business objects of the S-BPM process. The communication with the OData service is realized with the help of the OData4J library. It is possible to read data from the SAP system and use it in the S-BPM process as well as manipulate data in the SAP system (create, update, or delete).

When the prototype was realized, unfortunately no SAP system with OData support was available for testing. Therefore, it was only demonstrated that basic access to OData is possible from S-BPM processes.

This approach again needs Java programming knowledge, but has one advantage: OData is a standardized procedure for data exchange. If the OData interface is well defined and provided by SAP NetWeaver Gateway it is easy to use and integrate the functionality in the S-BPM processes.

15.4.4 Prototype Web GUI

The integration of the Web GUI into an S-BPM process is quite simple. The Web GUI as well as the GUI of the Metasonic Flow are browser-based. The Web GUI can be integrated directly in the process surface of the Metasonic Flow. The browser compatibility of the SAP Web GUI must be considered as it is not compatible with all browsers in versions.

The integration is different from the one before. The SAP interaction cannot be grouped in one SAP subject. The SAP transactions are called as an external application in the internal behavior of the subjects. It is as simple as copying the

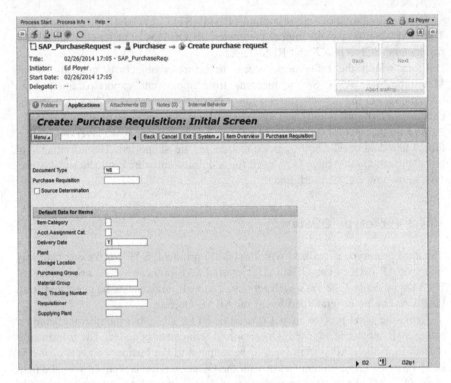

Fig. 15.5 Integration of the SAP Web GUI into an S-BPM process

URL of the Web GUI and adding some parameters for the call of a certain SAP transaction. Fields can be pre-filled with data collected from the previous process steps. The user simply sees the SAP masks integrated in the GUI of the Metasonic Flow; see Fig. 15.5.

The advantage of this approach is that it can be realized very simply. If a company has the Web GUI already in use, it is as simple as copying the URL of the SAP transaction to the relevant S-BPM process step and setting certain parameters. The disadvantage is that this approach is not as flexible as the previous ones; only the standard SAP masks are used. Adjustments at this point are only possible via the SAP system itself.

15.4.5 Prototype GUI for Windows

The integration of the GUI for Windows is quite similar to the integration of the Web GUI. The GUI for Windows cannot be integrated directly in the browser, but has to be opened in its own window. In order to achieve this a SAP shortcut file has to be generated, downloaded to the client PC, and executed. It is possible to jump into certain transactions and to pre-allocate fields.

Advantages and disadvantages of this approach are identical to those in the integration via Web GUI. Additionally, the user has to work two environments which can lead to confusions.

15.5   Results and Outlook

ERP systems can be integrated with S-BPM processes in various ways. To be able to integrate an ERP system it has to offer open interfaces as SAP ERP does. The so-far implemented prototypes do only cover 1–4 of the initially described ways of interaction (see Fig. 15.1). There is no way so far to describe and modify the internal processes of an ERP system directly; this must be part of further investigations.

Figure 15.6 summarizes the required process steps of the different integration approaches. The length of the shown processes is no indicator of the real effort. It depends on many factors such as precognition or process complexity.

The topic is of big interest to industry, as a follow-up project shows. Together with a large company from the financial sector (does not want to be named), a real application is planned. The use case there is a process that is normally performed with the company's SAP system. There are branch offices that don't have access to the SAP system. To enable them to start this process and to collect the necessary data an S-BPM process is used and the data is transferred to the SAP system. This helps to overcome the initially described problems with ERP systems. It empowers the organization to realize additional functionality while staying adaptive and agile for future requirements.

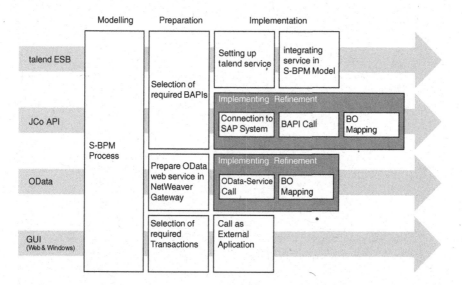

Fig. 15.6 Process steps for integration of S-BPM processes and SAP ERP

Acknowledgments The authors acknowledge the financial assistance of Metasonic in the development and evaluation of this project.

References

Fleischmann A et al (2013) Agiles Prozessmanagement mittels Subjektorientierung. In: Reinheimer S, Gluchowski P (eds) Agilität in der IT. dpunkt, Heidelberg, pp 64–76 (in German)
Leon A (2014) Enterprise resource planning, 3rd edn. McGraw Hill, New Delhi
Monk EF, Wagner BJ (2013) Concepts in enterprise resource planing, 4th edn. Course Technology, Boston
Müller S, Loeblich M (2013) Innovatives Business Process Management. ERP Manage 4/2013: 40–42 (in German)
Obermeier S et al (2014) Geschäftsprozesse realisieren: Ein praxisorientierter Leitfaden von der Strategie bis zur Implementierung. 2nd edn. Springer Vieweg, Wiesbaden (in German)

Appendix

S-BPM Model Construction

In the following the construction of S-BPM models is explained. We first introduce some fundamental concepts (eXPlanation 1–4) before showing various approaches to creating Subject Interaction Diagrams and Subject Behavior Diagrams (XP 5–14).

Fundamental Concepts

(XP 1)   A subject represents the behavior of an active entity.
(XP 1.1)   A specification of a subject does not imply any actor or technology that could be used to execute the described behavior.
(XP 1.2)   Subjects communicate with each other by exchanging messages.

Examples (XP 1): sales, information center, order handling, billing, customer, mediator, manager, patient, back office (Fig. A.1).

Examples (XP 1.1):

- An information center is a personal assistant.
- A customer is Uncle Charlie.
- Order handling is an Enterprise Resource Planning module (Fig. A.2).

Examples (XP 1.2):

- Subject 'Customer' sends subject 'Sales' the ordering message.
- Subject 'Billing' sends subject 'Customer' the billing message (Fig. A.3).

(XP 2)   A Message has a name and a payload.
(XP 2.1)   The name should express the meaning of a message informally.
(XP 2.2)   The payloads are the data (business objects) transported.

© The Author(s) 2015
A. Fleischmann et al. (eds.), *S-BPM in the Wild*,
DOI 10.1007/978-3-319-17542-3

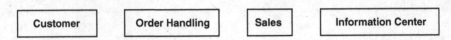

Fig. A.1 Sample subjects

Fig. A.2 Sample subjects and their instances

Fig. A.3 Sample subject-to-subject interaction

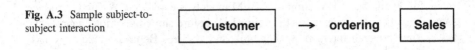

Subjects have internal behavior representations.

(XP 3)   Internally,

(XP 3.1)   a subject executes local activities.

(XP 3.2)   a subject sends messages to other subjects.

(XP 3.3)   a subject expects messages from other subjects.

(XP 3.4)   a subject performs all these activities in sequences—they are defined in a subject's behavior specification.

Example (XP 3.1): A subject calculates a price, stores an address, decides and provides a decision to others.

Examples (XP 3.2):

- A subject 'Customer' sends a message 'Order' to subject 'Sales' of various vendors.
- A subject 'Employee' sends a message 'Request for Clarification' to subject 'Manager'.

Examples (XP 3.3):

- A subject 'Customer' expects a message 'Order Confirmation' from subject 'Sales' of a vendor.
- A subject 'Employee' expects a message 'Clarification' from subject 'Manager'.

Examples (XP 3.4):

- A subject 'Customer' sends a message 'Order' to subject 'Sales' of various vendors. A subject 'Customer' expects a message 'Order Confirmation' from subject 'Sales' of each vendor.

- A subject 'Employee' sends a message 'Request for Clarification' to subject 'Manager'. A subject 'Employee' expects a message 'Clarification' from subject 'Manager'.

(XP 4)   Subject-oriented process specifications are embedded in some context.
(XP 4.1)   Context is defined by the business organization and environment it is part of.
(XP 4.2)   Context is provided by the technological infrastructure by which a business process can be executed.

Example (XP 4.1): Sales is part of Customer Services. Market data are imported from analytical market observers upon request by Service Development. Customer knowledge management is done in cooperation with an Internet Service Provider.

Example (XP 4.2) Sales is supported by an Enterprise Management System and a meeting management system to arrange personal consultancy. Customers access service information via a web interface connected to an embedded search engine.

Subject-oriented Business Process Modeling = Modeling Interaction and Behavior

The construction of a subject-oriented business representation is based on the behavioral entities or abstract resources involved in a business-relevant process. These entities are termed subjects, their exchanges of messages interactions.

(XP 5)   Subject-oriented modeling requires several activities, namely the specification of.
(XP 5.1)   the business case.
(XP 5.2)   the subjects involved in a process.
(XP 5.3)   interactions they are part of.
(XP 5.4)   the messages they send or receive through each interaction.
(XP 5.5)   the behavior of each subject encapsulating functions and interactions.

Example (XP 5.1): The business case is Order Management.

Example (XP 5.2): The subjects involved are: Customer, Order Handling, and Shipment.

Example (XP 5.3): Interactions are: Customer—Order Handling, Order Handling—Shipment, Shipment—Customer.

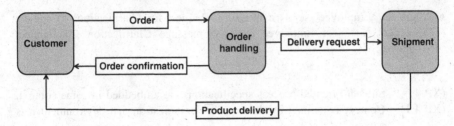

Fig. A.4 A Subject Interaction Diagram for an Order Process

Example (XP 5.4): The messages are: Order, Order confirmation, Delivery request, Product delivery.

Example (XP 5.5): A customer sends an order to the order handling department of a supplier. He is going to receive an order confirmation and the ordered product by the shipment company. Figure A.4 shows the communication structure of that process.

(XP 6)   Subject Interaction Diagram (SID).
(XP 6.1)   (XP 5.2) to (XP 5.4) constitutes a Subject Interaction Diagram.
(XP 6.2)   A Subject Interaction Diagram is the most abstract diagrammatic level of describing processes in S-BPM.
(XP 6.3)   For each subject of a Subject Interaction Diagram a Subject Behavior Diagram (XP 7) needs to be constructed for a complete and coherent S-BPM model.

Example (XP 6): The modeling process starts with identifying involved subjects and messages they exchange in a particular business case. The result of that step is the Subject Interaction Diagram (SID) or communication diagram as shown in Fig. A.4.

(XP 7)   Subject Behavior Diagram (SBD).
(XP 7.1)   (XP 5.5) for each subject constitutes a Subject Behavior Diagram.
(XP 7.2)   After the step (XP 6), the behavior of each subject is defined.
(XP 7.3)   A subject's behavior is described by three states (send, receive, internal function) and transitions between these states. Hence, when specifying the behavior of each subject, a sequence of sending and receiving messages, and activities to be set for task accomplishment, need to be represented.
(XP 7.4)   The description of a subject defines the sequence of sending and receiving messages, or the processing of internal functions, respectively. In this way, a subject specification contains the sequence of predicates.
(XP 7.5)   A Subject Behavior Diagram is the most concrete diagrammatic level for describing processes in S-BPM.

(XP 7.6)   Each Subject Behavior Diagram should detail a specific subject of a Subject Interaction Diagram (XP 6) for a complete and coherent S-BPM model.

(XP 8)   The states of a Subject Behavior Diagram represent operations.

(XP 8.1)   They are active elements of the subject description.

(XP 8.2)   States are implemented by services.

(XP 8.3)   State transitions are necessary to exchange and manipulate business objects.

Example (XP 7) taking into account (XP 8): Fig. A.5 depicts the behavior of the subjects 'Customer' and 'Order handling'. In the first state of its behavior, the subject 'Customer' executes the internal function 'Prepare order'. When this function is finished, the transition 'Order prepared' follows. In the succeeding state 'Send order', the message 'Order' is sent to the subject 'Order handling'. After this message is sent, the subject 'Customer' goes into the state 'Wait for confirmation'. If this message is not available, the subject stops its execution until the corresponding message arrives. Upon receipt the subject follows the transition into state 'Wait for product' and so forth.

The subject 'Order handling' waits for the message 'Order' from the subject 'Customer'. If this message comes in, it is removed and the succeeding function 'Check order' is executed and so on.

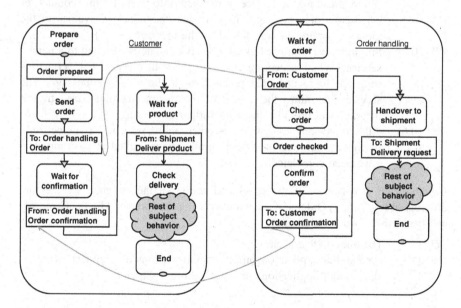

Fig. A.5 The behavior of the subjects 'Customer' and 'Order handling'

(XP 9)   Operations can be of the type 'send', 'receive', or 'internal function'.

(XP 9.1)   Internal functions deal with specific objects, such as required when a customer orders some products.

(XP 9.2)   As a consequence, at least one operation needs to be assigned to each state.

(XP 9.3)   Detailing the operations is not necessary at the modeling stage. It is a matter of an abstract object specification or of the integration of an existing application.

Example (XP 9): The operation could be represented by a transaction of an ERP system related to the regarded object, for instance, the update of an order data record.

(XP 10)   As we abstract from implementation details in the course of modeling, it seems suitable to replace the term 'Operation' by the more general term 'Service'.

(XP 10.1)   A service is assigned to a state and thus triggered and processed if the state is reached.

(XP 10.2)   The name of the states and the names of the assigned services can be different because several services can be used in order to define the required functionality executed in a state.

(XP 10.3)   The end conditions correspond to links leaving the state.

(XP 10.4)   Each result link of a sending state is assigned to a named service. Before sending, a service is triggered to identify the content or parameters of a message. This service determines the values of the message parameters transferred by the message.

(XP 10.5)   Similarly, each output link of a receiving state is assigned to a named service. When accepting a message in this state, that service is triggered to identify the parameters of the received message. The service determines the values of the parameters transferred by the message and provides them for further processing.

(XP 10.6)   All services are triggered in a synchronous way, i.e. a subject only reaches its subsequent state once all services called in a certain state have been completed.

Example (XP 10): Names of the states and names of the assigned services are different in Fig. A.6, as Order services process Order data prepared by the Customer and handled by Order handling.

(XP 11)   (Business) Objects are.

(XP 11.1)   data and/or applications affected by operations of a subject.

(XP 11.2)   data and/or applications processed through Services.

Fig. A.6 Subjects and Objects

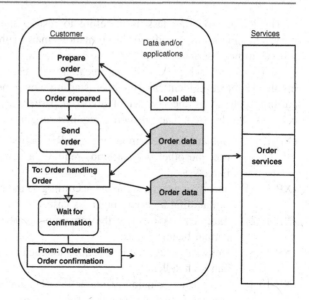

Example (XP 11):

Figure A.6 displays how subjects and objects are connected. The internal operation 'Prepare order' uses internal data to prepare the data for the order message. This order data is sent as payload of the message 'Order'.

(XP 12)   Implementation of Operations (internal functions).

(XP 12.1) Internal functions of a subject can be realized as methods of an object or functions implemented in a Service in case a Service-Oriented Architecture is available.

(XP 12.2) These objects have an additional method for each message. If a message is sent, the method allows preparing data values sent with the message, and if a message is received, the corresponding method is used to store the received data in the object.

Modeling the Other Way Around

Besides the stepwise refinement of subjects arranged in a Subject Interaction Diagram, another approach to modeling has been developed. It starts with an overall generic process model. This generic model represents some kind of chaotic process:

- Every party communicates with every party whenever he or she wants.

The initial modeling task is therefore to restrict the number of parties. This means modelers have to decide upfront how many subjects are involved in the process to be described.

In a scenario each party is communicating with each party; the behavior of the involved subjects is identical. However, starting with generic process templates that are only defined by the number of involved parties, a process can become more concrete step by step. The procedure requires several restriction steps:

(XP 13)   Subject-oriented modeling by Restriction. Modeling by Restriction (i.e. the other way around) requires a certain sequence of activities, namely to.
(XP 13.1)   specify a generic template according to the number of parties involved in handling a certain business case.
(XP 13.2)   name each subject of the remaining generic template for handling a certain business case.
(XP 13.3)   stepwise reduce the interactions for each subject until the business case can be handled.
(XP 13.4)   name each remaining interaction (i.e. message connection) between subjects which are required for handling the business case.
(XP 13.5)   introduce message types according to business case.
(XP 13.6)   adapt specification to subject behavior according to business case.
(XP 13.7)   refine the structure of the business objects transmitted by the various messages.

Example (XP 13): For the generic model the question 'Who Needs to be Involved?' needs to be answered. For Order management a generic subject-oriented process model with three involved parties fits the number of subjects a modeler has to

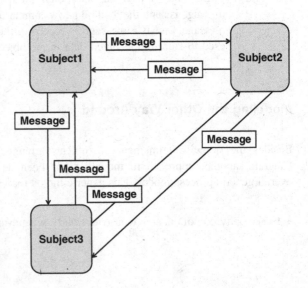

Fig. A.7 Subject-oriented representation scheme for a three-party process

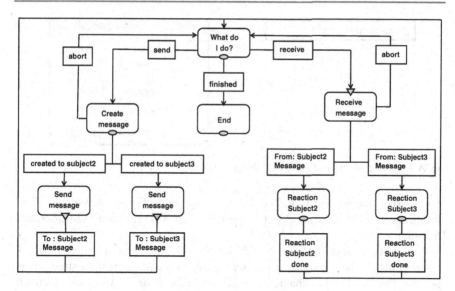

Fig. A.8 Generic behavior of the subject 'Subject1'

expect for the customer order process (Fig. A.7). Each of the parties exchanges messages with another party (Fig. A.8).

Each subject can send messages with the name 'Message' to any other subject any time. Figure A.8 shows the behavior of the subject with the name 'Subject1'.

In the select state, a subject decides whether it wants to send or to receive a message. To start a workflow, it does not make sense to receive a message because all the other subjects are waiting for messages. This means the start subject will start with sending messages and the message exchange can begin. Choosing the send transition, the subject goes into the state 'prepare message and select address' and fills out the business object that is transmitted by the message 'message'. After that, the subject decides to which other subject the message with the business object as content will be sent.

In the select state, a subject can also decide whether it wants to receive a message.[1] If there is a message for the subject available, it can be accepted and a follow-up action can be executed. It is not specified what the follow-up action is. This is like receiving an e-mail. The receiver can interpret the content of an e-mail and knows what the corresponding follow-up action is. The abort transitions back to the select state enable stepping back in case a subject has made the improper choice.

Utilizing the message 'Message', a business object is sent. The structure of this business object corresponds to the structure of a traditional e-mail with extensions like subject (attention: here the word 'subject' has a different meaning. It can mean

---

[1]This choice can make sense for a start subject; from the second time on, it goes into the select state.

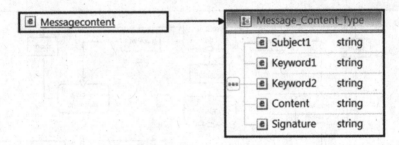

Fig. A.9 Generic structure of the E-mail Business Object

topic, issue, theme, etc.), keywords, and signature. Figure A.9 depicts the specification of the business object 'Message' in an XSD notation (XML Schema Definition).

The process specification is developed corresponding to the business requirements. In our example, these steps result in a communication structure as shown in Fig. A.10 and a behavior specification of the subject 'Customer' as shown in Fig. A.11.

With each restriction step, the behavior specification is becoming more stringent for the subject holders for their actual task accomplishment. Comparing Fig. A.11 with Fig. A.5 shows that modeling by restriction and construction does not necessarily result in identical models. Nevertheless, both models need to deliver the requested business results.

Fig. A.10 Subjects and exchanged Messages

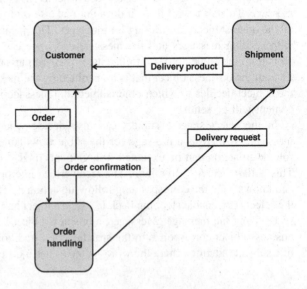

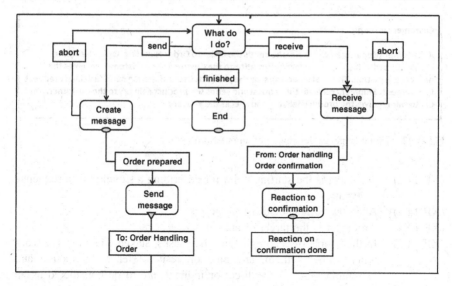

Fig. A.11 Instantiated behavior of the subject 'Customer'

The Third Way—Natural Language

Diagrams can also be derived from narratives, as in many cases people tend to describe their work structure in terms of stories rather than directly modelling it using diagrammatic representations. It turns out S-BPM modelling is structurally close to telling stories in natural language. Essential natural language constructs for constructing sentences, namely subject, predicate, and object, are sufficient for the representation of business processes in S-BPM.

Subjects, predicates, and objects do not only correspond to natural language entities, but also support human communication effectively, both in written and oral form. In addition, humans use natural language structures as the primary means to ensure mutual understanding (Pinker 2007). In S-BPM we make use of it, as it facilitates understanding business process models, and sharing of these models.

The S-BPM modeling language captures the above-mentioned constituent elements of natural language sentences. Models describe structural properties and behavioral alternatives, including the interaction occurring in the technical and/or organizational environment. S-BPM models can be transformed step by step into an executable application in a seamless way. In order to ensure coherence of specifications, the exchange of messages determines the flow of control.

(XP 14)   Modeling the third way means representing parts of the observed reality in terms of natural language, as it allows universal use and is familiar to stakeholders through daily communication.

(XP 14.1)   S-BPM uses the standard semantics for sentences, comprising subject, predicate and object.

Customer Order procedure

A Customer prepares an order. He/she sends the order to Order Handling. Order Handling checks the order. It sends an order confirmation to the Customer. The Customer receives the order confirmation. The Customer waits for the product. Order Handling sends a delivery request to Shipment. Shipment receives the request and sends the product delivery to the Customer. The Customer receives the product delivery and checks the delivery.

Fig. A.12 Natural language description of an order process

(XP 14.2)   A subject is the starting point for describing a situation or a sequence of events.

(XP 14.3)   Activities are denoted by predicates.

(XP 14.4)   An object is the target of an activity.

(XP 14.5)   In the course of accomplishing their tasks, stakeholders receive work inputs, process them, and pass on results. Hence, interaction and communication, either direct or indirect, are to be considered as an essential activity of stakeholders or (IT) systems for subject-oriented modeling.

Example (XP 14):

Analyzing the text according to the standard sentence semantics, the following subjects, predicates, and objects can be identified—the predicates are given with the subject, as the subject encapsulates them in terms of functions (Fig. A.12):

• Customer—prepare, send, receive
• Order handling—check, send, receive
• Shipment—deliver, send, receive

Objects: Order, order confirmation, product delivery, delivery request.

Using this information, both the SID and SBD as shown in Figs. A.4 and A.5 can be constructed in a straightforward way.

Reference

Pinker S (2007) The Stuff of Thought: Language as a Window into Human Nature. Allen Lane, London

Index

© The Author(s) 2015
A. Fleischmann et al. (eds.), *S-BPM in the Wild*,
DOI 10.1007/978-3-319-17542-3

Printed in the United States
By Bookmasters